Ouida

**Tricotrin**

The Story of a Waif and Stray

Ouida

**Tricotrin**
*The Story of a Waif and Stray*

ISBN/EAN: 9783742807656

Manufactured in Europe, USA, Canada, Australia, Japa

Cover: Foto ©Andreas Hilbeck / pixelio.de

Manufactured and distributed by brebook publishing software (www.brebook.com)

Ouida

**Tricotrin**

COLLECTION
OF
BRITISH AUTHORS

TAUCHNITZ EDITION.

VOL. 1107.

TRICOTRIN BY "OUIDA."

IN TWO VOLUMES.
VOL. II.

# TRICOTRIN

THE STORY OF A WAIF AND STRAY.

BY

"OUIDA,"
AUTHOR OF "IDALIA," ETC.

COPYRIGHT EDITION.

IN TWO VOLUMES.
VOL. II.

LEIPZIG
BERNHARD TAUCHNITZ
1870.

# TRICOTRIN,

## THE STORY OF A WAIF AND STRAY.

---

### CHAPTER I.

IN the little kitchen of the river-house in the vine country an old woman sat beside her fire.

Her home had everything that her hardy habits stood in need of; there was abundance of wood in the log closet, there was abundance of brown sweet loaves in the bread-pot, there was ample winter provision in the red earthen pans and the shining brass dishes; there was a bright and pleasant comfort in the fire-glow, in the scent of the herbs, in the purr of the cat; and a sturdy, bright-visaged peasant girl of sixteen, a grand-niece of her own from a distant province, never left her day or night. Yet in the worn, brave, patient, sunburnt face, so old, so still, so dark, there was an abiding, unutterable grief,—a grief that never spoke.

In the long summer days she would creep slowly into the porch, under the great flowering boughs of the chestnuts, and stand for hours shading her eyes with her hand, and looking out to where the distant road ran through the vine-field,—the road that led to the great world.

In the long winter nights she would move toward the window, and draw aside its little red curtain, and sit for hours looking out to where the swollen river roared between its banks,—the river that swept westward to the sea.

Summer and winter she watched for that which never came: the earth holds no greater agony.

At times she would go up the stairway to a great, heavy walnut-press, full of curious doors and dim recesses, and unlock these, and draw them forth, and gaze at their contents; —linen and woolen stuffs, and furs, and many different heaps of gold: she never touched them, but she would gaze at them very long. And at other times she would sit under the chestnuts, or over the warm hearth, as the seasons of the year went by, with only that mute and hopeless pain upon her face, saying nothing, but only stroking the white head of the great cat, Bébé.

She knit, and spun, and eat, and drank, and sliced the onions, and washed the lettuces, and dried the thyme, and worked on, and served herself with industrious travail, as all the temper and the teachings of her life had made her do, while there was one lingering pulse of strength in her aged limbs. But she scarcely ever spoke; and the look in her eyes never changed.

It was only when she sank to sleep in the warmth of the sun, or the heat of the fire, that in her dreams words stole brokenly through the lips, whose sternness relaxed, and whose silence was broken. And the little Lorraine peasant maiden, bending over her, with pity, and with wonder, found those dream-murmured words to be ever the same:

"They never come back! They never come back!"

## CHAPTER II.

"I HAVE not sold one!" said a little Italian lad, with his soft brown eyes brimming over with tears: he was a half-starved delicate child of some ten or twelve years, with a tray of white images.

He was one out of the many thousands, bartered for a few coins, from their homes on the slopes of the Abruzzi or Apennines. A miserable home, sheds shared with the goat and the ass, with dried forest-leaves for a bed, and a piece of sheepskin for a garment, and a draught of sour milk for a meal: but which yet looked so happy and so fair with its sweet-smelling mountain air, and its long summer days, with the herds at pasture, and its play at eventime under the broad cork-tree, and its deep still hush of solitude, with the spring-loosened snows stealing down through the silence,—when the child had been torn from them all forever, and carried northward and westward, to suffer the anguish of cities, the desolation of the streets, the famine of home-sickness amid alien crowds.

He had not sold one: standing there all the day through in the gay, changing, thoughtless throngs of Paris. And he knew that if he went back to his taskmaster without a coin for all his wasted day, the blows would rain down on him like hail, and he would be flung into the noisome, pestilential darkness of the cellar that he lived in, without even the mouldy crust of bread that was by right his supper. Worse things even than this were done to him,—a young child in a strange land, with the seeds of mortal disease in him, sure to die and tell no tale: and he wept bitterly in the springtide sunshine that quivered through a million leaves in a million threads of glory on his head.

He had sold nothing, eaten nothing, not drunk even a drop of water since the sweet balmy April day had commenced; and on an organ near they had played an old Lombardic tune that his mother had used to sing to him in the little cabin under the rock, while the evening mists grew white and hid the valley below. And the air had made the tears start in his eyes, and the great sobs rise in his chest: that time seemed so long—ah, God!—so long ago! For a childhood that is unhappy is as a martyrdom without an end.

"I have not sold one!" he cried to the only living creature who that day paused beside him, to ask why a little, pale, thin, wretched child was in sorrow in a foreign city.

"Ah! You grieve because the world will have none of your toys?" cried his questioner. "Well,—that is the grievance of all of us. The woman will not have our love,—the public will not have our science,—the galleries will not hold our art,—the nation will not accept our policies,—one way or another everybody chafes because every one else will not take to his playthings. And the successful man is the man who knows how to turn his toys to the tastes of the moment."

The boy looked up, shrinking from the jest that seemed to him so untimely and so unmerciful; but as he met the eyes bent on him, he took hope from their sunny compassion. There was no pity in the words, but there was infinite pity in the look; and children and dogs regard the glance far more than the speech.

"I have sold nothing!" he repeated once more, wistfully, with the sobs stifled in his throat. "And you do not know what the Patron is when one goes back without money!"

"He beats you—eh?"

"Ah!"—the child gave a great shudder, a shudder of remembrance and foreboding intermingled.

"Of course he does. He sees the world thrash all who have not the knack of getting gold in it. He only follows the fashion. He would not beat you if you stole?—to be sure not; he follows the fashion there too. But you do not steal?"

"No! I am afraid."

"Well,—not a noble motive for abstinence, but a wholesome one in the absence of a sturdier. Retain it. And you have not taken a sou all this day through?"

"Not one!" sobbed the child, in a loud wail of terrified misery. "Not one! and he will thrash me till I cannot stand."

"Most men are in your predicament, save a few happy hawkers who know well how to trim their wares, and a few wise men like myself, who, having nothing to buy or to sell, contrive to live at our ease. Well, if I had the money to purchase your trayful, you should have it; since I have not, let me see if I can get rid of some of that trumpery for you."

Before the astonished and sobbing child had recovered

his amaze at an address that rang on his ear as so wantonly cruel, his companion had caught up the board full of white images, sprang on a bench under one of the linden-trees of the boulevard, and, raised thus above the passing populace, arrested its attention by his attitude and his challenge.

"Stop! all you who are useless drones in the city!" he cried aloud. "The industrious men may be off, they will not diminish the crowd very much!"

By one accord all the throng paused under the limes, careless how their stoppage incriminated themselves into his first category.

"Listen!" cried several voices. "That is Tricotrin there —ah! he is better than the theaters any day!"

And they gathered nearer about the lime trunk, curious to know what he could be doing there, with his board of plaster casts held in air, and his eyes laughing down on their upturned faces. They were used to him in many phases: from a Harlequin dancing at their barrière balls to a Gracchus leading them in years that were red with revolution.

Whether he danced with them, fought with them, laughed with them, or suffered with them, he was still their own— Tricotrin.

Rapidly one and another joined the first speaker, and the group grew, and grew, with the marvelous celerity of a city throng, and loitered about the linden-tree that sheltered the bench where their favorite stood,—the board of plaster toys resting on his left arm, and the broad blossoming boughs flinging their shadows upon him.

"Ah, my people of Paris!" he cried to them. "Look at these things—the little lad who owns them has not been able to sell one of them among you. How is that? You are not commonly loth to buy new toys; no nation spends its money sooner or wider upon playthings. The world knows that. Why,—we are the great toy-shop of Europe.

"These are brittle, you say? Well, there is no gainsaying it. And they soil with a touch! I admit it. And they are hollow within, only masks at the best?—there is no question but that is true too. I grant every one of your objections. But are they anything new against playthings? I guess not.

"Look at your pet toy 'prestige.' Is not that brittle enough? What a glittering, inflated, gold-bedizened, empty-stomached bladder, that a single blow from the cudgel of adversity breaks and shrivels into naught! Can you eat such a bladder, can you drink from it, can you feed hungry mouths on it, can you take voyages in it, can you trust it to be as sound and as solid as a nugget of ore, or as a loaf of brown bread?—of course not. Yet nine times out of ten you spend all your wealth on it, and you are so busy blowing with all your breath into it to send it higher, that you never notice the grave being dug at your feet, and your children being sucked down into it. Then how in justice can you urge that you will not purchase this plaster bust of Homer, because a crack will make it worthless?

"But they soil so soon, you say;—what is the thing you love best to play with at your leisure, whether you be a noble drinking his wines, or a cobbler stitching his leather, a duke yawning in a palace, or a lemonade seller lying in the sun? Why—a woman's name, I fancy. How you toss it up like a ball in the smoke-clouds of slander: how you pull the dainty down off it, as off a butterfly's wings; how you fling it from one to another, careless of everything except how you get your sport out of it! Well, I warrant you that not one of these little white vases, not one of these little white statues, can be smirched one-half so swiftly as can a woman's fair fame. And off these you can scrape the soil; but off that you can never again remove the stain you once have made on it.

"But they are hollow inside, you still urge?—fie, for shame! What a plea that is! Have you the face to make it? If you have, let me bargain with you.

"When all the love that is fair and false goes begging for believers, and all the passion that is a sham fails to find one fool to buy it:—when all the priests and politicians clap

in vain together the brazen cymbals of their tongues, because
their listeners will not hearken to brass clangor, nor accept it
for the music of the spheres:—when all the creeds, that feast
and fatten upon the cowardice and selfishness of men, are
driven out of hearth and home, and mart and temple, as im-
postors that put on the white beard of reverence and righte-
ousness to pass current a cheater's coin:—when all the kings
that promise peace while they swell their armories and armies;
when all the statesmen that chatter of the people's weal as
they steal up to the locked casket where coronets are kept;
when all the men who talk of 'glory,' and prate of an 'idea'
that they may stretch their nations' boundary, and filch their
neighbors' province,—when all these are no longer in the
land, and no more looked on with favor, then I will believe
your cry that you hate the toys which are hollow.

"Empty indeed these are,—these little heads of Cupid
and little groups of the Madonna,—but empty as they may
be, they cannot be so hollow as those things that I have
quoted, that you cherish, and adore, and purchase, and have
faith in! Brittle, quick to soil, and a mere shell, with nothing
in it! Why, my plaster cast has copied most exactly all your
toys of love and ambition! Come buy them, then! No excuse is left you. I have broken your excuses one by one,
like the fagots in the fable!"

"We will buy them, Tricotrin! We will buy them at
your own price!" cried twenty voices from the laughing
throng below him.

He knew well how to deal with them, with that Paris
crowd, so quickly moved to raillery, to wrong, to tears, to
sympathy, to rage, with swifter mutations than any other
crowds ever know.

"We will buy them! Throw them down to us!" they
shouted, thronging closer about the lime-tree, and looking
upward to his face on which the mellow sunset glow was
falling.

He held up his hand with a gesture to them to pause an

instant; and the ironic gay scorn in his eyes softened and a graver tenderness of regard shone on them.

"Wait an instant: not for my sake. For the sake of a better thing—humanity. See here,—this is one of the shameful scandals of our cities. A child torn from his home, divorced from honest labor, set to a pretended trade, that by it he may cloak theft; spoiled for an honest citizen, that he may pander to the greed of an overseer too idle to labor for himself. If it be thus with the green wood, what will it be with the dry? If it be thus that the young children are reared, of what sort will their futures be? Ah—we enlarge the prisons, and we multiply the law courts, and we leave the school and the cradle to chance! We let the spawning beds multiply their poison; and we wonder that devil-fish are all that swarm in our seas! This boy is innocent—as yet. But the choice is given him betwixt blows and theft, starvation and dishonesty. Who shall look for moral courage in a child to enable him to withstand where men succumb? Buy these toys at their own fair prices. You will do a good deed. But do it for the sake of the young thing that is in need and in hunger,—not for mine."

Their answer was a shower of silver on the bench where he stood, and twoscore hands were eagerly outstretched to seize and share the little casts and busts.

He parceled them out among the throng, and took the coins from each, that from each was due, for the plaster thing that had been given in exchange for it. The surplus he forced back upon the buyers.

"No," he said, as they pressed it upon him. "Give him his proper wage,—no alms. I asked for a kindly act, and you have done it. We will not teach him to look on sympathy as a mere goose with golden eggs, or he may one day kill the bird that now has saved him."

Then, as rapidly as he had mounted the seat under the lime, he sprang down from it, thrust the money in the image boy's hand, and was lost to sight within the doors of the wine-shop close behind his lime-tree.

The throng broke up. The people went on their ways; those who had obtained one of the white images, holding it tenderly as a precious relic. One very old woman from the seaboard of the west, fondled with rapt adoration a little plaster medallion of which the value was, at uttermost, two copper pieces.

"I will put it over my bed," she muttered. "It will keep disease away."

She was close beside the door of a carriage as she spoke; a carriage that had been checked by the throng at but little distance from the linden-tree; its occupant heard her and leaned forward.

"I will buy that medal from you,—here is a gold piece."

The old Vendéan, stupid and purblind, stared up with dazzled eyes. She had all the avarice of the French peasant strong in her; she was but a rag-picker groveling in perpetual filth; she lived miserably that she might have the miser's delight of hoarding a few silver pieces in an old earthen pot under the bricks of her stove. She had never owned so much as a broad golden piece all at once in her life; but she hugged her medallion closer, and shook her head in sturdy denial.

"I will not sell it,—no!"

"And why?"

The question was imperious and impatient, asked by one who was little used to brook or hear refusals.

"Because it came from Tricotrin," muttered the toothless, withered, palsied crone, as she tottered on her way through the crowd.

She did not ask or heed who had spoken to her; she hated all those who drove in chariots. It had been just such a carriage as this, rolling rapidly to a king's festival, that had passed over the fair, slender body of the daughter of her youth, and crushed to pulp the delicate brown limbs,—and left her in her old age no better love than the earthen pipkin under the stove-bricks.

The great lady who had proffered her the gold for her plaster bas-relief, drove onward with a pang at her heart.

"An old creature, that gleans her food from the gutters of the streets, is truer to him than I have been!" she thought.

## CHAPTER III.

IN a great palace of Rome a man lay sick unto death.

Unto death!—though none were suffered to know it save himself, though he made no moan at any one of the inward tortures that consumed him, though he reclined by his lofty casement watching the rising of the moon, in what his household deemed the mere lassitude of long weakness.

He knew that he must die; whether in this night, or not for another year, he could not tell, nor science tell for him; but he knew that his doom was certain—as certain as that the moonlight was streaming, white and limpid and clear as morning, through his vast, painted, silent chamber. But it was his own secret, and he had kept it. He meant thus to keep it until such time as the dumbness and grayness of dissolution should disclose it for him.

He was oftentimes racked with torment. The disease that had fastened on him is ever merciless, sparing not prince nor peasant; a vampire which, when once it has made fast its fangs, never leaves hold till its prey is slain. But he never suffered a complaint or a lament to escape from him. He was of delicate frame, of fragile strength; he had long been a scholar, an invalid, a recluse; none deemed it more than some slight increase of feebleness that bound him to his couch.

Into the mournful shadowy hues of his chamber, where, by his will, only the moonbeams shed radiance, there came a sudden golden blaze of light, a sudden odorous waft of perfume, a sudden flash of glorious beauty, that came out from the gloom as the sun from a cloud.

These came with the entrance of a woman, behind whom two little pages bore two silver branches of wax-lights.

She swept over the room as a swan sweeps over the water, and came to him, noiselessly, save for the soft shiver of her silken robes. She was beautiful, exceedingly; and on her face shone all the victory and proud security of a supreme power. As she moved, her diamonds gleamed on her breast and in her hair and in the folds of her skirts; she was attired for a costume-ball at the Palace of the Doria, and had robed herself as Marie Antoinette de France, diademed and ermined in the full ceremonial of royalty.

She came to him and laid her white hand on his.

"I trust you are better this evening?"

His eyes dwelt on her with an unutterable adoration.

"I believe so," he answered simply. "I think I shall soon suffer nothing."

Some accents in his voice attracted her; she regarded him more earnestly.

"You do suffer, I fear?" she asked.

"A little—perhaps. In not being able to go with you, for instance. But I am weak, that is all."

There are lies nobler than truth.

"How magnificent you look to-night, my empress!" he continued, while his large, dark eyes gazed on her with rapt worship. "You grow more beautiful every hour! But why have you taken that part for yourself? A discrowned queen has nothing in common with *you!*"

She laughed slightly, glancing at her own splendid vision in the opposite mirrored wall.

"No, indeed! But I am Marie Antoinette in her omnipotence, in her glory. Nay! I am more than she. I am France personified! My costume is perfect?"

"You are perfect—yes."

He deemed her so: this exquisite thing, whom he called wife, and in whose heart there was no throb for him, but only one passionate, all-absorbing love for his great rival of the world.

"You see this diamond arrived in time," she continued, touching the center stone of her necklace of unusual size and brilliancy. "I was so afraid it might be retarded on its way through the east, though a courier traveled night and day with it."

He smiled indulgently—as to a spoiled child.

"I bade them get it here, if any way possible, by this evening. You have now the largest jewel out of the European regalias. Those trifles are a woman's pride, I know."

A spasm, whose suffering he could not entirely conceal with all his fortitude, changed his color and caught his breath a moment as he spoke. She looked at him quickly.

"I am afraid you are more ill than usual? Had I not better stay with you?"

There were compassion and the desire to testify it in the offer; but he knew well that it was the accent of duty, not of affection, that spoke in it. He strove to smile again as he replied to it.

"Stay!—and leave the Dorian ball? Stay!—and sacrifice that superb costume for which your diamond has traveled, expressly, the whole way from Benares? Nay—I am not so selfish, my beautiful one. You are not made to be chained down to a sick couch in all your youth and all your loveliness."

"It is I who am selfish—not you," she said, hurriedly, in a momentary pang of conscience and of self-accusation.

"Selfish? Oh, no,—wait until I reproach you, to reproach yourself. Is it not one of the few pleasures that my life has known to be certain that you are happy? Go—you are late as it is; and make the world say once more, what it has so often said already, that all its kingdoms do not hold a creature so victorious and so beautiful as my wife!"

She smiled; her life was so steeped in flattery, that it seemed only the daily utterance of what was her natural due. She was rejoiced to go; she had felt fearful lest he might accept the offer that her duty had wrung from her. She stooped, and lightly touched his forehead with her lips, and turned with her soft, languid grace from his couch.

"You are right; it is late," she said, as she glanced at a timepiece, and floated away through the length of the chamber, the lights which her pages bore falling on the flashing jewels of the royal dress of France.

The world waited for her, the world and all its homage. And—for the husband whom she left there,—had he not his reward! Would not every man whose sight beheld her beauty to-night, envy his possession of herself?

It was enough; she had repaid him.

His eyes followed her with a terrible yearning love that hungered for one backward glance, one farewell word;—none came, she passed out without one lingering look, one last good-night. She was thinking of the world that waited for her in the Palace of the Dorias.

The lights passed away, the curtain fell behind them, the trailing of her train upon the marble floor ceased to break the silence. He was left alone. And he covered his face with his hands, and shuddered as with cold, the dews of anguish standing on the brow that her lips had brushed as lightly and as carelessly as the wings of a butterfly brush the face of a corpse. He would have borne the throes of ten thousand deaths to spare her one throb of pain,—and he was no more to her than the glittering stones that shone on her fair bosom; nay, not one tithe so much! Honor, affluence, gladness, luxurious ease, imperial pomp, and all the homage that the world will only render to those who can command it, had come through his hand to her. Through him she was throned on high, where perpetual summer and everlasting sunlight were her portion, where the storm of calamity, and the chill of poverty, and the scorch of shame never more could touch her. Through him, the desire of her soul was given unto her; and the crown of greatness was set on her proud brows in lieu of the brand of bastardy, and of the thorn-wreaths of vain ambition, and of disappointed effort. Through him all things that she had craved had become hers without price or penalty. And his reward was that men grudgingly counted the years of his life that were set as a barrier betwixt them and her loveliness! And that to this exquisite thing,—cruel without intent and unwitting of the pain that fed her pleasure, as infants when they catch at butterflies,—he was only as the treasury from which the gold that was needed for her triumphs came, as the mine whence the jewels of her regalia were drawn, as the magician whose wand summoned around her the splendors of an enchanted world.

He lavished all that the earth held upon his idol. And she—she was not so much moved by all his priceless gifts as in the days of her childhood she had been moved by a single branch of dog-roses, a single horn of silvered sweetmeats from another's hand.

She was radiant, thoughtless, mutable, capricious, surrendered to the indulgence of every whim, and forgetful of the hand from which the power of such indulgence came,—it is ever on natures such as this that love is poured out most abundantly; natures that rejoice in its effect, but no more heed its root than the bee heeds the roots of the flower-bell that it despoils of its honey.

In her heart he knew not one pulse beat for him.

In her absence he knew not one thought turned to him.

In her future he knew not one memory would be faithful to him.

And this bitterness was greater to him than all the bitterness of death.

For he suffered also that jealousy which, arising in noble natures, will never stoop to suspicion, but yet it is the inevitable offspring of that possession of a beloved life, which is not also possession of the soul within that life.

He did not fear the safety of his honor. She was proud, she was truthful, she was of high courage; such women do not carry shame to their husbands' hearths. But—she was so young, she was so beautiful, she was so hourly besieged by all the honeyed eloquence of passion, and he—he was left here, old ere his time, powerless to attract or enchain her, gray, weary, hopeless, paralyzed with a piteous disease. When he bade her go forth into the world where her lovers wooed her ear, and every whisper that stirred the air was a whisper to forget himself, he reached that martyrdom of the soul of which the world knows naught, but which surpasses in its fortitude and in its torture every martyrdom of the body.

The night was very still; through the lofty casements the lustrous Roman moon shone white; the great chamber was hushed like a grave. He lay there long with his face hidden, and no sign of life within him, save now and then a quiver of his limbs as the canker of death within him dealt him some sharper blow.

A dreamy sense of exhaustion and of peace slowly stole on him, stilling his suffering, but stilling with it the life in his veins. His attendants, alarmed at his long silence, drew noiselessly near, and fearing to disturb what might be merely peaceful sleep, stood inactive round his couch. His physicians, hastily summoned, saw that it was sleep indeed, the sleep that knows no awakening. They raised him, and his eyes unclosed with the old, gentle smile they knew so well.

"This is death?" he asked.

"Seek the duchess—quick!" they whispered low; but not so low that the words failed to catch the ear of the dying man.

"No, no!" he murmured. "Tell her nothing. It would spoil her pleasure!"

And his last breath faded from his lips in that last thought for her.

He lay dead in the moonlight that streamed about him —fair, cold, pitiless, radiant as the life that he had cherished.

In Rome, on the morrow, men, speaking together of the last of the once-famous Dukes of Lirà, said that he had made no mark upon the world save by his strange marriage with his beautiful wife; and laid many wagers as to who in Europe would be likeliest to marry his fair duchess.


## CHAPTER IV.

THE noon sun shone on some few breadths of corn-land lying on a southern hillside above a winding road, where one little white, brown-roofed châlet alone stood looking down into the small, cool, dark-blue lake that slept below.

The corn was brown and ripe; the circle of the seasons had brought the harvest time again; the wheat was full in ear; and, with the yellow riches of the neighboring gourds and the fruit of some goodly olive-trees hard by, would give wealth enough for a peasant of the Pyrenees to be well content withal. Yet the owner of the nook of arable land upon the chestnut-clothed slope was weeping piteously, like Rachel refusing to be comforted, like Rachel having lost her son into the twilight of an unknown fate.

It was the grief of grand'mère for Antoine; it was the grief of a million mothers when the sickle of State-Lust gathers in the budding corn of the young lives they love; it was the grief of which Theroigne de Mericourt was ignorant when in answer to the reproach—"Why will ye women breed in servitude, why are ye not as the desert beasts, that losing liberty are fruitless?"—she replied, "Did not the child smile in his mother's face for all that Nero or Tiberius reigned?"

Under Tyrannies the children may smile, because they know not what Birth has brought them; but under Tyrannies the mothers weep. And in revolution the reddest hand, the voice most shrill and pitiless, are the hand and voice of a woman.

This woman, old and feeble, lamented for the son of her elder years whom the conscription had taken—taken from his peaceful mountain home, and his pastoral games, and his corn raised with so much labor on the arid soil just as its harvest crowned his toil.

She stood on the stone sill of her little dwelling, and beside her stood a man in the loose linen shirt of the people, with a violin under his arm and a little black monkey playing at his feet.

"It is the conscription!" she cried, wringing her hands—slender hands, for she had been city born, and could not aid herself as could the sturdy women of the southern land. "The conscription! See how the government devours us. All the youngest, and bravest, and best, drawn away to rot in the battle-fields!"

"Chut! good friend," said her companion's mellow voice, that was in itself a sound of consolation. "Blame not the government. Blame the war-lusts of men's souls. Look you,—if the people governed, I doubt not but they would be as cruel. A republic and peace we say—ay, we shall get them, perchance, in paradise. Not here. The people everywhere are hot and hasty and blind in judgment; they would rush into wars the instant that their jealousy or their vanity smarted. And then the youths would go to the slaughter. See how it was with them in the days of Argonne and Jemappes."

"That may be," moaned the bereaved mother. "But they would not take the lad from the plough, the boy from earning his grandam's bread, the child with the down on his cheek from the herd of goats that was all his store. They would have pity——"

"On their own class? Possibly. They would stay at home themselves, and send the poet, the scholar, the artist, the statesman, out to the storms of the grape-shot? Oh yes! But would that come nearer justice, my friend?"

"I do not know!" sobbed the woman, inconsolable. "I only know Bernal is gone!"

"Ah!" murmured Tricotrin. "That is all most of you know of justice,—how she looks through your own little eyelet-hole! Listen here, Aimée Herbalez, we have all our burdens; but it depends on ourselves how long we carry them. The conscription is hard, that I grant you; and were the bodies of men well trained to arms, and their minds to tolerance, there need be no conscription, because there would be no war. But while the world wags as it does, men must be patriots, and every patriot must be a soldier if necessity arise. And Bernal was a lad of spirit; he would not have been easy in your little nook all his days. Who knows?—he may carry the Bâton in his knapsack? There was a rough peasant boy once, down in the south, in whose fate it was written to sit on the throne of the great Gustavus,—and his race reigns to-day. Who can tell what Bernal may not reach?"

"He would be as far from me if he were a king!" murmured the despairing Herbalez. "It is good of you to talk so, and it is true that the boy was well pleased to go into the army, promising to get covered all over with orders. But, ah!—they talk of the stars and the crosses, and they die in a ditch!"

"Supreme truth! Thousands rot at an Austerlitz, and one man goes home a conqueror. If I kill a single creature for a bag of gold coins, I am guillotined as a murderer; if I kill a million creatures for a diadem of gold, I am worshiped as a hero. Singular arithmetic and ethics! But hark you——"

"They die in a ditch!"—wailed the woman. "My bright innocent boy!—he is gone into the hell of Paris, where he will forget his God and me; and they will draught him out to that hideous Cayenne, where they say no strong man can breathe and live."

"What regiment have they drafted him into?"

She told him between her sobs.

"All right! Only the second battalion will go to Cayenne. I know something of that regiment's commanders,—for that matter I did them a turn one night down an African defile, when it went hard with them against a band of plunderers. I will see what I can do to get Bernal left with the

first battalion at Toulouse. Toulouse is not so far but you
can look at him now and then. So take heart! The boy
shall come back here with his lieutenancy if we can get him
one; and—meantime, your corn is spoiling!"

"What matter the corn!" she cried, impetuously. "What
matter the corn, if you can save my boy? God reward you!
You are ever like sunshine in a desolate place. You are ever
full of generous thoughts!"

"Chut! In my own life I suck the sweetness from my
cocoanuts, and only eat the flesh of my dates, like the wise
Arabian lad; but when I see my fellow-creatures persistently
eating their cocoa-husks and their date-stones, and getting
no other nourishment, I do my best to set them right. And
the corn?"

"Ah, it is a terrible thing about the corn," sighed the woman, losing her ideal grief in her practical care, through
that necessity which is at once the slave-driver and the
solacer of the poor. "Bernal was just going to reap it; and
the neighbors in the valley have their own business, and I
am a weak, useless thing, and one night's storm would lay
it and kill it——"

"Assuredly. I will get it in by sunset."

"You!"

"Well! Why not? Have I not worked in the fields before
now?"

"But that was in play!"

Though he lived with them and like them, felt with them
and like them, there was about him that which the people
of every land instinctively obeyed and yielded to as the
sovereignty of one above them. Superstition, growing out of
reverence and love, gave him many strange attributes and
lofty antecedents; and to behold him one day claim the kingship of the world would not have been too great a glory for
him in the sight of the peasantry that worshiped him.

"In play? Indeed, no. I worked for a wage. I am indolent enough, good Herbalez, as you know; how many hours
I lie in the sun as lazy as a lazarone! It will do me good to

get in your wheat. Corn will talk to us, if we listen, better than most men,—what sermons in the full ripe ears that have sprung out of a seed that had looked dead; what poems in the blue cornflower that grows among the wheat like the poetry that springs through the busy lives of men; what rebukes in the brave, patient lark that builds so boldly, though the reaping-hook may cut her little body in two! Come, give me the sickle, there is no time to lose; by the violet of the skies there is a rain-storm due before to-morrow."

With fervent thanks she gave him the classic tool, and stood awed and wondering as he went to the work. To the literal mind of the woman, which was unpoetic but yet superstitious, it was easier to believe that miracles happened, and that the wheat and the blossoms really had tongues for him, than to follow the fantastic fancy which for him filled them both with meaning.

He was soon in the little field,—belted in by the chestnuts, and sultry with the ardent sun of August,—in a corner of which he put down his knapsack, his blouse, and Mistigri, who being a spoilt little epicurean, sat among the cornstalks, disdainfully biting a wheat ear now and then, and making a grimace at it.

"This is the way, Mistigri," he murmured to his single confidant and companion. "When dark hours are down, work through them. No exorcism charms like labor. Men's souls were never made to dwell in night shadows like the owls. To repine for one's self is something so narrow and mean. While one has health, and strength, and sight, and liberty, is it not rank blasphemy to say one has not happiness? Ah, Mistigri, there was a beauty in the Mexican's cultus that is missing from the modern creeds. To toss wine heavenward, with kisses, when the sun rose—that meant Gratitude and Rejoicing. And then Christians went with fire and sword, with the Bible of the Jews and the Inquisition of the Spaniards, to massacre all those bright worshipers by way of teaching them a better religion! Paf! Give me the Pagans!"

Mistigri nodded assent, being a little Pagan herself; and Tricotrin bent himself to his work, the hot sun shining on the brown corn, the yellow-winged orioles flying through the light, the poppies and cornflowers bowing under the sickle, the little bright-eyed mice scampering off, as their nests were laid bare, into the chestnut wood belting the field.

He worked fast and unremittingly; he was glad of the labor. Down below there, far away in the valley, were some delicate spires and mighty towers bowered in wood. They were the spires and towers of the Château de Lirà.

As he worked, four gay equipages, with outriders all aglitter in scarlet and silver, passed at a rapid pace below, along the road winding at the bottom of the slope. He paused to gaze at them, shading his eyes with his hand.

"That is our Châtelaine," said the widow, who had come out to bring him a jug of red wine and a roll of bread. "That is the beautiful creature I told you of—the great duchess."

"Yes," he answered her simply; and he took up his sickle, and went to work afresh, while the sound of the horses' feet still rang on the rocky road below.

"This is the first summer season she has been here," resumed the woman, sitting down with her knitting on the ledge of the wooden pale. "The duke never came here after his marriage: that took place far away south, out of France. We heard of it, and the people were well pleased; they hoped to have great gayeties at the château once more. But it was not so; they were always in Paris, or in foreign countries: we heard that he died abroad, and she did not come at all; never until this summer, and now,—now,—she makes up for the long absence! Such extravagance, such pleasures, such hundreds of guests, such a life—such a life! They do nothing but feast themselves like princes, and my boy Bernal is drawn for the wars!"

She dropped twelve stitches in her knitting-work,—like many other democrats who leave long gaps in their own work, because they must stay away from it to rail at an Order.

"She is not generous to those that are poor, then?" he asked, bending still at his work.

Bernal's mother shrugged her shoulders.

"I do not suppose she ever remembers that there is anybody living who has not cakes, and wine, and oil, every day! Generous? What do you call generous, Tricotrin? They roast a hundred fowls, I have heard tell, in her kitchen every day; they drink wine that has real sparks of gold in it; they laugh, and sing, and saunter all their hours away; they sleep in satin sheets—so they say: what good is that to us? If you were to go up and ask, for your very life, you could not see her. I did try, when my boy was taken: well! how was it? A servant spoke to another servant, and that servant sent a page, and the page mocked me, and sent another, and that other went to some great man with a silver chain on him, who rebuked me, and told me I was a rude woman, but I might go to the kitchens and ask for food. Food! they would have given me broken bones when I had lost Bernal to the army! No,—she is a fair thing; she has a face like the sun, but she is cold, she is hard, she has no thought for the people. Tricotrin—if the Revolution came again, I could find it in my heart to see her stripped and scourged, and made to eat the bread of bitterness. Look how she enjoys while we suffer!"

The old rankling jealousy, natural, yet so cruel, that lies at the root of all social antagonism, was acrid and almost savage in the words: he did not answer her, but reaped the corn in silence, while she knitted on, striving to recover her lost stitches; but the gap that had been made would not close,—in eagerness for a revolution of the future she had spoiled her labor of the hour.

There are many reformers like the Widow Herbalez.

By sunset the little golden store was reaped and set in sheaves,—the graceful sheaves of English form, with withes of wild convolvulus, and scarlet heads of poppy, bound up within the wheat. He was free from his self-imposed duty; he left the great white Pyrenean dog of the place on guard among the little harvest, and went down the hillside, pursued by the blessings and the thanks of the conscript's mother. "Gratitude is a lively sense of favors to come;" and she knew that she must look to him to carry it for grinding to the water-mill in the village below, where the foaming mountain river grew quieter, and watered peacefully green stretches of meadow-land.

There, in the valley, beneath his feet, not more than a league off, were the towers of the château, and the wide, dark masses of park and forest woodland; with lakes, and islets, and rocks, and streams amid them, and in their front the glorious panorama of the mountains.

From the center tower of the pile was floating the scarlet standard of the Lirà; with the golden hawk, with outstretched wings, of their insignia, glittering in the rays of the setting sun.

He descended the hillside with the lithe swiftness of the mountaineer, and passed through the scattered homesteads of the little hamlet, that were chiefly gathered about the side of the river, and had their white walls hidden under thickets of myrtle and olive.

The day's toil was over: the young men and maidens were playing the rough wrestling games of the district, or dancing the Moresco dances, that still linger there as the sign of the Saracenic days of yore: the old women were sitting spinning, nodding their gray heads together, amid the babble of their grandchildren; they were all very poor; they all led simple, homely, patriarchal lives; but they were happy, their youth had the gay grace, and their old age had the smiling content, that belong to France alone.

He scattered among the children a basketful of cherries that he had bought on the hillside, of an old woman who was seeing her ruddy store likely to rot away for want of a buyer in that lonely place: then he went from one group to another with cheerful words, as his habitude was, and gathered the wishes and wants of the little community. Both were humble enough:—a goat for the sake of its milk; a hank of flax for the spinning; a purchaser for the overripe melons; a necklace of priest-blessed beads; a smile from the bishop as he passed on his mule through this, his far-distant, and rarely visited flock; an acre more ground to some young lover's small patrimony, so that he could wed where he loved: all these in the little world played the part that crowns, and honors, and riches, and fair fame, and fierce passion played in the great world unknown to them.

One young child, beautiful as some mediæval painter's seraph, with that angelic spiritual regard which belongs to southern climes, pouted with a pretty scorn at her playmate's cherries, and came and leaned in grave disdain over her mother's knee.

"Dost thou not care for the fruit, Angelique?" asked the mother, reproachfully, smiling the while at Tricotrin, who stood by.

The child's fair face clouded with petulant disdain.

"No! I want more gold toys, mother!"

"Ah!" said the woman, half smiling still, but sadly. "Thy chain has spoiled all thy pleasures! A week ago, look you, our duchess up yonder saw Angelique as she passed, and laughed and tossed her a gold jewel off her wrist. It just fitted the baby's throat; but it has made her so vain, there is no telling how to please her now."

Angelique lifted proudly her little fair throat with the gold links glittering round it, her eyes shining and rapturous.

"I will not play with *them!*" she said, tossing her head toward her playmates. "They have only strings of yew berries or dried peas!—and she never called them beautiful!"

"Hush, hush! A careless word does mischief," murmured her mother, deprecatingly, to Tricotrin. "To give it to the child was very good, very generous, but the gifts of the great are——"

"Honey that moulds into poison! Your Angelique was happy in her necklace of yew berries, and now, the lust of gold is grown, and gold does not grow like the yews. She gives much,—your Châtelaine?"

An old woman—very old—lifted blind patient eyes where she sat under the chestnuts.

"She saw me sitting in the sun, in the park, the other day, and she spoke softly to me, and she shook her purse into my lap,—I counted twelve pieces, and Vevette found them every one of gold! She is an angel."

"Caprice!" muttered an old charcoal-burner. "Only a caprice, like the chain to little Ange. Her stewards tax us for every rotten twig of wood, till we can scarce keep body and soul together. She is a tyrant."

"We have only gourds and a stray onion to chew," muttered a herdsman, "and her dogs eat the fat of the land. She is an aristocrat."

"Her flowers have fires all the winter, and we shiver and starve."

"Her life is a fairy tale; how should she know what it is to have only a knob of black bread once in twenty-four hours?"

"She spends all her substance in Paris; and then her foresters grudge us a quail we have killed with a stone!"

"Her outriders lamed Bertrand's child for life, and she was laughing in her carriage,—she never saw, she never heard."

"Her fêtes cost a million francs a night, every night of last week, and they say each tree that was lit up cost as much as would keep a man for a twelvemonth."

"But it was beautiful; we could see the light here!" pleaded a handsome young goatherd. "And she has a face like God's own people!"

"She gave me my chain!" cried little Angelique.

"And my twelve pieces!" muttered the blind woman.

"All that will not put a slice of beef in our pots, with the garlic; nor yet mend Bertrand's boy's broken knee," said the charcoal-burner, gloomily, in summary and conclusion.

Tricotrin, standing under the chestnut, heard in silence; then wished them good-night, and walked on as Mistigri leaped to his shoulder.

"Ah! little one," he murmured to her. "How the hotbed of the world has heated and strengthened the faults and the follies!—yet the higher nature lives still, and the gift goes to the child, the gold pieces to the blind woman. Will it ever wake wholly and reign again? Yes, perhaps:—if ever she love!"

Meanwhile, under the chestnuts, the blithe talk of the aged women grew silent: the little Angelique pouted apart, vexed with herself for having scorned her share of the cherries; the charcoal-burner sat moodily musing of things of the old Revolution of which his grandsire had told him; the young herdsman would not join in the Sarabande, but wandered away thinking of the face "like one of God's people," that belonged to his proud Châtelaine, and gazing wistfully upward at the lights that began to gleam through the wood of the château.

The bright and light-hearted content and communion of their lives had been dimmed and been broken:—the world had sent amid them the visible presence of its devil-empress, wealth.

He, himself, went onward through the valley, through the deep belt of the woods, through the avenues of the park. The whole front of the antique building was lighted, and the painted oriels gleamed ruby, and amber, and soft brown, in the dusky evening, through the green screen of foliage.

The fragrance of the orange alleys, and of the acres of flowers, was heavy on the air; there was the sound of music borne down the low southerly wind; here and there through the boughs was the dainty glisten of gliding silks:—it was such a scene as once belonged to the terraces and gardens of Versailles.

From beyond the myrtle fence and gilded railings which

severed the park from the pleasaunce, enough could be seen, enough heard, of the brilliant revelry within to tell of its extravagance, and its elegance, in the radiance that streamed from all the illumined avenues.

He stood and looked long; hearing the faint echo of the music, seeing the effulgence of the light through the dark myrtle barrier.

A very old crippled peasant, searching in the grass for truffles, with a little dog, stole timidly up and looked too.

"How can it feel, to live like *that?*" he asked, in a wistful tremulous voice.

Tricotrin did not hear: his hand was grasped on one of the gilded rails with a nervous force as from bodily pain.

The old truffle-gatherer, with his little white dog panting at his feet, crossed himself as he peered through the myrtle screen.

"God!" he muttered, "how strange it seems that people are there who never once knew what it was to want bread, and to find it nowhere, though the lands all teemed with harvest! They never feel hungry, or cold, or hot, or tired, or thirsty: they never feel their bones ache, and their throat parch, and their entrails gnaw:—these people ought not to get to heaven, they have it on earth!"

Tricotrin heard at last; he turned his head and looked down on the old man's careworn hollow face.

"'Verily, they have their reward,' you mean? Nay, that is a cruel religion—which would excruciate hereafter those who enjoy now! Judge them not; in their laurel crowns there is full often twisted a serpent. The hunger of the body is bad indeed, but the hunger of the mind is worse perhaps; and from that they suffer, because from every fulfilled desire springs the pain of a fresh satiety."

The truffle-hunter, wise in his peasant-fashion, gazed wistfully up at the face above him, half comprehending the answer.

"It may be so," he murmured. "But then—they *have* enjoyed! Ah, Christ! that is what I envy them. Now we,—

we die, starved amid abundance; we see the years go, and the sun never shines once in them; and all we have is a hope—a hope that may be cheated at last. For none have come back from the grave to tell us whether *that* fools us as well."

So saying, he heavily shouldered his creel of truffles, and turned away sadly.

Tricotrin turned also, and laid his hand on the rush basket and swung it over his own back.

"I will carry it home for you," he said to the feeble old cripple. "We will have some more words together: and you shall give me a night's lodging."

"Willingly! But I have only a wattle hut in the forest!——"

"What matter? I can sleep outside it, under the pines. I have done that oftentimes. There is no more fragrant bedchamber,—not even where great ladies rest."

He glanced back at the distant gardens where the lights, and the music, and the guests of the evening festival were.

"She is happy: what matter that she forgets?" he thought, as he went back with the old woodsman into the shadow of the pine and the chestnut forests.

The little hut stood hidden in one of the deepest recesses of the great sylvan growth which, watered by innumerable subterranean branches of the river, that was fed with every spring-tide by the melted snows of the mountains, resisted the withering scorch of the southern suns. It was a small rough place, bare as a hermit's cell, and strewn with dried water-rushes; truffles were scarce in the district, and for them there were swifter and abler seekers than the cripple of eighty years.

He had been born in the Lirà forests, and had lived in them all his days, first as a charcoal-burner, then, when his strength failed him, and he had broken his knee down a ravine, by seeking for the dainty root that savors the rich man's banquet. Of any world lying beyond them, he had but the vague conception of a child: days and nights, and months and years had all gone by with him under the broad fans of the pines and the chestnuts, the seasons only measured to him by the budding of the rosy leaves and the falling of the golden cones. Yet he was patient, and laborious, and wise in his own way, like one of the gentle beavers that built their wooden cities in the lake beside his home.

"You have always lived alone?" Tricotrin asked him, as he sat at the hut door, smoking, as the moon rose and silvered all the delicate colonnades of the pine stems.

"Not always."

"Not always! How is it then that you are so now?"

"How does it always happen when we outlive those we love? Men are foolish who grow old."

"Rather,—men are foolish who hang on other lives! You had children once?"

The old man came forward into the moonlight, and sat himself down on a broken tree-root; he was very grateful to the stranger who had pitied him, he was glad to break his accustomed loneliness and silence by speech.

"I had one child; and I had a young wife whom I loved well. How many years is it since then? I cannot tell: another life, surely,—it looks so long ago. Madelon lived here, —yes, here. It seems strange to think of now. She was so pretty, and so brown, and so blithe; just like one of the robins. And she was always singing; sometimes I hear her voice among the leaves still. We buried her under that pine, —the one with a cross cut out on the bark,—but I always fancy myself that her soul passed into one of the birds. She was always fond of them; they were always fluttering about her. Is it possible, think you?"

He did not wait for an answer: he did not wish his fancy disturbed.

"Madelon had a little daughter; I did not care so much for her. It seemed cruel that when *she* died that life stolen from hers lived on?—you know what it is that I mean? Well, —the child,—Madelon, too, she was named,—grew up; and I was very gentle with her because she had no mother. They said in the forest here, and up at the château, that she was much lovelier than my Madelon had been: it might be so,— she was not so fair in my sight. The child was always happy, singing, too, making chains of berries and flowers, and looking at her own face as she saw it in the lake water. The great people up at the château—this was forty years ago, and more, what I talk of now, and they were very gay and brilliant there then, just as Miladi is now—took a fancy to her, and she went away with one of the princesses, in her service they told me. I was very loth,—I was all alone,— and she had the voice of my Madelon. But she wept, and fretted, and raved, and said she should die in the forest: what could I do? She was just like a bird in a cage; and if I had kept the cage closed she would have given me no song, and men would have said I was cruel. So she went,—pretty volatile thing. Went where?—that is what I cannot tell. She was as blithe in her flight as any young pigeon. I suppose she was happy. The seasons went by; those chestnuts four times were all pink with their buds; four times the brown fruit dropped out of their pods. I never saw Madelon all that time. Day after day I went to the château; I could hear nothing: she was with the princess, they said. I suppose the world is very large, is it not? By-and-by that great lady came again to stay at the château; I saw her face as she rode past one day. By dint of much prayer and entreaty I got to see her,—it was hard work for weeks to do so,—when I spoke with her she could not understand me; those great people have a different tongue to ours; but she was very gentle, and I could see she grieved for me, and she told me through her servant that she had lost sight of Madelon some years: that the girl had been with her but a brief season, and then had grown bad,—bad,—bad,—and had gone to be a rich, wicked woman, with the gold of the nobles. I do not know what I did, what I said, I have forgotten; it is long ago. But they told me I fell down in some fit; and it is true that after that time I was never strong, and my left arm, I could not lift it again. I never blamed the man that misused Madelon, look you; if a woman-child have no heart and no soul, and longs to be vile because she is dull in her home, why,—she is like the nightshade flower, she will bear poison let you plant her where you will. I never blamed him; but I was glad that her mother was dead. And—do you know one thing?—the birds have never sung blithely since."

"Never to you," Tricotrin answered him softly. "And you have heard no more of her?"

"No more. She never came back. Why should she? I am only an old lame man, and for the birds and the trees and the flowers the girl never cared. She was not like my Madelon, who loved them. Yet I am wrong to say I never heard again: I did hear once, twenty or more years after. There came a letter to me; I cannot read, I took it to the curé down in the village yonder, not the one that is there now,—the dead one. He read it out to me: it was from a sailor somewhere in what they call the Riviera. It was a simple kindly letter, to tell me that he was going to wed a pretty child; who he thought was my grandchild by what he knew of her mother's history. The letter had been ten months in finding me; it was ill addressed; the priest replied to it for me, but I never heard again. So whether it was true or not I cannot tell."

"Might I see it?"

"Surely. I have kept it by me."

He went into his hut, and after some minutes' absence, returned with an old yellow paper.

"Here it is. You can read, I dare say?"

Tricotrin took it; and read: it was barely a decipherable scrawl, very clumsily and laboriously written; pathetic through its gentle and homely simplicity. It set forth in few words that the writer was about to become the husband of an orphan girl who was known to be the bastard-daughter of one of the nobles of France, though brought up among the fishing people; it went on to say that her mother had never been seen on that shore, but, dying lately in Paris, had bequeathed her some jewels, a little gold, the declaration that she was her offspring by a princely lover, and the injunction to endeavour to learn whether an old man of the name of Aubin Ralcor was still living in the forests of Lirà; this was signed Madelon Ralcor, commonly known as Pearl Rosalba, and had been dictated from the dying bed of the testatrix. The sailor also wrote that he would die of starvation ere ever he touched the store of gold and gems; but that he earnestly desired to seek out, and be as a son to the old man Aubin Ralcor, whom he supposed the grandsire of his beloved: he subscribed himself in kindly appearing phrase— Jean Bruno.

The letter fell from Tricotrin's hand upon the mossy ground: he sat in silence, gazing out down the silvered avenue of pines: this homely tragedy touched him at every turn, and moved him with its deep-rooted sadness that had darkened three generations. What cruel play of fate's caprices had thus lodged the peace of these men of simple soul, and honest love, in the hands of these women, whose impulses led them from innocence, whose instincts launched them toward vice:—who saw only a wearisome sameness in the passion that clung to them too fondly; who had no other thought than to cheat it, betray it, forsake it? Born from the simple peasant-girl whose grave was made under the cross-marked pine, they had uprisen, like upas-trees, destroying all who rested near them: the old eternal mystery of guilt begot of innocence, of Commodus begot of Antoninus.

He folded up the page and gave it back to Ralcor. What avail was it to deal him the fresh pain of such a story as the sole one he could tell of Bruno's wife—of Coriolis?

"A well-meant, tender letter," he said. "Did you never hear more from him?"

"Never. The priest answered for me, as I say, for I would willingly have seen Madelon's daughter. But whether he ever had the reply or not I cannot tell. No news came from him. It is best so, perhaps. I would rather be left alone with the forest. It knows me as they never could do."

"And is there nothing you desire then?"

"No. I shall be glad to die, that is all."

"And leave your forest?"

"I shall not leave it. They will bury me there by the pine. It will be the same thing, only quieter. To live hardly is all well enough when one is young;—only a crust—what matter? One has the spring of the deer, the heart of the eagle, the speed of the hound. But when one is old,—it is not worth while. The mill takes so much labor to turn; and so little corn comes from it."

With these words he rose, and bade his stranger friend good-night, and went within, and fell upon his knees before his little wooden crucifix, roughly made from two pine-branches, and prayed with the guileless faith of childhood;—half senseless, half sublime.

Tricotrin remained without, in the bright calm moonlight of the forest aisle.

The belling of the deer sounded down the wind; the soft owls flitted through the dusk, the glow-worms glimmered underneath the moss: and far beyond across the woods in the great château, the light, the laughter, the dance, the song, the love-jest passed the hours away as though there were no such memories as crime, or grief, or shame, on earth.

"She is happy," he said, half aloud, to little Mistigri, as he looked at the far-off towers of the mighty place, and mused at the tragedy hidden beneath the simple and obscure lives which on their surface bore only the rough illiterate homeliness of a sailor's and a woodman's toil. "She is happy; what matter the rest? She would have gone to the evil of these women, Mistigri, if she had stayed with us; not for love of the sin or the shame, but for love of the 'great world' she craved, for escape from the peasant-life she detested: she would have been like Madelon, like Coriolis. True: there is scant worth in an honor only reared into growth under the hothouse shade of fair circumstance. But those frail things of womanhood are no stronger than flowers: they grow straightly, or crookedly, as they blossom in fresh air, or foul; and if we only care for a rose we lead it up to the sunlight, we do not stamp it down into the swamp in its bud. I was a coward, perhaps; I feared that her life should ever reproach me. If we had seen her fallen, wretched, cursing men, and by them cursed, what remorse we should have felt—you and I—Mistigri? And yet——"

And yet?

Were the pomp, and the pride, and the careless glory, and the graceful contempt, of the life that she led, so much nobler after all than the sin of Madelon, than the shame of Coriolis? Was not their root the same passion though their blossom was triumph where the other fruit had been bitterness? The one grew as the palm, whose stately height and lordly crown of greenest leaf towered in perpetual summer, the idol of every passer-by: the other grew as the belladonna, whose purple brilliancy of flower turned into the poison that bore death to all toyers with it, cursed aloud as men left it on the highway to be trodden down by each strange foot: but they sprang alike from the same soil of ambitious desire, they were alike fanned by the same winds of impatient and feverish longing.

The one carried a green crown of honor; the other but acrid berries of slaughter; yet the sap feeding their veins was the same—it was the passion of the feminine instinct for pleasure, for gain, and for homage.

The passion that has cursed the earth since the primeval age; as the Hebrew poets saw, even in the days of the world's youth, when they created its parallel and parable in the metaphorical poem of Eve, in the allegorical picture of Eden.

## CHAPTER V.

AT noon the following day he went up the vast flight of steps that led from the gardens to the doors of the magnificent feudal pile, palace and fortress in one, that crowned the brow of the hill throned amid its darkling pine woods.

"The Duchess de Lira is within?" he asked of a group

of footmen, clad in scarlet and white and gold, lounging inside the courts, that were like the great courts of Versailles.

One of them raised his insolent head with a low laugh.

"The duchess left here early to-day; she is gone to the royal marriage at Madrid."

He turned and passed away down the great marble stairs, without answer.

"What could that fellow want with our lady?" said the footman to his peers. "If she had been here she would never have seen him—a strolling player with a fiddle at his back."

## CHAPTER VI.

THE snow fell once more thickly over the roofs and streets of the City of Paris.

In the little by-lane of the Latin quarter wherein Mère Rose had dwelt, all the quaint angles and gables and jutting angles were white with the fallen flakes; all the leaded dusky panes were glittering yet dim with frost; the empty linnet's cage had icicles around it, in lieu of the lime or the lilac bough that had used to hang above it. Mère Rose was dead; and the linnet was dead also. The casements of the coffee-house were closed against the sharpness of the cold; there were no music in the streets, no laugh on the crisp air, for the populace of this quarter were exceeding poor, and suffered greatly in the winter-time; across the road at the window where the grisette had been wont to sit, sewing her rose-colored skirt for a students' ball, the shutters were fastened, the owners of the dwelling were gone to prison for debts that they owed for bread and vegetables.

Though it was the first morning of a new year, there were no mirth, no gayety, no greetings, little movement, in the passage way: there were only a ragged child raking in the snow for bits of offal, and a fat, pampered cat, the savage pet of a butcher, watching to seize a bird, whose half-frozen, heavily-weighted wings dragged it slowly through the descending snow.

Tricotrin stood at his garret lattice and looked down awhile upon the desolation. It was the day of the city's uttermost rejoicing; but there was no rejoicing here.

Even the elastic mirth of the national temper was killed under the cold and the hunger, that came with a season of almost unexampled severity.

Like the attic of Teufelsdröckh, "in the highest house of the Wahngasse," it was his watch-tower whence he "could behold all the life circulation of the city." With Teufelsdröckh he could say, "I look down into that wasp nest, or beehive, and witness their wax-laying, and honey-making, and poison brewing, and choking by sulphur. From the palace esplanade where music plays while serene highness is pleased to eat his victuals, down the low lane, where, in her door-sill, the aged widow, knitting for a thin livelihood, sits to feel the afternoon sun, I see it all."

Saw it—with that far-reaching, clear, penetrating vision which belongs only to that mind which men, for want of a better name, have called the poet's; which by the infinitude of sympathy attains to the infinitude of comprehension; which understands all, because it feels all things; and which withholds the largeness of its justice, and the insight of its tenderness, as little from the palace as from the hovel, from the throes of ambition as from the travail of poverty.

He looked out, from his attic window, upon the snowy morning:—the ragged child fled away with a scream as an old tin pot was flung at his head from a doorway near, with a shower of curses; the cat bounced on the frozen, fluttering bird, that gave its life up with scarcely an effort at resistance.

A little way farther on, the child, having been punished while innocent, deemed it as well to be guilty, and snatched a roll from a baker's stall unperceived, and darted out of sight with his theft; the cat having been successful in killing her prey, choked herself with the broken bones and bloody feathers, yet beat off with tooth and talon a weakly kitten that crept timidly near her for the scraps of ruffled plumage that were left.

"So the year begins!" he thought, "with two fables set in motion,—the famine that is turned to guilt by unjust punishment, the greed that success makes savage and venomous. Between them they make up the world! And here, one pities the lad, one is enraged with the cat, but neither our pity nor our rage will make up the lost loaf to the baker, or the lost life to the bird. There is the toughest puzzle of the problem. Neither our compassion nor our anger are of much use after all."

The half-entangled metaphorical fancies drifted idly through his brain, as the baker discovered his missing roll with outcries and lamentations, and the cat dealt its feeble fellow a final stroke that sent it shrieking into a cellar.

Thus the year commenced on the chill, bleak, biting morning of its first day.

He turned from the lattice as a small, pale, black-eyed maiden brought him his coffee and roll. He gave her a little piece of silver.

"Here, Flore—take that to your friend, Réné, over the way. Tell him I saw a lad run off with one of his loaves just this moment; and I know he can ill afford to lose it with wheat at the price it is, and his two old people to keep all the winter through."

The girl nodded, and went off, willingly and with a bright laugh: the baker was a favorite with her, a good-hearted laborious youth from the Cévennes, who had hard work to maintain, singlehanded, two helpless aged women, one blind, the other paralyzed,—his mother and grandmother, who, if ever his breadshop should be closed, would be turned out upon public charity. Réné loved the black eyes of the little Flore right well: but there was no chance that he could marry her, while those two old women should sit on either side of his stove, needing all the warmth its scanty fuel could yield.

He got no gratitude, and no thanks for it: the two women muttered and crooned against him, day and night, because the room was so small, the tiled floor so cold, the coffee so rough, the sugar so scanty, the bread so stale, the soup so flavorless: but he went on uncomplainingly with the execution of his duty to them, in that almost unconscious self-sacrifice which is one of the best and purest things found under the "sulphur-chokings" of the lives of the poor.

When the girl was gone, Tricotrin broke off a great piece of his own roll, and scattered it in crumbs upon his window-sill, and on the stone ledge that ran beneath it: the robins and the sparrows soon fluttered to the feast.

"There!" he said to Mistigri, with a laugh. "Do you see, little one? That is just about the measure of all we social philosophers ever contribute to the redressing of the world's wrong-doings—save one starving songster out of a million, and amend one theft out of ten thousand millions! A fine thing to crow over and be proud of, truly! Perhaps the cat is the wiser moralist of all of us, after all,—'I am fat, I have talons, I can be cunning and strong at once, and therefore I can be successful,' she says. 'Why should a little wretched bird, half dead already, with drenched wings, and maw empty of food, not perish to give me a succulent morsel?' That is the cat's argument: it is the argument of the *tyrannis* everywhere. And the birds, somehow or other, always leave the safety of their high roof-tops, and their ambient air, to come down where the cat sits; because, though within reach of her claws, they thus get warmth, and crumbs, and wool for their nests, where she is. And so the nations ever leave their liberties, and their simplicities, and their hardy freedoms, and the roof-tops of their republics if by chance they have ever flown so far, to cluster round some fierce *tyrannis*, subtle and strong in one; because though they are pecked and slain by talon and fang to sate insatiate greed, they find food easier to be got, and the wherewithal to line their nests more abundant, where a despot feeds his mob into a proletariat, than where there were only the freedom of the air and the elevation of the mountain-tops. The cat kills, aye; but each foolish bird deems that he himself will have the good luck to escape her, and each comes down to fatten on the refuse she has left on her plate as a lure for him. There is always the cat for the sparrow—the *tyrannis* for the republic,—that once has learnt to covet!"

And with that piece of political apologue to Mistigri, he gave her a cup of hot milk, from which she drank with dainty lady's ways, and which she enjoyed more than she did the political moralizing, and betook himself to his own breakfast.

It was noon; and he had long before given his new-year greeting to the household, and tendered and received the simple gifts which, in this quarter, carried alike a pleasure and a sincerity unknown where gold went by handfuls to the buying of treasures made worthless and wearisome by hackneyed custom.

There was one gift that had made his own heart quicken with a throb of rejoicing.

It had come to him late on the previous night, brought by the hands of a sturdy youth of the shores of Finisterre, who had wandered, in self-will, and on the spur of a young man's vague ambitions and discontent, up to the great city; with some such seething impatience and aspiration in his soul as were once in the lion-heart of the farmer's son from Arcis-sur-Aube. It stood now above the stove, in the lofty whitewashed barren garret, wherein the Greek Canaris had once been fed and succored, and the Waif of the Loire had once dreamed her dreams over her roasting chestnuts. It was the model of a ship, cut out of oak that was dark as ebony from long burial beneath sea-water: it had been carved with exceeding skill and patience, with no better instruments than a rude clasp-knife and an oyster-shell ground to a fine edge; and had been polished with the sands of the shore till it shone like black marble, where it stood against the whitewashed wall.

On it was cut:

"RIOZ TO TRICOTRIN."

It had been the work of several long winters, shaped to the measure of the beating sea, fashioned to the dies iræ of the storm wind.

To every other eye it was a toy, something clumsily made, perchance, as by a fisherman's rough hands and ill-suited tools; the mere model in old wreck-wood of a fishing-smack. But to him it bore a story of a life redeemed, of a life conquered, of a life saved from the hell of its own passions by justice and by patience—a story of self-conquest as great, of self-denial as strong, of travail with temptation as bitter, of expiation in pain as long-enduring, as were ever symbolized by the white crucifix above cathedral altars.

It had come far to him; come from that iron-bound, furious, terrific coast upon the western waters, where he had dwelt for three years asunder from the world, and away from all its beauty and its joy, that he might drag one human life from the blackness of its guilt as he would have dragged it from the seizure of the waves.

It had come far to him from that old Armorican shore; and it had moved him strangely; speaking to him with a voice that he alone could hear.

"Chut! Mistigri," he said softly, as his eyes fell on it where he sat. "I was wrong to say there are only the cat and the sparrows, only the tyrannis and the proletariat;—are there not ever, if we will only look for them, some battle to be fought, some patience to be needed, some vileness to be wrestled with, some greatness to be rescued? Bah, little one! If we only all remembered that, and occupied ourselves with that, we should be doing more good than by raving about the cat's talons, and blaming the sparrows for not living on hilltops like eagles!"

Mistigri finished her milk, inattentive to his discourse; in her secret heart she sympathized much with the cats, little with the sparrows, not at all with the eagles. Mistigri had been reared in the atmosphere of republicanism; like many democrats by education, she only really admired the "tyrannis," and had she lived in the days of Dictatorship, would have sat upon Sulla's shoulder.

Tricotrin rose, put on his loose coat of furs, thrust her gently into its breast pocket, and went out into the snow.

The kitten which had been driven away had returned, and having eaten up the blood-flecked feathers had set itself to watch upon its own account.

"There!" murmured Tricotrin to the monkey. "You see that is always the way—it is never the *tyrannis* that is the sole evil; there are always the blood-suckers that seize what the chief talon has spared, there are always the followers and imitators who multiply one evil into a hundred. The hill-tops are cold, my good friend-sparrows, but believe me they are far better."

The proletarian sparrows, however, disregarded him, and continued to put themselves within cats' reach, for sake of the crumbs of food left on the platter, as he turned out of the passage-way and took his road to cross the river into the aristocratic quarters of Paris.

These were thronged, busy, mirthful, glittering, with the gay crowds of holiday-makers and gift-buyers; he paid no heed to anything he saw upon the way, not loitering as his habit was for jest, or act, or indolent amusement with the humorous of the town, but pressing straight onward into the patrician parts he sought.

His eyes were eager, anxious, clouded, sunlit, all at once: like the eyes of one who goes to what is half anguish and half ecstasy.

He paused at length before the massive metal gates of a great court.

In years long gone by, when, in scorching midsummer weather the blood of men had been heated to fever-heat, and broken into sanguinary act as over-ripe grass breaks into flame, a great mob had beaten in with maddened blows those strong-wrought brazen gates, and forced themselves into the court within, and spread over it like a flood, and sworn to sack and burn all that they beheld. And they had been driven back by him, scourged with his scornful rebuke as with the stripes of a whip, as he saved the Lirà Palace from destruction.

Now he went thither—doubtful how he should gain admittance through the flippant, idle, insolent herd of lackeys and of pages that lounged through their indolent days in its halls and corridors.

"Your duchess is visible?" he asked of them, as crossing the great court he entered the first hall, lofty, vaulted, all of white marble, with only touches of dead gold and of deep purple to break its purity and vastness.

"She is come from Spain; but she will not be likely to receive you!" said one of the group of pages, with sneering impudence, glancing at the new-comer, whom he recognized as a mad bohemian, whom the people cherished, but who was never seen anywhere save in hovels, and wine-shops, and thieves' haunts, and artists' attics.

"That question is not for you to ask or to decide," said Tricotrin, tranquilly. "Go—and tell your mistress that I am here."

"And who may 'I' be?" scoffed the page, incensed at the tone and at the words.

"Tricotrin," he answered simply. "Play no longer with phrases; do your errand, and bring me word what her pleasure is."

The page loitered, sorely inclined to test the patience of his adversary under insolence and torment; but something fearful of such self-indulgence, sent the message through other servants to her chamberlain, who took it sullenly, not without reluctance and wonder; though he was aware that the new-comer had been held in high esteem by his late master, and had done him great service in days of revolution.

The chamberlain passed through several chambers, picture-cabinets, and reception-rooms, and entered at length an apartment looking on the gardens at the back of the hôtel; an octagon, all azure, and silver, and tempered light, and delicate fragrance, with walls after Boucher, and the laughing Hours imitated from Correggio dancing in a joyous band around the ceiling.

Sunk among cushions was the most lovely woman of her time and of her court. The fire gleams flashed on the silk folds of skirts, whose negligence was the supreme perfection of art: her fair hands glowed with rings; and as she glanced at a book that lay upon her lap, she toyed with a Polichinelle, whose bells were of gold, whose tambourine was circled with pearls, and who had cost that morning seven hundred francs.

Around her were strewn jewel caskets, bonbon boxes, bouquets, playthings, marvelous in ingenuity and extravagance, fans of every make and of inconceivable costliness, all that fancy could fashion, and riches be wasted on; as though every shop in Paris had been emptied there, in the lavishness of the new-year offerings. And at a third of them she had not looked.

There is a wild and wayward destiny in life which ever loads fruition with satiety.

Lost in languid, sunny, victorious musing, she did not hear her servant's entrance until he had approached her, and spoken the few words of the message with hesitating deference, and scarcely concealed expectancy of a refusal.

She started slightly, and over her face swept for a moment a shadow of annoyance, mingled with another feeling that her astute attendant could not analyze. Both were instantly banished; she answered with tranquil indifference,

"Certainly. Admit him here."

Her chamberlain backed out from her presence, filled with a curiosity that he dared not utter. A few minutes went by, then into her chamber was ushered,—one, who to her conscience, her memory, and her life, was a Reproach.

He bent his head before her, and stood still, without advancing, while the attendants closed the door behind him.

She, with a flush over the fairness of her brow, rose with her hands outstretched, her rich silks and laces trailing round her, her loveliness shrined in the dazzling heaps of her strewn new-year gifts. Her first impulse was of proud shameful pain; her next of conscience-stricken and awakening loyalty.

He shaded his eyes one moment with his hand with the gesture of one whom the sun blinds, then came to her and took her own hands in his in silence. There was no one near to witness how a bohemian was received by a great lady.

"Viva!"—that was all he said; but in the single word was a caress and a benediction beyond all that longer utterance could have given.

She, a proud and splendid woman, in the plenitude of power, and the dauntlessness of empire, shrank slightly as she heard it; it was fraught with all that she would have buried in oblivion forever; it recalled all that galled, and fretted, and embittered her cloudless and haughty life. With that word came back to her all the shame she burned to ignore and forget, as though it had never been; it brought with it all the echoes of that early and innocent affection to which she had so long been faithless and disloyal.

She was cold, while she knew coldness so base; she was restless under his gaze, though she knew that so much love looked on her in it; she was stung with impatience and with false pride, though she knew that in him she saw the savior of her existence.

It had been years since she had beheld him, and in those years the power of the world and the poison of vanity had eaten far into the purer gold of her nature.

"It is so long since I have seen you!" she murmured, as she drew her hands from his hold gently, and sank among the cushions of her couch, turning her eyes upon him.

"Nay,—not longer than is best," he answered her, with a tremor in his voice. "You had seen me oftener had you missed the sight of me. But that was not probable; not possible."

She hurriedly began to utter the denial that courtesy compelled and gratitude required.

He stopped her with a gesture, slight, but of authority.

"Hush! No disclaimer against truth out of courtesy to me. Think you I cease to know your heart better than you know it yourself? You forgot me; it was natural, inevitable. Why not?—why not?"

There was an unconscious pathos and wistfulness in his accent; as though, against himself and his rights which arraigned her, he pleaded excuse for the negligence and the ingratitude of the one who owed him her rescue from the grave.

Her eyelids fell; her forehead flushed; the imperial coquette felt humbled in her own sight.

"You deem me very base," she murmured.

"Base? No. Only,—a woman! Long ago did I not tell thee how it would be with me and thee? I knew the world's work. Thou didst not,—then. But *I* do not blame thee, Viva."

His phrase had changed insensibly into the familiar "thou;" and his eyes, as they dwelt upon her, had the yearning love of lover, husband, father, poet, all blended in one passion,—a passion mighty as death, and which would live and die, holding eternal silence.

Her cheeks burned as she heard, she breathed quickly with agitation: at the sound of his voice the old, warm, reverent tenderness stirred from its embers in her heart; and yet,—it seemed so hard that one should live who knew what she had been, it seemed so bitter that one should look on her who could remember her the child of charity!

He watched her, reading well her thoughts; and gazing at the marvelous change wrought in her; at the perfection, as of some superb tropical flower, to which her early promise had expanded, at the magic whereby the fair child that he had known had altered into this magnificent patrician.

A young girl, lovely as a poet's ideal of Gretchen, had been crowned by the Loire-side queen of the vintage-feast: but a woman, superb as a sculptor's dream of Aspasia, was before him now. He gazed at her long, then turned away as with a sudden pang of unbearable agony.

"Good God! How changed you are!"

She smiled, a dreamy, haughty, careless smile. She knew it well, and was proud of the change that to him was so bitter. Yet something in the phrase jarred on her: she had so long tried to forget that she had ever been otherwise than what she was now, that the trial had brought success with herself, and self-persuasion had almost induced self-deception.

And she did not heed, or did not even divine, the anguish that change bore for him.

It was never betrayed. She knew well that he loved her: but she never dreamed how he loved her. It was a martyrdom, without even the reward of recognition.

"I could scarcely be otherwise than changed," she answered him musingly. "Do you know—do you know—it seems scarcely possible to me that I could ever have been the child *you* knew and succored?"

"Does it?" he replied, gently; for he never lost gentleness to her, however deeply she might wound him. "That is very natural, I dare say. Yes; it is inevitable you should be changed; and in much more than mere form. You have a lofty station, Viva!"

"Yes,"—her delicate brows contracted; the Duchess de Lirà, whom none ever addressed save by titles of dignity and reverence, could have wished that familiar pet-name of her childhood, that relic of her foundling's estate, dropped out forever into oblivion.

"You have the whole of the Lirà properties?" he asked.

"Every acre; every sou. He had not a living relative. He could will them where he would." .

"His was a great nature—a noble nature."

"He was most generous,—yes."

"Did he suffer much?"

"Not much—I trust. He died in my absence; but calmly, and painlessly, they assured me."

"You regretted him?"

The color flushed her face again.

"Not so much as I ought; I knew that well at the time. I regretted his mother's death far more. I grew to love her well, and she loved me—"

"But so did he—God knows!"

"Ah, yes!—far more than I merited, you would say. That I am sure. But one cannot love merely *because* one is loved, you know? He was most good, most gentle, most thoughtful for me, and I owed him very much; but—"

"He was nothing to you! No; you have had too much tenderness in your life to know its worth. You are surfeited with it, and it is valueless. Had you had but a few crumbs instead of such abundant banquets, you would feel very differently. Bread is tasteless to the rich man; but bread to the poor man is as the apples of paradise. He was aware that you cared nothing for him?"

"He must have been so. I never used dissimulation. They made me very happy, and I liked them—thus; but I never professed attachment I did not feel. Besides—I have no belief in that idyllic folly they call 'love!'"

"You have not?"——she had no belief in love, while over her life watched a love exhaustless, unrepaid, purified to sublimity, and free from one murmur of reproach against her!

She looked quickly up at him.

"Of what are you thinking?"

"Shall I tell you?"

"Surely."

"Well—I thought that the foundling, who was mine, would have flung back, as disgrace and insult, the bribe of a silver coin that should have been offered her to purchase a single kiss from her lips. But the aristocrat, with whose life I have nothing to do, had so little of that true pride left, that she saw no shame in bartering for gold and rank all her youth, all her beauty, all her soul!"

The simplicity of the words had a grand rebuke, a rebuke that stung her keenly. She had enough still in her of the temper which had made her loathe her young lover's golden toys, to make her now feel every barb of the censure to the quick.

"You blame me because I am married!" she murmured, with an impatient irritation.

"Because you married without love. The woman who does so sells herself as utterly as, and little less basely than, the courtesan."

She gave a languid gesture of offence. Truth lay in his words; and unwelcome truth, with its severity and its nakedness, was an outrage that never approached her graceful presence.

"You speak strongly on a singular subject," she answered, coldly. "I am not accustomed to such language. I view marriage as the world, I believe, views it; and at the time of my own you were informed of it, and you offered no objections——"

"I bade you do as you desired. It was not for me to stand between you and the magnificence you coveted and could obtain. You knew what I thought, full well. But I have not come hither to upbraid you for that which is past. I pitied the man who spent his whole soul on you, and bought your loveliness through his wealth, and found that, squander what he would, he could not buy one throb of tenderness, one pulse of warmth! I pitied him from my heart——"

"Others envied him!"

There were all the insolence of supreme vanity, all the sovereignty of supreme triumph, in the accent with which the brief phrase was uttered.

"They might do so. I was not among them," he answered, gravely. "He purchased a bird without a song, a rose without fragrance, a sun without warmth. For—he bought your beauty without a soul! And you left him to die in your absence!"

Her white, delicate teeth bit the lower lip of her bow-like mouth. She moved impatiently, contemptuously. She,—whom none ever crossed or contradicted in her slightest whim or caprice,—to be arraigned and censured by a wanderer, a bohemian, an outcast! For thus in her thoughts she classed now the redeemer of her life.

"You are angered because I say this thing," he pursued. "I will say more. You chose to wed with him because he was noble, he was of great riches, he could give you a lofty station——"

"Who else would have done so?" she interrupted him passionately. "You forget! I had no name, no parentage, though means were found to hide this, and give me in semblance foreign origin; there was not another of such rank as his that could have wedded one under such social ban as mine without exposure of it; there was not another who could have concealed the truth from the world as he could, nor from whom it could have been withheld."

"No; and therefore for that cause you sold yourself to him. I repeat the word that galls you so greatly. But it is precisely because this man loved you so tenderly, so generously, so patiently, that your sin against him was so dark. You took all, and repaid him nothing in the only coin you had to give; and when he died you were only—in your heart—content to be so soon left free, to be so soon unchained to enjoy all the possessions that he gave without the burden on them of their giver's life."

She was silent; but the hand which had let fall the Polichinelle beat impatiently on the mosaic table beside her couch, and a shadow of vehement offence, mingled with something of repentance and of consciousness, darkened her fair and serene face. She knew that he read her soul with all his olden accuracy; she knew that he spoke what was but the simple truth.

She glanced at him, and felt steal on her the wonder

which, since she had known the world, had often come across her mind, as to whence arose that strange and strong unlikeness betwixt his fortunes and his bearing.

She — grown keenly critical, scornfully indifferent, and very difficult to impress — was struck as she had never been with the authority, the dignity, the kingliness of his manner, the pure accent of his voice, the careless grace of his movements. In her early years this question had never occurred to her. She had had no standard with which to compare him: now she wondered, in this first moment of his entrance to her, whence he came, how he had become what he was, — this man who was without grade and without home, who lived among the peasantry, the populace, the fisher-people, who was an itinerant and a socialist, yet who had about him a command monarchs might have envied, and a beauty that painters might have given to an Agamemnon.

Once, when she had still been his, the story of his life had been upon his lips to tell her. The impulse had been repressed, the tale remained untold forever.

"Why did you never come to me while my husband lived!" she asked him suddenly.

Now and again she had seen him; seen him as he sold the Italian boy's images to the populace, as he stood outside the gates of the Tuileries that she quitted, as she rode through a German pine-forest, as she drove through a Lombardic city, as she watched the Roman Carnival from her balcony, as she glided over the ice of the Neva to the music of her silver sleigh-bells. She had seen him often — ever with a strange flush, a strange pang, a strange emotion of mingled sorrow and delight, tenderness and shame. But from the time that he had heard of her marriage, he had never approached her.

The unloved lord who, heaping all his treasures on her, yet could not win one soft thought from her, divined through sympathy the reason of this absence. She never did. So little did she comprehend his motive that she, in all her eminence, in all her brilliancy, felt oftentimes a pained and passionate anger that this man, whom still in her soul she loved as she had loved no other living creature, should thus withhold himself from witnessing her glories.

"Why did you never come?" she repeated, with imperious persistency. "The duke held you in warm esteem, in high honor—you know that!"

"I do not think my absence lessened either his esteem or his honor. I never came to you because—because—no matter why! I acted as I deemed best. You need not question that."

She was stilled and vaguely disquieted by the reply. Even yet, despite the lapse of years, he possessed an influence over her that no other had ever attained.

"You lead a brilliant life?" he pursued, desirous to turn aside from the subject on which she pressed him.

"I lead the customary life of my station."

She hesitated a moment; the thought crossed her mind, could not she pay by Power the debt that Gratitude had left unpaid? Was there no benefit possible from her high position and vast influence that might strike the balance between them, and do something to lessen that weight of obligation which it so galled her proud throat to bear?

But the mere thought looked insult to him. She did not dare to utter it aloud.

"I saw something of the fashion in which you seek to make the hours fly, down at your castle in the south," he continued. "I arrived there too late to have an interview with you there. You were gone to the royal marriage in Spain; but I heard much of you on your estate, much of the magnificence of your hospitalities——"

She turned her head with that smile wherewith she was accustomed to deal as she chose with the souls of men.

"Do not be content with hearsay of them. Let them be shown to, and tested by, yourself. That will give me far more pleasure."

It was a courtly, graceful, elegant utterance; but it struck cold as ice to his heart. There was no warmth in it; there was only the polished suavity of conventional courtesy.

"I have never sat at any gold-laden table. I shall not commence with yours," he said curtly. "Why let us deal in this hypocrisy? You know as well as I—I as well as you —that it would only be irritation and ignominy to you to see me among your guests. You could not account for me; you would have to present me as 'Tricotrin, the bohemian,' you would be compelled to admit that I had no friends except the People,—no, I know your nature far too well, and that of the world you live in, to impose any such penalty and penance upon you. You see—I can have some sympathy with the class to which you belong—I can even sympathize with its false shame!"

The contemptuous bitterness of his answer stung the latent truth in her into life; she was pained by it, and the natural frankness of her temper broke into speech.

"Ah!" she said, with involuntary self-scorn, "there you do *them* wrong, not me. If I had been born and reared in their rank, I should not know that 'false shame.' The Order never has it: it is far too proud of itself. An hereditary prince may shake hands with a beggar, he cannot lose rank thereby; it is the new-comer into honors and splendors who dares not imperil his fresh titles by touching the beggar, lest the world cry, 'see—he runs to his brother!'"

He looked at her earnestly.

"You have the acuteness and the sarcasm in you to see this," he said, "and yet——"

"And yet I am no better than what I satirize! Is that an uncommon fault in your Juvenals and Voltaires and Swifts? So—you heard of me in the south. What do my people say?"

And despite the momentary self-dissection in which she had lashed herself scornfully as an alien, and adventuress, in the great order to which she now belonged, there were all the royalty of possession, all the negligence of command, in the intonation of those words, "my people." In such a tone might Maria Theresa have spoken!

"Your people?" he echoed, with a certain ironic disdain

that cut her pride hardly. "Well, they talk of your splendid entertainments; you do not give them much else to talk of, I believe, except it be of the extortions and oppressions of your stewards."

"Extortions! Oppressions! I never heard of any."

"Doubtless. How should you hear? If a wood-cutter or a charcoal-burner, grimy, starved, and half clad, found his way on to your terraces to accuse your great servants of peculation and tyrannies, which would he be likeliest to get —a blow from a lackey's wand if he did not shuffle away quickly enough, or a polite ushering in to your audience-chamber?"

She smiled a little, but vexatiously.

"Well! Would you have my rooms thronged all day with a mob of foresters and burrowers in the earth?"

"There is a time for all things. There can be hours set apart for such hearings. It is just that barring out of the unjustly-oppressed from the audience-room, when they are only armed with an appeal, that brings, sooner or later, the clamorous mob, armed with clubs and pikes, into the banqueting-hall. It is not the nobles' fault, it is the fault of their hirelings: for none are so brutal to the poor as those who have once been of them. You have the same stewards that the Duke de Lira employed, I suppose?"

She colored a little.

"Not in the south. The person he had left in office there opposed my will in one or two matters: one does not pay servants to have them dispute, discuss, advise, and finally disobey. I discharged him; and obtained one who knew his place better."

"Who gives you lip-service and the form of obedience that lies in servility; and makes your name hated throughout your estates, by wringing subsidies from the poverty-stricken for his own private purse: yes—I dare say that is knowing his place better! As modern enlightenment goes. But— despite your sanction of his reign—I shall be glad if you will take some pity on an old truffle hunter in your woods. He is very old, and lame; can live only a few years at most; and having dwelt on the Lirà estates from his birth upward, may claim to have the trouble of keeping his body and soul together made somewhat easier to him. Besides, he has a piteous story."

"Assuredly. I will direct them to see that he wants for nothing. Will you give me his name?"

"It is Aubin Ralcor."

She noted it down on the little ivory tablet hanging by its gold chain at her side. She did not ask the old man's history, so he left it unrelated. He felt that the memory of Coriolis must still be painful and unwelcome to her.

"You know, I have been but little in our own country," she pursued, as though in apology for her ignorance of the necessities of the poor upon her lands. "We were occasionally in Paris, but far oftener abroad. The year after the duke's death I passed in retirement in my villa upon Como. The only time I have been at the castle I have been surrounded for a few weeks only with a circle of guests that left me little time for thought. This summer I entertained the king of——but you know all these things?"

She broke off somewhat hastily, with a sense of anger, that nothing in her dignities or in her splendors could move him to surprise at, or to veneration of them.

"Yes," he answered her. "There is nothing in your life I do not know."

"But how? I have met you so rarely."

"That may easily be. You would probably have discerned me, had your thoughts been of me. Anyhow I have watched you—many times. But I do not want to talk of myself; here is your oldest friend whom you have not yet seen."

She started as the monkey sprang forth from where it had slumbered in his pocket: the sight of the little animal recalled so many memories in such vivid intensity.

She covered her eyes with her hand for awhile, and breathed rapidly and with emotion. She was once more a child on the banks of the sunny Loire: she saw once more

the innocent and lowly home from which she had gone
without one backward glance of gratitude or of regret. She
was moved more keenly than she had been for many years.

But her life had taught her to conquer and conceal all
agitation; she was quick to recover her habitual calm and
negligence.

She stretched out her jeweled hands full of sweetmeats
from the new-year boxes.

"Ah, little Mistigri! She is still alive! How old she must
be by now! Mistigri, will you not eat my sugared almonds?"

Mistigri was either shy or cross: she would not be cajoled
into touching one of the dainty, pretty, colored crystals of
sugar: she did not recognize her old playmate, for whose
rescue she had once voted with her filbert, in this brilliant
aristocrat who held her out these bonbons.

"Mistigri does not know you," he said quietly, stroking
the little black averted head. "Well! the world of Paris has
emptied itself upon you in your new-year gifts. And what
pleasure do they give you—all these jeweled cases, all these
splendid trifles?"

She smiled: the smile that in his eyes had no light.

"Pleasure! Do you think me a child still, to take pleasure
in those bagatelles; they are only custom."

"Ah! And yet to have such things of custom, or the like,
men will barter their honesty and women their honor. That
is droll! Which is the richer? he who has but little but enjoys all, or he who has much but with all is sated? A few
years since how your heart panted for such 'bagatelles.' Yet,
then a wreath of river-lilies, a leaf full of wild strawberries,
made you glad. Which was the richer—your present or
your past?"

"Which? How strange a question! There can be little
doubt, I imagine. Though I have lost a child's love for new-
year presents, there are many——"

"Costlier toys? Men's love and peace and honor? Yes:
there are, for women such as you. But, Duchess Viva, once
you broke and trod upon a grape garland, and when you had

destroyed it, wept vain tears over the bruised leaves. Take heed you never do so with a life."

"The poor grape garland!" she said, with a careless, low laugh, avoiding the rest of his speech. "I remember it, and my foolish passion, too; but it reminds me to ask you—the dear old woman—'grand'mère,'—is she well?"

"Yes. She is well," he answered gravely.

"She has always had my money—my presents?" she asked hurriedly, a hot flush coming and going on her face.

"Yes: she received them."

"And was pleased with them? I sent them regularly, but she could not write to tell me whether she liked them."

"You remember the walnut press in her little bedroom?"

"I think I do—yes."

"Well; in it lie all your gold and all your gifts. She would not pain you by returning them: but neither would she use alms from one who, for so many years, has never cared to look upon her face. You have yet to learn that money cannot heal a wound that negligence has dealt; and that there are some debts which cannot be repaid in coin."

The color deepened in her face, conscience in her warred with irritated pride.

"That is absurd," she murmured. "I never forgot to supply her with what she needed——"

"She needed nothing, except the one thing you never gave her."

"I should have gone to see her," she said rapidly, with an unconscious accent of apology and self-excuse. "But—so many things engaged me; at first I was so entirely under their rule, and latterly I have been abroad so very much. I will go down and visit her soon—as soon as the days are somewhat brighter."

"You have said that long: and—she has eighty-nine years. The spring does not always bring new life to the old and leafless trees."

She was silent: he had stirred her heart, but he did not move her pride.

He took up the Polichinelle, true to his habits of saying no useless words; and he was reluctant to seek for the brave old woman the remembrance that was not instinctive and born of gratitude.

"My old friend Punchinello?" he said, "all jeweled and gold-laden, too: well, puppets as empty, and less harmless and mirth-giving than he, have eaten up the nation's gold often ere now. A handsome puppet, moreover, which all crowned marionettes are not."

"I bought it for a little Russian prince—the son of great friends of mine."

"Ah! And it cost?"

"Seven hundred francs."

Tricotrin shook the toy lightly, till the little turquoise-studded bells rang a chime.

"So, Punch!—you lie in a silk and eider-down box, and cost seven hundred francs. Fie, fie! Why, you are almost as costly and useless as a king!—you, too, who have made fun for the people everywhere ever since the days of Rome. Punch—the Russian boy will break you in ten minutes; and outside the gates yonder I met a girl, once your mistress's playmate, Edmée Roxal, whose son lies dead in her arms because she had not money to buy him a loaf. Contrasts are sharp in this world, Punch! and the populace that you have wagged your head for through so many generations has always got steel or shot if it ventured to find that out, and object to it once in awhile."

She looked up; and shook hurriedly out a shower of gold from her purse.

"Edmée Roxal!—her child dead of want! How fearful! Give her these!"

He put them gently back.

"No. They are not wanted now. Money will not buy back from King Death. And—for Edmée herself; she lies in hospital, delirious, clinching the stiffened limbs of the infant to her breast. Neither you nor Polichinelle can help that:

only—when you give so much for him and his kind,—think of these things, and of your safe haven from them!"

"But we never do think of these things!"

There were carelessness, regret, impatience, apology, all in the words: she, beautiful, luxurious, adored, had wholly ceased to remember that a time had been when "these things" would have been her portion also, in all their cruelty and nakedness, had not his hand been stretched to rescue her.

"True," he said, simply, "you never do."

To him it was not possible to recall that time to her; since, to awaken her soul to gratitude for the mercies of her fate, he must also have called on gratitude for himself.

"But when this girl—Edmée—is well again, let me give her all that can comfort her!—give it through you!" she said quickly. "You will say nothing of who I am——"

"I promised you silence long ago. I never justified you in supposing that my promises were given to be broken."

There was a sternness in the answer that moved her with a certain sense that was almost as of fear: the greatness, the singularity, the mysteries of this life, that had so long been interwoven with her own, bewildered her: she could not comprehend them.

He rose; and stood before her, gazing at her with a look under which her eyes sank. Little by little she had been drawn away from him, till between them scarcely a bond remained. The thought crossed him—would he after all have been so selfishly in error, so blind through the mists of passion, if he had kept her, through her ignorance, in his own hands, under his own law and love? Would he not have made her happiness purer, her life truer, her future safer, because nearer God, than they now were; brilliant, imperious, pampered, exquisite creature though she was? She was great, she was lovely, she was content, she was unrivaled; but where was that "divine nature" wherewith he had once believed her dowered?

"Where are your thoughts now?" she asked him once

again; restless beneath that fixed and melancholy regard which she could not meet.

A sigh escaped him as he answered:

"Pondering whether the Duchess de Lirà, great in all magnificence though she be, may not after all be poorer than was the child Viva, happy in the simple wealth of the honey, and the chestnuts, and the violets from the woods!"

"I could wish you could permit me to forget that such a child ever lived!"

The impatient and cruel words were uttered, heedless how they struck him, in a moment of haughty wrath that this obscure and nameless past could be quoted against her, that in her path of roses this one thorn should be still beneath her feet. She had ever clung passionately to the belief of some mighty origin having given her birth: for the last years she had shut out from her own sight the remembrance that she had ever been other than she now was. She spoke on the spur of pride, selfishness, offended dignity: she did not feel the baseness and the cowardice of her utterance.

His mouth quivered under the fullness of its snowy silken beard.

"Have I seemed to remind you of it? Forgive me. There is nothing for *you* to remember;—farewell!"

He bowed his head; and laid down upon her hands a cluster of white and purple violets; lovelier amid the darkness of their broad round leaves, than all the jeweled trifles of art and fashion strewn about her.

"Others give you gold and diamonds," he said wearily. "I have nothing but these. Only,—remember for once enough of your childhood to take them from me as I give."

He turned quickly from her to spare himself and her all need of answer; but the love which had once lived so strongly in her heart was not wholly petrified into death; the nature which had been so long attuned to his, could not but vibrate in some measure to his touch.

She rose swiftly; the look of bygone years in her eyes, the accent of bygone years in her voice. She stretched her hands out to him with all the sweet and contrite grace of her early penitence and supplication.

"Oh! do not think me so vile as I make myself seem! I have not forgotten; I never forget in my heart. It is the world that makes me sin against you; the coldest, vainest, basest, weakest part of me. I know how cold, how false, how guilty I must seem to you; and I have been so! But these flowers are dearer to me than all their jewels, and for my crimes to you I hate myself. To meet you thus,—to be severed from you thus,—to live as though I owed you nothing,—as though I had forgotten your matchless goodness, your infinite mercy,—I think that I must be the guiltiest thing on earth!"

All the ingenuous contrition, all the wayward inconsistencies, all the native tenderness, all the warm and sudden self-reproach, which had been characteristic of her childhood, were on her now, shattering down the pride of an imperious egotism. For the moment she forgot all that had divorced them, for the moment she was to him all that she once had been. For that moment an ecstasy glistened in his eyes,— to die the next.

He took her outstretched hands, and touched them once, lightly, with his lips:

"You have no sins to *me*. And—if you had, did I not long since promise you pardon? Your better nature is not dead in you; cherish it still, it will be greater riches to you than your gold."

And then, he turned and left her.

With the violets lying in her lap she sat long, motionless, and alone.

"Have I deserved to be what I am?" she questioned, the rare voice of remorse speaking in her soul. She knew only too well that she had not.

Yonder, in the vine country, in the little river-house, the woman who had nurtured and fostered her in her infancy was left to loneliness, and sorrow, and old age, unsolaced.

Across the Alps, in the City of the Dead, was the solitary

mausoleum of the husband to whom she owed every renown, pleasure, and glory that now illumined her life, and whose vast, mute, boundless love had served her in tenderness and in humility, unrecompensed even by a caress as fond as that she gave her dogs.

And out from her presence had just passed the man to whom her whole existence was one long ingratitude.

"Have I deserved to be what I am?" she thought. "Have I not been base—base—base?"

And she knew herself to be so.

All her life, since the time that she had voluntarily gone from him, had been one long ingratitude against him. She knew it whenever she paused to think; but thought had so little place in her shadowless life.

All things had gone well with this fairest daughter of Hazard. Accident, which seemed her progenitor, had been ever her protector. Fortune and all its chances had been gracious to her.

She had left her early life as far behind her as the beautiful, glittering, ephemeral winged insect of a tropic summer leaves its larvæ bed, in the closed cup of a poppy or a lotus, as it wings its way high into air and sunlight. That she— she so great, so worshiped, so irresponsible, so widely courted, so habituated to idolatry and power and all the ways of wealth—could ever have been that Waif and Stray whereof he spoke, seemed as impossible to her as it is to the full-plumed aphis glancing in the sun to recall the season of its chrysalis slumber.

She!—the most beautiful woman of her world and of her age—had once been that foundling child, reared by a peasant, succored by a bohemian, dwelling under a cottage roof, and made happy by a gleaner's treasury of scattered cornstalks, by a peasant's gold of honey and yellow gourds, by an infant's jewel store of morning dew-drops and of blue forget-me-nots!

It was bitter to her to think it; to have the memory of it forced upon her; and she paced to and fro the length of her chamber, with restless, uneven steps, as she remembered that, thrust this fact away far down into oblivion as she would, the fact still lived, and could not be destroyed: with all her wealth, with all her empire, this fact was stronger than herself, and could not be abolished by her will.

It was the one canker in her ever-blossoming roses; the one ghost within her joyous palaces; the one bitter drop in her wine-cup's ruby light.

The canker was at her heart, the ghost within her walls, the bitterness upon her lips, in this moment when the odor of the snow-born flowers wafted the memories of her buried childhood to her.

Life had been so fair to her. The years had gone by in one continual blaze of triumph, in one continual hymn of rejoicing. She was great; she was unrivaled; she was satiated with offered love. What else could make the paradise of a woman? From the hour when she had cried, "The fairies have remembered me at last!" the fairies had never again deserted her.

From the hour in which her selection had been made, all things had led her to her new existence, all things divorced her from her old: and no sigh for all she had abandoned ever grated on the ear of those who had made her what she had become.

The haughty temper and far-reaching vision of the aged aristocrat had environed with scrupulous care this child of Chance, in whom her prescience foresaw the future bearer of her name.

She had bent all her skill and all her energies to conceal from the world that the creature she adopted was the offspring of Hazard, nurtured on alms; and to make of her a woman so perfect that the most critical should discover no flaw in her grace or her beauty, in her acts or her thoughts. And she had been perfectly successful. Swiftly and easily, all the precepts that an unyielding pride could teach, all the impress that an exquisite elegance could make, were stamped on the facile wax of a temperament already akin to them.

To Viva, nothing of greatness seemed either new or strange. Rank was no King Cophetua to her, and she no beggar maiden. She was only a long-dethroned princess rightly reinstated in her sovereignty. There was no need to dread her self-betrayal. She wore her purples as though born to them; and even her patrician instructress was compelled to murmur to herself, "If a bastard—surely one of some imperial race, such as there sits not in these days on the fool-filled thrones of Europe."

Travel, culture, change of scene, learning made graceful and alluring, all that could be brought to the moulding of her mind and tastes were given her. She was kept in seclusion and in foreign countries some few years; she was baptized by the Church with a long bead-roll of saintly names, the priests not questioning their liberal patroness; she was changed into that brilliant empress which education and wealth, and an artificial atmosphere, and all the pomps and graces of wealth, can make out of any lovely, vivacious, and impressionable child.

At times, even the cold, and courtly, ever-sarcastic old woman could have wished for a shade more warmth, a touch more earnestness in this glittering volatile thing that radiated round her, and seemed never to be moved to any sense of debt or gratitude, but only to the buoyant exultant sense of victory and of fair fortune. But she wished for them in vain: the only one who could have wakened them was banished.

And, unconsciously, in her sedulous destruction of that one pure, ardent, early tenderness in the young girl's heart, she shaped the weapons of her son's martyrdom.

When at length the silent passion that he had struggled against so long as mere selfish and vain desire was conquered, and spoke, and offered all its matchless possessions, its magnificent gifts, they were accepted with the smiling indifference of a fair, pampered, ambitious creature, who conceived that the donation of her own loveliness balanced all debt between them, yet who, insecure in her singular fate,

5*

saw in this alliance the sole possible passage to the security of power.

"I shall be the Duchess de Lirà!" she thought, with a haughty smile; if she thought also with a shuddering sigh, "And I must be his Wife!"

The sudden illness and death of her protectress hastened this union to which she willingly consented, instinctively grasping the sole scepter that was stretched out to her; only seeing the kingdom that lay before her of omnipotence and pleasure, and triumphant vanity, and sure deliverance from all future chance of obscurity or humiliation. The marriage sacrament was administered beside the death-bed of his mother, that no breath of slander, no rumor of injurious wonder, might ever touch the fame of the one who henceforth was to bear a title illustrious for centuries among the princes of the earth.

And the tidings, traveling far from the Austrian city where they tarried, went in the sweet spring evening to the house of Mère Rose.

Attained ambition on her lips was no Dead Sea fruit; but an enchanted apple, ever fresh, ruddy, luscious.

For her sake her lord went forth from the seclusion he had so long preserved, and even approached a court which he abhorred as the court of an usurper, that he might show her to that great world for which she so long had pined. She became the idol, at once the leader, the reigning beauty of her sphere.

Her husband, content only to minister to her wishes and her will, grew the slave to her idlest caprice, and was grateful for her slightest smile. For a second time an immeasurable devotion was laid subject to the rule of her mutable fancies; this time, yet more than the first, it utterly failed to move her to any sense of its priceless value, it was only regarded as a means to the end of her own gratification.

Intoxicated with homage, applause, indulgence, extravagance, pleasure, she did what to few it is given to do,— she realized her wildest dreams. She had but to wish, and she possessed. She had but to look, and she vanquished. Her conscience was stifled, her memory was killed, her heart never beat but with the throbs of vanity and triumph; love had no peril for her, for she had against it the shield of an all-absorbing self-love.

She lived as exclusively in the present, and as absolutely for herself, as the brightest humming-bird that ever wantoned above roses.

She had once had purer visions: these had all perished. Her moral ruin was not less rapid and complete than were her social ascent and her absolute domination.

So she lived her life; and on the night of the Dorian ball her husband died, in silence and in solitude.

For the hour the impression which that death made on her was vivid, and her self-reproach poignant.

But then she was free,—absolutely free.

"Light-wedded, and light-widow'd, and unaware of any sort of sorrow."

She passed out once more, after the briefest retirement that custom could sanction, into the noonday blaze of the world she had quitted, tenfold more potent now than ever; for now to the sorcery of her smile was added the sorcery of her gold, which men were also free to strive and win.

No living creature dreamed that in the great French aristocrat there beat the same pulses that had throbbed in the young limbs of the Waif and Stray.

To keep her unseen until time and culture had so changed her that there was no fear of her recognition by the keenest eyes that had ever beheld her, had been the first care of her powerful guardians. Estmere, and the son of Estmere, she had never met; and when one or two of the young nobles who had been at the banquet of Coriolis, and might have recalled some likeness in her to the child whom they had there beheld,—their memories had been too filled with the fair forsaken faces of women for them to heed the resemblance, or to suspect the secret of the one before whom they bowed so low in homage.

Vague mystic rumors did indeed float about concerning her: but the hand of her imperious protectress had been strong enough to lift her high above suspicion; and many expedients had been found and used, with keenest tact, to supply all flaws, and smooth all strangeness, in her story.

Yet, although all others had so completely forgotten, she could not utterly forget;—not utterly, with those white and purple flowers lying in her hands.

That time had been, when these things, and such things as these, gleaned from wood and pasture, had been her only treasures; when she had owned no more home, or heritage, or food, by right, than such as the bird, forsaken of its flock, can make and find from tufts of grass, and pods of seeding flowers, and any wind-blown alms of nature. That time had been; if she had kept its memory in her heart in gratitude, an amulet against all evil thoughts, a cross to recall to her all those who suffered, a rosary whereby she had counted her faults, her follies, and her better deeds, it had been blessed to her.

As it was,—cast scornfully and cruelly aside, as some detested thing for which she prayed oblivion and annihilation,—it might some day rise up and have its vengeance on her.

And at rare times she feared this, with a fear wholly foreign to her high-couraged and imperious temperament.

The fear was kindred to that which will pursue and move a monarch, whose passage to his throne has been hewn with an iron blade through the granite of gigantic crime, and whose steps have waded through the blood of a murdered people to reach the diadem of his desire.

Was it not over the lifeless bodies of slaughtered loves that she, also, had passed to her victories, and to her kingdom?

## CHAPTER VII.

THAT night, at one of the greatest houses of Paris, the most exquisite woman of its courtly assembly bore in her hand a massive cluster of simple blue and white violets—violets, full of a wild forest fragrance, amid the exotics blossoming there.

"Are they for the sake of the Past madame?" asked of her an old Marshal, whose youth had known Marengo and Jena, seeing in them the emblems of his Chief.

She turned her eyes on him with a look her lovers had never seen in them.

"Yes! They are for the sake of the Past!"

Those around her wondered eagerly and in surprise what Past this could be of which a creature so young still and so eminent could think with such regret; with her it could not be they knew a Bonapartist memory.

When she went forth to her carriage, one watcher standing by, unseen, among the crowds, caught a glimpse of his violets in her clasp of jeweled gold. And summer dawns had not been sweeter to him than the bleak and stormy night became,—she had enough of the love of her childhood to treasure his flowers thus!

The remembrance of him, slight though it was, sufficed to send back warmth and gladness to his heart; he gave a martyrdom of tenderness, accounting it as naught,—he was touched to passionate thankfulness by this one trivial act.

Thus great natures ever give, and ever receive:—pouring out their gold like water, and into their garners receiving dross in exchange.

## CHAPTER VIII.

WHEN her carriage had rolled away, Tricotrin also left the gates, and went far away through the Quarter of St. Martin, up toward the thieves' nest of Chaumont.

The thrill of joy which had quivered through him as he had seen the violets in her hand and in her bosom, faded into the depression which ever follows a hope that is unutterably sweet, yet wholly baseless, and which springs up only to perish in all the glory, and all the fragility of the evanescent flower that only blooms for a single day.

She remembered him and her childhood,—that was something. But she was divorced from him forever; and could no more return to him than the fruit, gathered in for a prince's table, can return to the moss-covered branch, where once it hung in a country orchard.

He had known that this would be so; he had foreseen it as the inevitable sequel of that choice which had removed her to the world for which she had longed. Not now for the first hour was its truth before him. He had seen it with each time, through the many years of her separation from him, that he had looked upon her and had watched the actions of her life. But it had never struck on him so strongly or so vividly as when he had beheld her that morning; as when, in every gesture, and smile, and glance, in every languid movement, and contemptuous reply, and negligent grace, he had seen how wholly the gay, wayward, innocent, transparent child, that he once had sheltered, was lost in the patrician woman of the world.

He had kept aloof from her. It had been too keen a suffering for him to provoke it. He, who cast all pain from him on the impulse of a joyous nature as he would have cast an adder from his arm, could not voluntarily seek the torture that her presence was. He took heed that she was content; he assured himself that her own desires were the guide she followed; he kept vigil, how constant and how deeply penetrating she did not dream, over all the changes of her life. But, once having seen that it was well with her, once having learned that in her servitude to ambition she only embraced the success that she craved, he sought her presence little.

During the years that her husband lived she never saw the face of the man she had forsaken, though, once or twice, amid deep garden ways in Italy, or on the waters of old Teutonic streams, she had heard—or had thought that she heard—the music that she had loved in the days of her childhood. And in such moments, under the spell of that sweet and distant melody, her eyes had filled with sudden tears, and her heart with sudden yearning, and the vague sense of a loss, irrevocable and endless, had come over her.

Their lives had drifted asunder, as two boats drift north and south on a river, the distance betwixt them growing longer and longer with each beat of the oars and each sigh of the tide. And for the lives that part thus, there is no reunion. One floats out to the open and sunlit sea; and one passes away to the grave of the stream. Meet again on the river they cannot.

His heart was weary as he went.

Could he have served her he had been content. But what need or what call for service could there be in this fate so royal, so shadowless, so eminent, so coldly and so radiantly clear? She had wealth, and had the world at her feet; she had empire, and had no wish unfulfilled; she had youth, and had all things that render youth glorious. What space in such a life was there for love to fill? She had need of nothing. She had the armies that conquer, she had the sorcery that transmutes, she had the smile that makes fate smile back in answer. What appeal in such a life was there for aid or succor?

Once he had promised her that though she should return to him sin-stained, wretched, broken-hearted, driven from every refuge, and shrinking from every glance, yet would he not forsake her, but would shelter her with his tenderness still. But a sterner trial than this tore the strength of his love at its roots. He had to stand outside the golden gates of her paradise,—forgotten.

Not rare on this earth is the love that cleaves to the thing it has cherished through guilt, and through wrong, and through misery. But rare, indeed, is the love that still lives while its portion is oblivion, and the thing which it has followed passes away out to a joy that it cannot share, to a light that it cannot behold.

For this is as the love of a god, which forsakes not, though its creatures revile, and blaspheme, and deride it.

His heart was weary within him as he went through the dreary way; the night was bitter and full of storms. The snow-clouds hovered unbroken, but the wind was wild and chill as ice, and ever and again a gust of rain swept with shrill passion over the half-frozen ground, and dulled the few lights burning.

He had come into the quarter of the poor, and into the hotbeds of crime, through the maze of crooked streets and swarming tenements that were alive with guilt as an ant-hill with its insect-swarm, while, furthermost, the cavernous rocks of Chaumont sheltered every sin and every lust in their hideous recesses.* It was ever thus that he exorcised his dark hours. Yet, to-night, the heart-sickness of every poet and every leader of the world was on him, too heavily for even the justice of truth, or the purity of labor, to have worth in his sight.

"What avail?" he thought. "What avail to strive to bring men nearer to the right? They love their darkness best,—why not leave them to it? Age after age the few cast away their lives striving to raise and to ransom the many. What use? Juvenal scourged Rome,—and the same vices that his stripes lashed then, laugh triumphant in Paris to-day! The satirist, and the poet, and the prophet strain their

---

* It is needless to recall that this vile place has been by the late Imperial works changed into a spot of healthful recreation and great beauty.

voices in vain as the crowds rush on; they are drowned in the chorus of mad sins and sweet falsehoods! Oh God! the waste of hope, the waste of travail, the waste of pure desire, the waste of high ambitions!—nothing endures but the wellspring of lies that ever rises afresh, and the bay-tree of sin that is green, and stately, and deathless!"

Yet—though in that hour he saw the vanity of labor, the futility of effort, the helplessness of truth against the massed evils and armored insincerities of the world, as men in their hours of loneliness must ever behold them,—yet, he went onward into the Gehenna whither his steps tended.

Above, and hidden in the huge dens of the rocks, assassins, and brigands, and ravishers brooded and glutted over their golden spoil or their writhing prey; and in the horrible streets that lay below, naked children and half-naked women fought and tore at each other like mad dogs, songs of riotous blasphemy were crossed by the din of drunken combatants, and hideous misery with hideous obscenity struggled which should be king regnant there.

The rocks towered up against the black starless skies, silent because, screened in their caverns, men, who had changed to devils, hoarded stolen treasure, and stifled telltale shrieks, and crushed out panting life all noiselessly, and strove to find some new variety of lust. But in the quarter of the town beneath them there was a loud tumultuous hell, in which sex and age were alike forgotten, and confounded in one pit of shameless shame:—a pit where human lives were pent together in gasping droves, as if they had lost all semblance of humanity; where one vast caldron of iniquity seethed on and on forever, forever fed afresh. It is in such social bodies as these that the cancer of the world throbs and poisons all that it infects, and taints even that which is in health—a cancer whose sole attempted cure is now and then a random cut from the knife of evil power, that leaves it wider spread than ever, covered, insidious, deadly with the germs of an eternal death.

As the imprecations, the screams, the yells, the laughter

worse than any curses, the songs that had so utter a depravity in them, the cries of young children under brutal blows, beat on his ear where he approached Chaumont, a great softness, a great pity came into his eyes.

"God-forgotten, they call you!" he murmured. "Rather man-forsaken."

He was unarmed; he penetrated into a quarter where death waited for any honest man who durst venture his life there; he came among ravening wolves, to whom murder was pastime, and cruelty joy. But he walked on, with the careless courage of his nature. Fear was as far from him as from any eagle of the Engadine; and, moreover, these wolves were as faithful dogs to him, caressing his hand where they bit through to the bone of every other. To him they were tame, and were loyal. He lashed them with scorn; he scourged them with reproach; many a time he seized their prey from out their very jaws; he stood between them and their passions; and he braved them openly in their maddest rage. But they never lifted their weapons against him, and in their most furious moods he was sacred to them. They knew well that there was love and not hate in his soul; and they unconsciously revered what they could not comprehend,—this courage which only feared sin, this pity which could embrace even guilt, this manhood that had every strength, and boldness, and liberty that they honored, and yet was so pure from crime, and so stainless from shame.

He knew that he was safe amid them. Had he not known it he would have gone thither just the same. It was not in his blood to study caution, or dread peril; many a time, with his back against a wall and the haft of a knife against his chest, he had kept a score of desperate brutes at bay, refusing to relinquish them their victim. And he who loved sunlight, and mirth, and the smile in women's eyes, and the gay recklessness of artist life, and the beauty of a summer world, came into the hells of great cities on that simple, unflinching duty to humanity, which was a law the bohemian and the wanderer never broke. Those whom the world cast out he made his brethren; and, if once in a thousand times of trial it was given him to raise a sinking soul from the abyss into the purer upper air of earth, he was content; he earned the only wage he asked.

"They shudder when they read of the Huns and the Ostrogoths pouring down into Rome," he mused, as he passed toward the pandemonium. "They keep a horde as savage, imprisoned in their midst, buried in the very core of their capitals, side by side with their churches and palaces, and never remember the earthquake that would whelm them if once the pent volcano burst, if once the black mass covered below took flame and broke to the surface! Statesmen multiply their prisons, and strengthen their laws against the crime that is done—and they never take the canker out of the bud, they never save the young child from pollution. Their political economy never studies prevention; it never cleanses the sewers, it only curses the fever-stricken!"

A hideous clangor broke in on his ear as he went, lost in thought, and unheeding the din that he knew so well, worse than the roar of a million wild beasts. This clamor was shriller, viler, more horrible than common; it caught his attention, and lifting his head, he saw at some little distance a red resinous glare.

"Murder is being done; they are never so joyous over aught else," he muttered, as he hastened his steps. He was no optimist to deem his wolves slandered sheep; he knew them as they were, in all their blackest, hardest, most hopeless guilt.

He soon came within sight of the fire; a bonfire blazing in a pent dark court, and throwing its glow on the rocks beyond, while about it hundreds of living creatures swarmed, and shrieked, and sang, and raved, and danced in a saturnalia of devils' joy. A rabble of brigands with bare chests and great arms black with filth, of women disheveled, unclothed, yelling like furies, of gaunt beggars with their filthy rags flying in the wind, and their long lean knives glancing in the air, of children leaping and screaming with delight, surrounded the pile of blazing wood that burned only the fiercer for the falling hail that hissed in its smoke. And above it, hung there to consume by slow degrees, suspended by an iron chain knotted about his waist, and fastened to an iron spout in a wall, swaying in the wind, and uttering awful cries, swung a living human figure.

This was the bacchanalia they enjoyed in the bitter wintry night.

"Ah-ah! How bright he will burn!" screamed a little five-year child, dancing in ecstasy at the finest firework she had ever beheld.

Tricotrin gave a glance at the blackened form, as its chain-halter cracked and shook in the wind: then threw himself with a leap like a stag's among the throng, seized a knife from the hand of a boy ere the lad could resist, sprang on to a broad stone coping on the wall, stretched up, seized the wretch by his waist-chain, cut the cord that knotted the iron links to the projecting spout, and dragged him down on to the ledge where he himself stood. All was done in an instant, ere they knew what he did: they were silent in supreme amaze.

Then a roar broke from all the crowd as with one voice; a roar like a herd of hyenas cheated of their carcass-prey; they loved him in their own fashion, but they loved slaughter more, and they hungered fiercely for that splendid human bonfire.

"Give him to us!" they yelled, while twice a hundred knives glittered in the glare.

He stood above them, on the stone, above the stifling, resinous, scorching pyramid of flame: the creature he had rescued lying at his feet. All his life and ardor had flashed back into his face with the need of action; his eyes blazed with scorn and passion; his white abundant hair blew backward in the wind; his fearless gaze unflinching met the glare of the upturned, bloodshot, thirsty, murderous eyes.

"Give him to you!" he echoed in their own parlance,

which he spoke with rapidity and ease. "Am I vile as yourselves, think you? What was his offence?"

The rush of thundering voices hissed out, as with a single breath, the story of the criminal; a new comrade, a puny creature, stealthy as the cat, timid as the hare, who had joined them for awhile, only to spy on them and to betray them to the law: a traitor that deserved ten thousand deaths drawn out in years of torture.

Tricotrin heard; the red light fell upon him as he looked down on the riot that seethed beneath him, and on the knives that menaced him if he did not yield.

"A dark guilt, truly," he said with brevity, as his mellow voice rang clear through the din. "But *you* are not fit for its judges. Fine fellows, indeed, to sit in the judgment-seat— you who would be shot or guillotined, every one of you, if you but had your deserts. What do you call yourselves— devils, tigers, or men? You have no claim to the last name! A spy is a thing as foul as a viper, I grant; but not to be burnt alive for all that, and you are too utter blackguards yourselves to have any right left in you to punish. Two hundred men, too, against one—glorious equality! For shame, you hellhounds; I knew you were brutes when the bloodthirst was on you, but I did not guess till now you were cowards!"

He knew how to deal with them,—as Dumouriez dealt with his mutinous battalions. The fiery scorn, the contemptuous invective, the dauntless censure struck them dumb, where other words would have excited their mockery, or inflamed their passions. The silence did not last long; they were in furious hatred of their prey, they were in ravening longing for their sport; they closed nearer and nearer, stretching out their gaunt hands to seize, and lifting their knives in the air.

"Give him to us!" they shouted again, with awful blasphemy upon their tongues. Any other than himself they would have hurled down and torn in pieces, as hounds tear offal.

He laughed aloud; with haughty defiance flashing on them from his eyes.

"Give him to you? You think I am a huntsman, to fling the fox to the pack? Off, you scoundrels!—sheathe your knives, I tell you; do you hear? You want my life?—I dare say! You are murderers, and that is your trade. But I do not mean to die in your hell: I should find no worse where devils rage, if the priests' tales be ever so true. This man shall be mine. I say it. You know I never break my word."

The tumult raged higher and higher, swelling out like hoarse roar of the sea.

"Give him to us!" they screamed. "The fires shall have him, and not you!"

He stood unmoved; a brawny giant flung himself across the flames, leaped up by the stone ledges, and made a lunge at the body of the spy. But Tricotrin was too rapid for him; he dealt the brigand one blow, straight in his chest, and the man fell like an ox under the pole-axe.

There was a moment's pause of stupefaction; they were superstitious of his power, they endowed him with more than mortal force. But the women, ever foremost in cruelty and riot, ever hounding on to war the men who might choose peace, mocked and mouthed at their males for cowardice, and yelled with shrillest oaths their horrible cry.

"Give him to the flames! His blood or yours!"

He looked with changeless calm upon them still; the hot flickering glare of the fire lighting up the majestic height of his stature, and the dauntless, scornful grandeur of his face, on which there stole a certain wistful saddened pity.

He had thought that these brutes loved him.

"Poor mad wild beasts!" he murmured. "You know not what it is you do. You can kill me, doubtless, if you will; but you cannot make me look on to see you steep yourselves in slaughter."

The roar hushed, like the roar of sea waves sinking down into calm: silence fell on them with a great and sudden awe,

A sublimity that their minds could not reach stirred their souls from this serene courage, this offered sacrifice, this refusal to forsake them, though they forsook themselves. A gaunt, bull-throated, sanguinary, brutal brigand,—type of the *populares* of all time, from the mobs of Marius to the mobs of Marat,—thrust his knife down into his girdle with a curse.

"Let him have his way! He may thrust a pike through me and I will not say him no."

There was a throb of human blood under the bullock hide, there was a pulse of manly softness under the wolf skin. He was a butcher of men; he had drawn his knife across more than one panting throat; he lived by riot and pillage; but his temper answered to courage, and he had an instinct that reverenced greatness.

He was the leader among them, whose word was law, and whose argument with rebels was a rope: the crowd dared not revolt by more than a sullen savage groan. Tricotrin flung his bright glance over them.

"Patron Mi-Minoux, that was generously spoken. You give me this man?"

A roar of baffled rage broke from the throng, in which the loudest voices that led were the voices of women. But Mi-Minoux stayed it with a gesture.

"A thousand devils seize you! He deserves more than this from us," he shouted. "Tricotrin—take the damned beast's life; for your sake I say, not his, the hound!"

"For mine—and for your own."

He stretched out his hand to Mi-Minoux; the soilless hand that had never been stained with bribe or blood, or even the insincerity of a false greeting, meeting the one that was black with a thousand crimes, and red from murder's work. Over the Patron's dusky brutal face a tremor and a light passed quickly; he drew his own hand away as though it were burnt with fire.

"Hell and fury! *Mine* is not fit!"

Tricotrin looked on him with the smile that had such infinite pity.

"Chut! Why not! We are both men!"

Then, standing still on the stone ledge, with the drooping, huddled figure of the spy lying in a shapeless mass at his feet, while the bonfire burned dully in the rushing hail, while the flames and the wind sank together, and the people grew very quiet, hushing the children who cried aloud for the spectacle they had lost, his voice rang, clear and sweet as a bell through the thieves' quarter,—

"Children! You give me, to-night, gifts more precious than silver and gold. I thank you from my soul. I would not barter this single life that you spare to me—vile though it be—for all the coins of monarchs' treasuries. You were wild beasts when I found you. Nay! a millionfold worse. For the beasts do but slaughter for hunger, as we kill the calf and the lamb; and the beasts never slay their own kind. You were worse than the tigers are; but still—my tigers were human. They let go their prey out of love for me. Ah! Why will ye not have as much love for yourselves! You are fools, though you deem yourselves wise: fools in the election of Crime for your god. Does that god bring you aught but blows! Will he feed you with aught but ashes! Will he clothe you with aught but fear, and shame, and fever, and fire! Ye are fools in the god that ye serve. Ye are slaves, though ye deem yourselves free. What life does your deity give! To fear like wolves; to burrow like moles; to be hunted like foxes; to be shunned like lepers; to endure months of famine for sake of one hour's gorged and loathsome debauch, like the vultures that only find sweetness in carrion. To be netted at last like a fox in a gin; to have your limbs cramped in irons; to be fettered, scourged, shaven, yoked together like coupled hounds; working like the mill-horses for no reward in one endless circle; sleeping on a plank, growing old in a cell, without the chance of a hope, without a woman's kiss, or a man's laugh, without a draught of wine, or an hour of liberty:—that is the life your god gives you! That is the fate you deem freedom! How long will you worship so blindly?—so long as you are born in darkness; so long as you are begotten and bred and reared in ignorance and iniquity. You lay your children, new-born, in the red iron hands of your Moloch. You fill their mouths with curses ere yet their milk-teeth are shed. You snatch them from their mothers to send them out to your god's hideous service. You give them life, only that you may cause to be brought forth fresh spawn of sin to curse the world that you hate. You bring the young children your women have borne to see a man burn for their sport: if they kill you when you are old and useless, and cumber their path, will it be the children's fault or your own? Slaves yourselves, why will you bring the new lives into bondage ere yet they can tell what the liberty of innocence means? Fooled serfs of a false god, whom you worship because his altars glitter with the tinsel of vice, why will ye bind your offspring down beneath the tyranny of your vile religion? You think I use language too harsh? Oh, my people! You would have taken my life a moment since because I would not stand by to see you steeped afresh in blood; will you never believe how gladly I would lay it down for you if it would ransom you from suffering and sin?"

They were silent as they heard.

The passionate eloquence of the poet, winged with living truth, pierced their souls as he spoke to them. Vaguely the meaning and the greatness of his words reached the dullest and vilest life that cowered there. Women, sexless and shameful, shuddered and beat their breasts that had nourished thieves, and cursed aloud their kisses that had rewarded murderers with kisses sold for stolen gold. Men, dogged and brutal, dropped down their heads, and shivered where they stood, and wondered in their poor untutored brains, that struggled against such mists of poisoned ignorance, whether indeed he who arraigned them thus were man or god.

It was only the little children who crouched beneath the

flame pillars of the fire, who murmured in their baby-throats against him, because he had cheated them of the burning, and had not let them hear the music of the death-shriek.

He heard, and stooped, and raised up one of those who muttered in lisping revolt against him. The child was only a few years old; but from out its elfin eyes the thirst of inherited lust already glistened, and on its parching mouth the heat of the drunkard's desire was already set.

"Look!" he said to the silent people, while his eyes rested on them with a regard of tenderness and of compassion unutterable. "The child hungers for the sight of a death agony: your blood is in his veins, and he can have no choice but to be vile, for have you not made his pastime murder, and his cradle-song a curse? You have created him only to slay him,—are not the beasts of the desert holy and full of mercy beside you? Women—as these creatures come to the birth, it were better to tear them from your breasts, and dash their brains out upon the stones of your streets, than have them become like this. He is not a child—this thing that clamors to see a living creature burn. He is a budding seed of awful crime, to which your passions had dared to give the breath and force of life. And through him your sin will pass down through generation after generation. Have you ever thought what it is that you do when you beget these lives that grow up, like rank grass, from corruption!"

The great multitude was silent: even the hellish creature that had mouthed and mocked at his feet, was quiet and touched with awe, not knowing the meaning of the words, but moved, unwittingly, by the solemn and dread sweetness of the voice above him.

Through the mob of murderers, and ravishers, and thieves, and forgers, a shiver ran like one deep sob.

Without another word he went down from the stones where he stood, and passed away through their midst, leading the condemned with him.

## CHAPTER IX.

CHRYSOSTOM, when he protected Eutropius under the shield of his eloquence, could not have had more disgust for the vileness of the one he had saved than had he now for the spy that he had rescued from the fire. Without asking he guessed his guilt; the guilt of a criminal turned informer, and chastised by those he had endeavored to betray.

At him, he had not even glanced; and the unhappy creature had not once lifted his aching lids, but moved on with trembling steps through the furious driving of the sleet and wind.

When at length they had reached a solitary place where none were in hearing, his protector loosened him, and faced him.

"If Iscariot had lived, he might have redeemed his crime. There is no sin that shuts out hope. What are you? and how came you there? It may be I can aid you."

The traitor he had rescued looked up at him with blank scorched eyes, that still saw nothing save the glare and ebb of the flames from which he had escaped.

Tricotrin scanned his face; and his own changed. He stood motionless, looking on the charred, shrinking, half-naked form before him.

"Again!" he murmured. "Again!"

The other did not hear or note him; feeling, beholding, listening to naught save that roar and leap of the bonfires which seemed still winding around his limbs, and crushing his breath with their clouds of smoke. Of his rescue he was scarcely conscious; he had followed the hand that had guided him, by a dumb instinct: he was senseless and paralyzed with the past fear; he was like a moth caught by some gentle hand from out a flame, and loosed, maimed and blinded, upon the darkness and coldness of the night.

"Again!" murmured Tricotrin; "how vile we are at our best! If I had known I might have left him to his fate!"

All the light, and the pity, and the sublimity that had been upon his face when he had addressed the multitudes, and driven them back from slaughter, had faded; it was dark, and gray, and weary, the fatigue of rising passions, and the despair of a soul that could not reach the heights it strove for, following the inspiration and the tenderness and the strength that had been on it as he had arraigned the murderers.

He uttered not one word, but stood gazing down upon the blackened, quivering, helpless thing, whose life would have gone forth in fire but for him.

They were alone: dark leaning roofs of empty buildings rose upon either side, like the steep slopes of caving cliffs; the winds shrieked through the narrow passages; the sky above was leaden and starless. The creature, looking upward,— with his sight still dazzled, and hot as with the horrible scorch of the flame upon it, and with his brain still maddened from terror,— caught the eyes that rested on him, and knew them, and trembled, and covered his face with his bruised, bleeding hands, and cried out that the dead had arisen.

Above him, like the Saint Michael of Guido, stood the form of his savior; the shadows changing on his face, fiery, fleeting, lightened, darkened, swift and varying as the thoughts at conflict in his heart.

On the earth, the Greek, Canaris, writhed senseless; shuddering in epilepsy, foaming at the mouth, beating the air with frantic gesture, struck down, as by a stroke from some avenging angel, by the gaze that had looked at him with the look of the dead.

The night had grown still more inclement. The pattering hail had changed to a storm of rain, whose great drops froze as swiftly as they fell. The air was ice; the winds were hurricanes; the cold was growing with every instant more intense. Left upon the frozen ground, half nude, convulsed, insensible, the wretched creature lying there must have perished no less surely than had the flames consumed him.

He was beyond the pale of human kinship, beyond the right of human pity,—a traitor who had turned against his comrades, and striven to betray them to the law, so that his own wretched life should be, by the law, set free.

To the man who looked on him, he was yet more than this; he was a foe whose poisoned fangs had bitten deep into the frank, free faith of boyhood.

Yet, with the same mercy as he would have raised a dying, leprous-eaten wretch, Tricotrin lifted up the criminal from the earth, and passed onward.

"Doing otherwise—how were I better than they?" he thought.

From the active deed of murder he had that hour withheld the people. It was not for him, whose lips had spoken their rebuke, to yield himself up to the instincts of their vengeance. He went on through the ice-storm, over the whitened, frozen ground, heavily cumbered with the convulsed limbs and twisting body of the unconscious burden that he carried.

Once, ere this, he had given this man the "chance" that he had coveted; and out of that chance he found to-night that the lost wretch had coined only deeper crime, viler ruin, lower degradation. Yet, he gave him still another. The baser, the weaker, the guiltier this life, the more need was there that it should have breath and space left to change and become cleansed if such amend were possible.

There was nothing stirring in the howling winter night that already trenched on dawn: he met none to aid him in his errand; the only sound was the steps of the half-frozen patrol some way from him, and the soldier he could not summon. To give up this thing, that lay insensible and rigid across his shoulder, to the hands of the law was not the reading of duty that he followed.

Painfully, and by slow degrees, he toiled on through the beaten storm that turned to ice as it fell upon his face and form. At length he reached the gaunt walls of the nearest hospital, with its lamp burning over the entrance-way, the flame dashed to and fro by the fierce eddies of the gusts that shook its iron cage and blew the ice-rain past it in white clouds.

He knew the religious refuge well: as one of those few places upon earth where to suffer is deemed sufficient passport into pity, and where no other title of admission is required than the canker of disease and the woes of necessity.

He rang; the great bell boomed mournfully through the stillness. He leaned the figure of the man against the porch and gazed on it with an infinite pain in his eyes. It was huddled together, sunk in the swoon that had succeeded the convulsion, helpless, pitiful, miserable beyond all words.

"Had you been true in the years of our youth, how would it have been with us both now?" he thought;—and all the strange, wild, cruel dreams, which rise with the memory of a fate that has been within our grasp, and has been seized from it, and broken asunder, and cast into the abyss of irrevocable losses, arose before him as he stood outside the walls of the hospital with the senseless body stretched in the gray shadow at his feet.

The boom of the bell died on the silence. The iron door slowly unclosed. He was familiar there; and the Brethren were wont to call him, in the bitterness of winters such as this, their Alpine dog, their St. Bernard of search and of succor.

"I brought him from the thieves' quarter. He is not dead," he said, briefly.

They took the ghastly burden within, to where were warmth, and science, and care, and rest; and he turned and went backward into the storm, refusing to enter there.

He was not conscious of the violence of the winds, or of the perilous ice-blasts of the rain. His memory was with the past; he wondered how it would have been with him had one lie from the lips of that dying wretch not changed the current of his life in boyhood—one act of baseness from the traitor, who had come at last to the burning play of the thieves' awful mirth, not driven him in youth to exile.

Greatness, and power, and the treasuries of wealth, would have been his. The laurels of fame would have filled his hands in lieu of the wild flowers of gipsy wandering. His pleasures would have been taken in palaces instead of under the tawny roofs of fishers'-cabins, of village-hostelries, of painters' sketching-tents. His wine would have been poured from chalices of gold or silver in place of the drinking-horns of careless artists, and the brown jugs of bright-eyed maidens. His name would have been on the lips of the world instead of in the hearts of the people; and honor would have blown loud clarions in his path where love now laughed in his eyes and song now rang on his ear.

Regret had never touched him.

Those heights which he had left, had ever looked to the gaze that was bold and true as the eagle's, only as the sand mounds which the children of the world held in their ignorance to be golden thrones.

The diadem which he had laid down had ever seemed to the forehead that was warm with the suns of the south, and proud with an unstained truth, and caressed with the sweet lips of women, but a leaden fardel of weary weight, that men only bare because fools called it a crown.

The ambitions that he had forsaken had ever appeared to the mind that was steeped in the colors of the poet, in the passions of the lover, in the indolence of the wanderer, in the gayety of the reveler, but as ropes of sand, whereby those who deemed that they climbed to the stars fell back into the pit of oblivion.

He would not have exchanged his life for a kingdom; and envy of those whom men called great had never left its evil breath upon him. He knew too well the penalties that make the air in which such men soar so arid, and drench so weightily with the dank dews of satiety the wings of all those who fly on high.

Regret had never touched him.

Never—until this night when he had beheld the violets he had given in the white breast of a woman.

## CHAPTER X.

LOST in deep thought he noted nothing as he moved homeward from the hospital, until in one of the lonelier passages his eyes were drawn to a dark strange figure coming through the drifting snow, that froze as fast as it fell; wandering with a dreamy uncertainty in the gait, yet advancing with a curious resolve and swiftness. The man was dressed in heavy blue fisher's clothes, his beard was very long and rough, and blew in the strong wind, his eyes gazed out into the darkness, painfully bright and yet unutterably weary.

Tricotrin had seen that same form oftentimes since he had seen it first under the tawny sail of the Loirais hay-boat. In dark, quaint, old-world nooks of man-forgotten towns; in the hot yellow glare of southern cities at noon; on the olive-shadowed roads of the Riviera; in the great brown cumbrous barges, on rivers crowded with summer-soil; in the deep glow on cool, dim, silent churches with the amber shadows and the yellow lights sleeping on their noiseless footways: seen it ever in the same wandering quest, ever in the same mute solitude.

His voice rang through the frosty air: "Bruno!"

The sailor paused, and looked around, with a vague memory in his eyes: in a certain sense he had grown to recognize that voice better than any other's, though he would glide away from all companionship, and suffer no pursuit. He knew it, something as the dog, whose heart is in his own dead master's grave, will know a voice that ever speaks tenderly to him, and never seeks to draw him away from the tomb.

Tricotrin laid one hand on his shoulder.

"You have not found her!" he had learned that it was more merciful to treat the delusion as a truth.

The sailor's eyes turned on him with a look as bewildered

and as utterly heart-broken as the eyes of the dog at the grave of his master.

"Not yet. It is long;—it is long!"

A great sigh shook him as he spoke. It was long;—it was over twenty years.

"The years pass swiftly," Tricotrin answered him with the grave gentleness which had won him something like trust and love even from this poor, hunted, stupefied mind. "The years bring us age. May it not be she is dead?"

"No. That is not possible. If she were dead her soul would come to me."

Bruno's eyes were bright with this strange faith which lived in him and could not be stirred; this faith which was the tempest-tossed relic of that barbaric creed of his childhood, which drew his tired steps to the altars of the churches in a vague worship, half superstition, half heart-sickness.

Tricotrin looked on him in silence; what words would allay this hopeless grief, or dull this endless loss? Her soul! —the soul of that soulless thing who had but senses and passions, and who had no god but the gods of gold and of lust!

"I thought I saw her—look you!" whispered Bruno, suddenly, while his voice sank very low. "Last night,—a few hours agone,—I came on a place where the men and the women dance on the ice, and the torches burn, and the sledge bells ring, and the great trees are all alive with fire and silver. You call it the wood of Boulogne? Well,—I thought that I saw her. Through a casement, in that wooden house on the lake, where the lights glitter all night, where the devil sits laughing to see men do his work. It was her face!—it was among many; they were shouting, and singing, and pouring red wine down their throats, and the face turned and looked at me with her eyes—oh, yes!—with her eyes. But do you know what looked through them?—*a devil*. Through her eyes he jibed me, and mocked me, and vaunted his vice and his lusts. Then I knew that Satanas had bade him take her likeness to tempt and to torture me. And I had strength to flee; I fled all night through the woods, through the darkness, through the ice and the snow. Will it be so in hell? Will they curse us by putting their vileness in the shapes we know purest and loveliest?"

He paused abruptly; the man who heard him stood silent, touched with a pity beyond all words.

The devil the forsaken husband had beheld had been the woman whom he believed pure and unsoiled as the snow that fell round them!

"Come with me, Bruno," he said softly. "Come with me if for to-night only; you are cold, and fevered, and worn out; you are ill, though you know it not. Come!"

The sailor shook his head; with the dogged dreamy resolve settling over his gaze.

"I am not ill. And I must seek her."

"But you have sought her so long?"

"Yes. It is long—how long! I cannot count. But that is no matter, you know; when I find her we shall forget that. I must not rest. I would not sleep; but that sleep comes on me at last and kills me, body and brain. I never sleep but just at the dawn. I cannot tell why, but I feel she is in less peril when the sun first breaks. All things are waking, and they are merciful,—the beasts and the birds. There is mercy in their eyes that no men have,—but you; and they suffer; that makes them pitiful!"

He paused once more; the strange, wild, tender thoughts straying through the chaos of his shattered reason.

"Come!" urged Tricotrin gently. "We will seek her together!"

But Bruno drew away.

"No—no—no," he said absently. "I must be alone; always alone. You see;—we do not know where she is; she may be ill, and desolate, or a beggar mayhap; she must be like a stray lamb on a bleak mountain side, alone, in the width of the world. And you know the lamb will only come to the shepherd's voice; another's scares her. And something tells me I am near to her now: the end will soon come."

There was a light like the pale radiance from stars upon

his brown attenuated features; but the stars were not shining, the sky above-head was black with leaden snow-burdened clouds: the light was the light of a martyr's hope; holy, pure, divine.

He moved swiftly away, with a backward gesture of the hand, mournful, appealing, commanding, that entreated not to be followed, and that could not be disobeyed. His footsteps fell silent on the softness of the snow; his form glided away like a wraith, soon lost in the bush and the gloom.

Tricotrin stood long and looked back at the vault of darkness into which he had passed.

"Twenty-four years!" he thought. "And he has never wearied! What is my bitterness beside his?"

Then he went onward, back to the gayer quarters of the town; and, as he went, he passed the open portals of a world-famous theater. The flood of gaslight streamed out upon the dazzling snow; the audience poured out with it, in a flood of glowing color; the throng was full of laughter, and all their voices were singing snatches of a new mirthful carol of Auber, heard within that night for the first time, and bright as the wines and the loves that it chanted.

"How she sang, how she acted, how she danced!" shouted a student. "She is as lovely as ever she was,—is Coriolis!"

## CHAPTER XI.

"Love! Love! always of love!—how tired I am of it!" she thought, casting aside the latest of the many letters that vainly wooed to new nuptials the Duchess de Lira.

A poet dying in a garret, a revolutionist pining in a dungeon, a man heart-sick with foiled ambition, a woman scourged from the world's pleasures by the world's opprobrium, a wife with no sphere save the narrow space that her hearth-fire lit —these might need it, these might glorify it. But she!— What had she to do with this comrade of beggars, this consoler of transgressors! It was an incense that perfumed her path, a wreath that her foot trod in passing, a passion-flower that was twisted among the gold and gems of her diadem:—no more. What cause had she to stoop and share a thing so common, and so commonplace, that touched the lips of gipsy-girls, and smiled from the eyes of artists' mistresses, and sang its songs under cottage eaves, and made fair the dreams of toil-worn peasants? This tale told so continuously on her ear, grew very wearisome: it was a melodious monotone, but its changeless monotone was tiresome.

Love had indeed done all things for her. It had been around her all her life: her servitor who ministered uncomplainingly to all caprices, her treasure-house from which she drew what she would, her wishing-ring whereby all the powers and joys of an exceeding greatness had become hers, and overborne the accident that had cast her, a bastard or a changeling, upon fate. But she held it in gay, languid, light contempt. It was a thing so easily won with a careless smile, it was so easy to retain by an indolent word, it was a spaniel as fawning and faithful under blows as under caresses—in fine, it was such a fool, that she held it in scorn, like all things cheaply purchased; and although it was her one great creditor, without which she had been bankrupt and a prisoner in the jail of bitter circumstance and hard destitution, she scarcely gave it a grateful memory, never a reverential thought.

She esteemed it, as his mistress,—beautiful, callous, exacting, avaricious, contemptuous,—will esteem the man who gives her all she has, and is content with all her wayward moods, and adores her so blindly that he never perceives that he is only her tool, her purse, her dupe! To need love one must need sympathy. Sympathy was indifferent to her: she was perfectly successful, and success is sufficient for itself.

The lying murmurs of the slanderous world had attributed many loves to this woman, so magnificent, so young, so seductive, so tempted, so negligent of her lord, and so early widowed. But that world was at fault as its conclusions most often are: she had never loved. She only loved—herself: and so fair was the sovereign whom her mirrors displayed to her that she had never once felt inclined to change the allegiance. In one sense, indeed, she had loved the man whom she had voluntarily forsaken: loved him with a fondness and a strength she had never otherwise known; but that affection had never been strong enough to combat the sunny selfishness in her; and for several years it had been so commingled with self-reproach, distasteful humiliation, remorse, and the consciousness of ingratitude, that she had grown to thrust it away from her as often as it moved her.

She was dreamily but entirely content where she reclined, with the fire and the wax-light playing on her: they who are thus, but seldom recur to the past. The fruit we have eaten is only sweet in its recollection when that which our hand holds is bitter and rotten, and on the boughs of our orchard there is no blossom that promises fresh wealth for the spring.

She had so many things of which to think. Past scenes of triumph in gorgeous old palaces of Vienna and of Rome; present days of empire in this peerless Paris where she reigned. Treasures of art, and of beauty; of the looms of India and the jewels of Asia; of painter and poet and musician; of land and water and castle-crowned landscape, that were all inalienably hers. Caprices which, if she had them to-night, would become the fashion to-morrow. Ambitions for rule, for dominance, for the celebrity of the State as well as of the salon, which were sufficient to give zest and pleasure to the passing of life with the aroma of some one thing attainable though as yet unattained. All these floated in gorgeous hues through her thoughts; as, when she had been a child, had done the tales of the fairies when she had watched a flock of blue-warblers flash in azure through the sunshine.

She had youth, she had wealth, she had power, and dominion, and freedom, and success: what room could there be for remembrance of a long-buried time when she had been nameless, and homeless, and motherless, and friendless also, save for one friend who never begrudged, never reproached, never wearied.

Once, in the allurement that the actress possessed for her, he had dreaded for her with a terrible fear the life of temptation, of seduction, of diamond-crowned evil, of those women whose loveliness is as the curling snake which clings but to destroy, and whose sweetness is as the poisoned honey culled from the brilliancy of African flowers. If she had gone to it;—gone through its glittering portals to its bitter end, and known shame and starvation, and the painted misery that shrinks even from the pitiful eyes of the street-dog;—she would have remembered better far, and the days of her childhood would have been to her even as a paradise whose closed gates were guarded by a flaming sword, and whose light would have looked as the light of eternal suns that could never again stream on her. In her wretchedness and desolation he would have been remembered and avenged,—in her joy he had no place.

Beside these letters of the passion which she mocked, she had much correspondence to glance through where she sat in her dressing-chamber resting for a half hour, ere she should attire herself for a costume-ball at one of the embassies:—from the last of such entertainments she had been summoned to find a husband lying dead in his great Roman palace whose latest word had been, "do not spoil her pleasure."

But of this she did not think.

One letter she perused a little more earnestly than she did those of honeyed flattery, or eager worship; it was from her steward at her château in the south. It was full of humble apology and regret at having been unable to execute her most august commands.

"Unable to make my theater in the south court!" she murmured aloud, as she read. "Intolerable! If he cannot obey me in the possible, and the impossible, I will displace him with some one who will."

A line farther down caught her sight: she saw that the command he herein referred to was touching, not the new theater for her autumnal gathering, but the old truffle-hunter, Aubin Ralcor. The steward wrote that he had been found dead on his bed of leaves that morning; the steward regretted that death should have been so discourteous as to precede and prevent madame's wishes: but death was such a democrat—it would not even respect madame's orders. The steward proceeded to say that the theater in the south court should assuredly be ready in the autumn, as madame desired: death could not interfere in this case, for if it carried off a workman, he would with ease be supplied:—Providence was bountiful and made laborers invariably in excess of work.

"Poor old man,—it is a pity!" she thought. "But I am glad the theater is sure to be ready,—there are glass-houses by millions, but no one has had a glass theater. It will illuminate so well, and sparkle all over like a crystal."

She cast his letter after the others, and went to the appareling of her charms, on which she expended so many hours of her time, so many seasons of her meditation, in the same pleasure with which she had gazed at the necklet of the Prince Fainéant when all the little, chirping, waking birds beneath the eaves had seemed to tell her there was naught so fair as she on earth.

Princes and nobles told her that sweet story now: but it had lost little of the charm it had possessed in the swallows' first telling.

She was neither ignorant nor of slight intellect, as most vain women are; she had alike intelligence and wit of an unusual keenness, but she was for all that the vainest of all living things. She adored herself; she delighted in that exquisite face of hers to which she owed all her captivity of the world; she would draw the heavy burnished gold of her tresses through her hands; she would turn her head over her shoulder and glance at herself, Narcissus-like; she would gaze into the slumbrous night-like depths of her eyes, with a never-ceasing pride and rejoicing in her own loveliness.

Painters and sculptors had reproduced it in every manifold phase; but it was the one thing of which she never wearied:—the only thing.

And she required it this night to be at its utmost height; she desired it to be beyond even its accustomed measure: she wanted it to dazzle, enchain, subdue, appeal, inflame, astonish, and subjugate at once, and in even an unwonted force. For —this night alone for the first time—she knew that she would meet the man who, looking at her on the grape wagon of the harvest-feast, had said,

"She cannot be of the people!"

She had never met him hitherto, although the repute of his fame had often come to her. Those who had guarded her life had avoided him, not allowing her to divine any intent or perceive any purpose in their so doing. She had been little in her own country, not at all in his; and for several years he had been absent in the gilded exile of a great state duty, that he had accepted and executed in onerous service to his nation.

But she had remembered him with a curious tenacity of remembrance, in a creature so prone to swiftest oblivion of all things. She had listened with eagerness to whatever rumor had said of him, playing with his name as it will ever do with names once made of mark. She had often wished, with a curious mingling of fear and of desire, that he should return from his rule in the East, and cross her path once more.

She had no fear that recognition of her would ever awake in him. She was too utterly changed; even if it had been possible that any memory of a child seen once on a summer evening could remain with a man who was occupied with the full, earnest, arduous and lofty career of a statesman and diplomatist.

But she knew that she herself could never entirely banish the remembrance of how he had seen her; of how she had wandered through his picture-galleries, a nameless child; of how she had sat in his farm-servants' dairy chambers, and eaten of their honey and their bread, like any cowherd's daughter.

She knew that she could never wholly forget this; and the remembrance was acute suffering to her.

She would go into his presence the sovereign of his world, his equal, nay, his superior in rank, a beautiful, haughty, courted, idolized woman: and she would always remember that if only one of the lowest laborers on his land could recognize her and tell him the simple truth, he would know that in all her omnipotence and with all her attainments she was little better after all than a living lie to the world that adored her.

They had never met; they were to meet this night. And for that cause she aspired to make her beauty look even more than mortal, and for the sole time since she had seen her child's face mirrored in the brown depths of the Loire, was tempted to be almost discontented with that gracious and prodigal gift, and to desire that it should even be something yet more splendid than it was.

Why did she want this?—she could not have told. He would not know—never could know—that when he should look upon her now he should see the same features that he had once praised when he had ridden at evening among the vine-fields of his own lands. But *she* knew:—and she wanted to come with all the glory and magnificence of an empress before the man who had seen her last as a peasant child upon a vintage-wagon.

Proud as she was, Viva's was only half the pride of the born patrician; the other half was the pride of the Pompadours, of the Cabarus, of the Theodosias, who have sprung from the darkness of obscurity into the blaze of power. Her rank had grown as natural to her as it is to any legitimate sovereign; yet it was perpetually marvelous to her as it never can be to those who have enjoyed possession and dignity from their birth upward.

In one of the reception-chambers of the palace to which she went that night, a knot of those who guide the destinies of nations were standing conversing, at the moment of her entrance.

One of them leaned his arm on an ebony cabinet, and was turned slightly away from the brilliancy of the thronged rooms. He was of lofty and slender stature; very fair, with a grave, passionless beauty of feature, and an exceeding serenity and pride of bearing: a man to be singled out by the most careless spectator, whether in the press of a street crowd or the glitter of a throne-room,—a man who bore all the impress of one who had played a high part, and held a high name among the world's leaders.

The ministers speaking with him paused and broke off their discourse, and glanced through the rooms.

"There she is," said one of them. "Did you ever see so magnificent a creature?"

"I cannot tell. Her beauty remains only a rumor to me."

"What! You have never met her?"

"Never. I have heard so much of her that I have, I confess, somewhat avoided this marvel, the catalogue of whose charms has so often wearied me, and whose caprices I have known to interfere with the most serious deliberations."

"You are prejudiced. Wait until you have seen this sorceress. You do not know until then how beautiful a woman can be."

"Surely? I have seen so many beautiful women."

He spoke with a smile, but with a certain incredulous indifference to the subject which he was too courteous to express. Also, it was true that he had avoided, at such times as he had been near her presence, this woman of whom they spoke. He had heard nothing of her that attracted him; much that repelled. Her coquetry, her coldness, her neglect of her husband, her imperious volatile caprices, her wayward exercise of her wide power, her absolute abandonment to the utmost extravagance of pleasure: all these repulsed his taste in women.

"You are sceptical," said one of the statesmen beside him. "Look there, then—and believe."

He turned his head, and looked as they bade him.

Among the brilliant throng he saw her, diamond-crowned, diamond-winged, with a troop of little children of the highest races in the land playing before her and behind her as elves and fairies, as Pucks, Peas-blossoms, Cobwebs, and all the joyous band of Oberon, scattering lilies and laburnums, carnations and camellias in her path. It was summer still for her and them, though out in the streets an aged woman froze to death in an archway, from snow and from starvation.

"She is beautiful, indeed!" said Estmere, under his breath. At that moment she passed close by him, in the midst of her laughing cherubic fairies,—and their glances met.

She saw once more the blue, tranquil, thoughtful eyes that she had likened in her childhood to those of Arthur of England—eyes that she had never forgotten. And in her own there came a look of recognition, over her face passed a flush of surprise, of pleasure, and of apprehension all commingled. The look was gone, the warmth was faded, almost as soon as they had come, but he had caught them,—he who, to his own knowledge, never had beheld her. Others saw them also, and thought,—"Is it true that they have never met before?"

She floated past him in all the magnificence of her pageant: he never dreamed that, once ere then, looking at her when she had sat crowned with grape-leaves by the peasantry upon his lands, he had said of her—"*She* cannot be of the people."

The air of the world she dwelt in transfigures like the breath of the frost, and changes the wild-flower spray as though by magic into a glittering, chill, exquisite thing, dazzling as diamonds. But is the flower's fragrance any longer left?

A while later, and his presentation to her was offered in such fashion that he had no power left for the discourtesy of refusal: and as he bent before her and spoke in the melodious chill tones that she still remembered, she could not, with all her self-command, retain the perfect calm and negligence of her accustomed manner. And he, a man far too high-souled for vanity, and far too wearied to seek for conquest, wondered to himself what interest he could possess for this patrician coquette, to whom he was wholly a stranger.

He lingered a very brief while beside her; and passed onward, resigning his place to her more eager courtiers: for the first time she had failed to see admiration in the glance that had fallen on her, for the first time a chilliness of disappointed expectation touched her.

"The instinct of my childhood was a just one: he alone looks 'great,'" she thought, and in her soul she felt with bitterness, "And he alone sees no beauty in me!"

She often looked for him that night, but she saw him no more. He had quitted the palace very early.

"Is she not perfect?" one of his acquaintance had asked him that night.

Estmere had answered, "No."

"No! What does she lack, then?"

"Feeling. That woman lives only for herself."

And day after day, night after night, they met thus: and he greeted her and avoided her thus, with that ceremonious courtesy which is chillier than any rudeness or bitterness. Seeing him continually she yet saw nothing of him. If he had any sentiment toward her, it was aversion rather than homage; yet, from the high-bred serenity of his habitual manner, she could not extract so much flattery as would have even been found in censure or in insolence. He simply neglected her: keener affront, harder offence, there could scarcely have been against her.

The exception of this one man from her subjugation moved her to more interest in him than she ever felt for any of those who had been fooled by her glance and made wretched by her word. Although she, from a certain lofty pride in her, had been utterly untouched by any of the passion she inspired, she had never restrained herself from the fullest exercise of her sway over men's souls; she had never forborne from using the power that her beauty bestowed on her, using it with the uttermost witchery and enhancement that were possible. She had seen the extremes of passion, of devotion, of despair: she had studied the natures of her many lovers, till she had gained as deep an insight into their weakness as Coriolis herself could have attained. And Estmere alone escaped her,—the only man whom she had been tempted to meet with interest, to treat with reverence!

Nor could she have her vengeance for his neglect by mockery of him, by disdain for him. He was as far removed from her satire as he was from her seductions. There was that about him which hushed the vengeful ironies that rose to her lips. He had an influence over her that she could not resist, even while his studious avoidance of her most deeply incensed and mortified her.

He was "great," as her childish fancy had felt. Not by rank, or wealth, or honor, in which very many of her present world could far excel, and almost all could equal, him; but by the force of natural character, which gave an unstudied greatness to all his thoughts, motives, and actions; which lent a perfect and harmonious repose to his slightest words and movements; which rendered everything that was unworthy, insincere, untrue, or exaggerated, impossible to him; and which made base things show their baseness, lying lips halt in their falsehood, and unreal pretensions sink to their due insignificance before him. He was a statesman, an orator, a leader; and was great in all these; but greater in nothing than in the dignity and simplicity of his life, public and private: just, sincere, incapable of time-service, indifferent to every splendid bribe, gentle of temper, if severe in judgment, he won the reverence of all who came near his influence, and was honored even by the foes who resented the proud silence of his temperament and the patrician tenets of his code.

And it was precisely this character which attracted the mutinous, brilliant, uncertain, and imperious nature of this capricious and wayward woman. She was in her sweetest moods when he was near; she gave him her gayest wit, her airiest grace, her fairest smiles, and her most dazzling radiance;—all in vain.

Not the coldest word of admiration ever passed his lips to her; and she never once could change the calm, passionless, grave regard of the deep-blue meditative eyes that were like the eyes of the Roman Augustus.

## CHAPTER XII.

IN a miserable garret in the Quarter of the Odéon, a boy of eighteen lay on his little truckle-bed, prostrate with ague and with fever.

Although the winter had stolen into earliest spring, the weather was still bitter, and full of snow and ice, and sweeping northern winds. The youth suffered greatly. He was an art-student; the seventh son of a poor widowed woman, who kept a wretched wine and tobacco shop in the extreme east of France. He could have had no help from her if he had asked for it, and he was too proud and too tender of heart to ask, choosing rather to perish in this Paris, that had been the Eden of his desires, then to take one copper fraction from that scanty store of his helpless mother. He dreamed divine dreams of his own future, of the honors he would win, of the medals he would bear off, of the pictures he would paint, of the prize he would earn that would send him to study amid the greatness of Rome; and, meantime, he ornamented sweetmeat-boxes, as a means of livelihood in such days as his tertian ague left him free, and endured the daily agonies that killed Gilbert and Hegisippe Moreau, and still kill their kind—lads that an imperial nation has no time to count.

He was very ill, very miserable, very lonely; he was of a shy and silent temper, and had made no friends. His last coin was gone; he was too tortured by his disease to work.

He thought he should die, and die alone. And at eighteen both death and solitude are hard.

He was glad to hear a knock at his door—glad even though it were but his landlord, to whom he owed rent, come again to curse him for a sickly beggar. When he saw who it was that entered, his hollow eyes lightened with an exceeding joy.

"It is you!" he said, softly, with a sigh of infinite content and gratitude.

His visitant came up to him, and smiled, and spoke pleasant, soothing, cheerful words, and let a little black monkey leap out of his arms and play her antics on the pallet till they brought a wan laughter on to the boy's white cracked lips. Then he thrust some billets of wood that he had brought under his arm into the empty stove, and set light to them, and flung open the lattice for the cold but crisp air to enter; he poured some rich wine out of a flask he had in his pocket into a tin pot, and heated it when the wood had caught flame; he gave it to the lad upon the bed, with spices simmering in it, and a fresh roll of white flour to eat with it. Finally, he sat himself down beside the one little deal table, on which the brushes, and colors, and boxes waiting for ornamentation stood, and drew one of the sweetmeat-trunks to him, and began to paint on it, and gild its sides, and make it gay with flowers and fruits and birds, expending on it all the fair conceits of a luxuriant fancy.

The youth lay still and watched him with all the gratitude he was too weak to utter in speech.

Seven times in two weeks had his savior come thus; and restored life to him; had done his labor for him; and brought him the coins of his wage; had silenced the wrath and the complaints of the landlord; and spoken of the coming spring, and of the healing it would bear upon its wings. Spoken, too, of a cottage that he knew in the village of Barbizan, where, for a trifle a week, a lad might be housed and fed, and watch the great painters in their holiday, and have around him all the sweetness of the forest air, and see the primroses bud forth from among the moss, and the rabbits steal among the fern, and the tender leaves of the oaks unfold in the bright young year.

And when he had tried to thank him, and to ask him who he was and whence he came, his redeemer had laughed a little, and answered only:

"Tut!—I am Tricotrin."

And the boy, though but a new-comer into the city, had known all that the name spoke; and had asked no more.

His friend sat there through half the day, painting the lids of the boxes, wasting on them a hundred delicate graces, a hundred grotesque fancies, a hundred forms of loveliness and picturesqueness: because when genius abides in a man it will never let him do aught ill, but will ever thrust itself out in any work of his hand, be it of the simplest or the slightest.

He was only painting on sugar-boxes that would be sold for tenpence a piece. But the creative power in him called beauty into these common things, and he sketched on them as a king's painter sketches on a palace-cornice.

Twice or thrice he paused to give some food or some wine to the lad. Sometimes he went on with his labor in unbroken silence. Sometimes he called boyish laughter on to the youth's pale lips by gay drolleries of story or airy vagaries of wit. Sometimes he spoke—and this was oftenest —of that little nest in Barbizan, where so soon the breath of the spring would be bringing the birds from their nests, the foliage from the boughs, the roses from the briars, the wild hyacinths from the grass; and where he said that the boy should go.

Then, when he had done all the work that was there, he bade the lad a cheerful good night; left him with a big jug of milk beside him to ease his thirst; piled more wood on the stove; and went carrying the boxes with him, that he might get the payment for them, and put it in the hands of the landlord, who had sworn that if the rent went unpaid the youth should be turned out in the street.

As he went down the stairs a child met him, sent from the house that he dwelt in, with a letter received in his absence.

His face changed color as he broke the seal and read the one line within it—it was simply:

"Can you come to me during the day?"

He knew in whose handwriting that brief summons was penned—knew it, without the armorial bearings and the cipher that decorated the glossy sheet.

A thrill of hot delight ran through him. His heart beat quickly and joyously; his eyes flashed and lightened with pleasure.

She had not wholly forgotten!

He watched her life; but he scarce ever went into her presence. He had accepted oblivion, and he was too proud to assert a claim that she had forgotten. She was happy,—he let her be. If ever the time came when she knew what grief was, he would then go to her, not before.

But with her summons fresh joy flashed through him. He did not pause to speculate, to wonder, to doubt; he only cared for the fact that once more he had become a desire and a necessity in her life.

He did the duty to which he had pledged himself first. He turned down the street in which the bonbon box-maker dwelt, sold his merchandise, received a gold piece in exchange, and appeased with it the landlord's avaricious greed. Then he was free; and went with the swiftness of a greyhound whither she had called him.

His pulses were throbbing and his brain was dizzy as he was ushered into her presence. He did not know what he hoped, yet hope was strong in him. He gave joy away so often, with such lavish hands, to others, it could not seem strange to him one day that gift might be returned back into his own breast.

"You sent for me?" he asked, eagerly, with that radiance still on his face, as he approached her.

She turned to him with the instinctive coquetry of her nature.

"You never come to see me unless I do!"

The reproach was very sweet to him; the tone was like the accent of her early years.

"Why do I not?" he said, gently. "It is because such women as you do not have one want left for those who can only bring them love to fill up. You know too well that if you ever thought of me——"

He paused abruptly; in his code the one who stood as creditor for an unpaid debt of gratitude must never urge a claim forgotten by the debtor. Moreover, he who had loved her all her life through was too proud to speak to her of a love she had chosen to cast away, undesired, unrecalled.

"I do often think of you," she murmured, hurriedly. "Can you deem me so dead to all feeling? You! who were all the world to me once!"

"There is no need to remember that. Others have done much greater things for you since. But is there any service I can render you now?"

The unintentional reproach which lay in the inference that she must have some need of him or she would not have remembered him, escaped her.

"Service?—no," she answered, with a tinge of embarrassment. "Do you recollect Lord Estmere?"

He started, and moved slightly away; all the glow, and light, and warmth died from off his face; his eyes, which had dwelt on her with such gladness and such fondness, lost their radiance.

"Is it of him you desire to speak to me?"

"I have seen him again, that is all," she answered indifferently, conscious how insufficient must seem the cause for the action. "And—if I remember rightly, you seemed to know much of him. Is it so?"

"I know of him—yes."

"Then—do you know anything of him that the world does not?"

"Why do you ask that?"

"Why?" she said, impatiently, while, in her own despite, a flush of shame for the interest she had allowed herself to show for a man who gave her no homage and no admiration, passed quickly over her face. "It seemed strange to meet him in the world—that is all."

"You fear his recognition?"

"Oh, no! What have *I* in common with the child crowned in that village-wagon?" she interrupted him with capricious impatience, forgetful of the cruelty to him that lay in the scornful sentence. "I was only curious to hear anything you could tell me of him; because——"

"He interests you?"

She laughed with careless, contemptuous indifference; but he saw that her eyes fell, and that the flush was still on her face.

"Interest! I think nothing interests me,—except new diamonds! I mean, because,—I imagined, you must some time or other have come in contact with him. Was I right?"

"Lord Estmere and I are total strangers."

"Do you think any ill of him?"

"I believe him to be one of the noblest and most high-souled men on earth."

The answer was sincere, and given in the purity of truth; but it went hard with him, for all that, to give it utterance.

She looked at him silently a moment; swift in penetration, when she was not too careless to exercise the power, she saw that there was something withheld from her.

"Then—do you know anything of his life that the world does not?"

"Of his life? Nothing."

"There was some terrible story of his wife, was there not?"

"She was false to him—yes. The story is known to the whole world. She was a high-born woman, an exceedingly beautiful woman, and as sensual and as vile as any courtesan, at soul. He wedded her when he was but a youth; he adored her, I believe; and she—lived with him a few years only to dishonor his name forever for sake of a Greek slave in their household!"

"A Greek slave!"

"Well—with the nature and the vices of a slave; cowardly, timorous, false, and vengeful. The creature had owed all to Estmere's race,—a handsome boy of Athens, made first page and then secretary; an Adonis, pampered and caressed for his girlish loveliness; a graceful hound that first fawned and then bit! That was the paramour for whom Eustace Estmere was abandoned;—abandoned, I say! The sin was not half so openly sinned. It was the old tale of treachery and dishonor which did not hesitate to taint his own hearthstone!"

"But she is divorced from him?"

"Of course! But do you think that such a stain can ever leave a man's life as it found it? do you think the publicity of so close a shame can even pass away from a proud and a sensitive nature?"

"That is true; I forgot."

She thought of the grave fair face that she had once likened to the "King of the great Pendragonship," and of the anguish which in youth had gnawed at the heart of the man now so passionless and so tranquil.

She perceived that some chord she could not trace connected Tricotrin with the dishonor for which he felt so keenly. She remembered too, more vividly than she remembered most things of that forgotten time, the impatience with which he had heard her quote Estmere's praise of her after the vine-festival. She did not know that her young Faust of the golden toys had been the son of this dishonored wife. She did not know that he withheld that fact from her lest its disquietude should haunt and disturb her peace.

"Then you can tell me no more of him than this?" she said at last, with a certain disappointment in her voice.

He looked quickly at her.

"Of Estmere? No," he said, with bitter impatience. "What is it you can want to be told? His career lies before the world; he is a great man; and pays the penalty of such greatness in having the stare of a million curious eyes fastened on every dearest secret of his private life. Love betrayed him; he wedded himself to public ambitions. You can tell better than I whether they content him: if you take interest sufficient in him to make the matter your study."

She gave a restless movement.

"I imagine Lord Estmere has other aims beside happiness. I scarcely think any great man is likely to be happy; that belongs to peasants, to students, to youth, and provincialism. It is not much known in his world and in mine. If we are amused it is the utmost we ask. You do not think it possible that he should recognize me?"

"You fear it?"

"Fear it!" she echoed, as she rose with an impetuous movement, and turned her head instinctively to the mirror. "Fear it! Good Heaven! Of course I fear it—I should die of shame!——"

"You live on falsehood, then? A dangerous food—one sure, soon or late, to end in utter famine. But you need have no dread on this score. You were but a fair child then; now——"

"Now?"—she laughed softly, a low, victorious laugh of conscious power.

"Now—you know well enough what you are. Every man tells it you in eloquence that would be the most sickening tale you could hear were not vanity the sole passion that knows no satiety!"

She made no reply; a flush of resentment gleamed in her brilliant eyes, and unspoken words trembled passionately on her lips. She held them back by the lingering remembrance of the gratitude she owed him; she knew that she could not deny him the right of a speech that none else would have dared to utter to her.

He looked at her in silence many moments.

"You never think of a second marriage?" he asked, suddenly.

"Think of it!—I cannot choose but think of it! It is always being forced upon my thoughts! But if you mean do I intend one,—no!"

"And wherefore?"

"Ask me rather why I should!" she said, with a careless laugh. "What is there I could gain by it?"

"Gain is your only god, then?"

"That is very harsh! I do not think I am avaricious. But I have absolutely all that I can desire; I should risk jarring the harmony of my life, and I should add nothing worth adding to it by any other alliance. Besides,—my liberty charms me. I might marry for a throne perhaps; but there are none vacant just now!"

The levity and negligence of the reply grated cruelly on him!—she spoke of wedding with the sovereigns of the earth as though she were imperial born, to the man but for whose charity she would have been left to beggary and bastardy!

"You speak in jest," he said gravely. "Such jests are well enough in such a youth as yours, but if you have no other creed with which to meet the weariness of waning years and the loneliness of age, I pity you!"

"Pity me!"

She laughed in all the glory of her beauty, all the plenitude of her power, all the rich and full sufficiency of her existence!

"Yes, I pity you," he answered her, with that accent in his voice which had always stilled and moved her in her childhood. "Even from women as beautiful as you, time steals their charms; time brings satiety, lassitude, envy, and the disappointment of dead hopes; time confronts them with rivals, and takes the bloom from the cheeks, and the light from the eyes, and the gladness from the soul: in those days of darkness it will be ill with you if in the days of your youth you have only gained vanities that wither and ambitions that cloy, if you have not learned the sweetness and strength that lie in unselfish love and impersonal thought. You reign now—ah, yes! And I can well understand how your kingdom is so fair that you never remember how time like the sea eats away its bright shores, and how with each year it will grow less—and less—and less,—when once the season of your youth is passed. But what I fear for you, in your future, are the bitterness and the solitude that you will know, if—having disdained the anchorage of love—you shall be left alone on the rock of your pride, when your kingdom of beauty has sunk out of sight beneath the tide of the devouring years."

The voice that she had known so well; the poetic language that had used to move her heart like music had still their spell for her; she listened, incredulous and unwilling to be touched, yet stirred by the words against her own desire.

But the spirit of rebellion, the habits of mockery in her would not let her own to that reluctant emotion.

"You mistake very much, I think!" she said, negligently. "I do not believe a woman's power so evanescent; when youth goes there is intellect left. I am little of a student,—but the play of political power amuses me well. As for love,—pray credit me! that may be the Alpha and Omega of provincial life, it is merely one among a thousand other arts and distractions in the world that I live in. You may hear it made the be-all and end-all of existence at a peasant's bridal; but it wears another aspect in our drawing-rooms."

"I know. It is represented by vice, intrigue, ambition, and avarice! Madame de Lirà—think me as harsh as you will,—I confess that the courtesan, who dances in the paint and tinsel of her wretched trade, is not in my sight much the inferior of you great ladies, who wed yourselves for gain, and intrigue for aggrandizement from your bridal to your death-hour! I am not sure, after all, that when in your childhood I dissuaded you from entrance on an actress's career, I did not withold you from the more honest, if the less lucrative, position of the two."

She heard him in mute amaze, her eyes surveying with a

grand wrath the man who dared bring such bare truths as these into her presence: who dared force the nakedness of an unpolished fact upon the elegant artifices of her daily life. She said nothing; but with a bow, in which all her anger and all her dignity were mutely uttered, she swept past him and out of the chamber.

"Can nothing teach him what I have become!" she thought, with passionate forgetfulness of every other thing than of her own eminence and sovereignty.

It seemed to her almost a crime against her that a man should live who held it in his power thus to arraign and to insult her.

She forgot that she had summoned him; she only remembered that he had dared to speak to her—the truth.

When she had left him, he paced to and fro the deserted room, with his head sunk upon his chest, and his heart sick within him.

She had stung him far more deeply than she had dreamed: she had dealt him a blow she had been all unconscious of striking. He had come to her bidding with the gladness of a love eager to spend its loyalty in service, with the unselfishness of a tenderness, oblivious of its own claims, and grateful for mere remembrance; and he had been only met with the name of Estmere!

"Must he have all—even her thoughts!" he said, in the bitterness of his soul. The time had been,—nay, the time was still,—when, thinking of the career of the great noble, he had balanced its pain, its toil, its fretting ambitions, its early dishonor, its surrender to the fetters of public service against the freedom and the careless joys of his own life, and had laughed as he felt how free was the one from the cares of the other. Now for the first time there arose that which he envied Estmere.

For, the love with which he had loved the fair child who had wandered with him through the illuminated streets of the rejoicing city,—who had laughed with him among the vineyards of her river-home, and danced for him with the wild poppies in her hair, and sung to him as she bounded aloft upon the grape-press,—was love tenfold more passionate, because tenfold more hopeless, for this imperious and peerless woman who would almost have scorned to yield her beauty even to a monarch's embraces.

As he left her palace, the song so often on his lips was silent; his head, always so gallantly erect, was sunk; his heart was heavy within him.

He thought he had controlled this weakness in him;—but though passion when blessed with possession flies as fast as the hues of the rainbow,—passion, whose only food is pain, glows on and on, unblenched, like the red in an Egyptian sky, through the long years of drought and famine.

He bent his steps toward the religious hospital, where a few nights before he had left the dying frame of his enemy.

The words that he had lately spoken had recalled to him a forgotten duty.

"Is it better with him?" he asked at the entrance-gate.

"Scarcely. He will never recover, we think."

"I have three gold pieces on me; all I have: will you take them?"

"Take them? For this man?"

"Yes—spend it for him in such fashion as seems wisest to you; I will bring more shortly. If it be possible, employ what I can bring, so that when he goes forth once more to the world he may have a chance of purer life,—if that can be."

"You know him?"

"I know of him."

"And you are his friend?"

"No. His foe."

"His foe? And yet——? Well, it shall be as you say."

"I thank you. All I desire is,—never let him learn that it was I who brought him here, or that it is I who do this thing. Give him no burden of gratitude save to yourselves."

Then he turned away, and went on through the night once more.

They were well used to him, and asked him no questions.

Since he had saved this miserable life from dissolution, he deemed that he had a right to give it one added chance to cleanse itself from crime. But the hate that he bore to him as his enemy was none the less keen and burning, because justice to him as a fallen wretch outweighed it. "The thing which I should have done as just to a stranger, must I do as none the less just to my foe," was the principle which his actions followed. The laws of men were not the laws of life. Yet, nevertheless, he could have slain the Greek who lay yonder had he given rein to his passion.

"And the woman lived who could forsake Estmere for that Judas!" he mused as he paced the gloomy streets backward to the gayer quarters of the city. "Truly there are women who turn to evil as the swine to filth; and know no more than swine the pearls that lie beneath their feet!"

## CHAPTER XIII.

IN a by street, in an obscure quarter of Paris, there dwelt an artist who had suddenly achieved fame—so suddenly that he had had no time to change his abode, to meet his new visitant, Fortune,—a guest who has ever had a curious habitude of changing the broken chairs, the chipped pipe-trays, the lame-legged table, the lumber and the poverty of a painter's work-room, into costly couches, antique bronzes, ebony cabinets, eastern embroideries, picturesque color, and luxurious ease, but who not unfrequently turns out with the old rubbish, a witch-stone that she found there, called genius. Critics and connoisseurs rarely, however, detect its absence.

This artist, Paul Lélis, was not young when Fortune suddenly bethought herself of him; and he clung to his witch-stone; and he did not care to leave that old familiar nook high under the roof, where he had spent so many bohemian years—where he had known what it was to have to lie in bed all day in winter to keep from perishing of cold, to have to scratch little pictures for sweetmeat-boxes to get a mouthful of onions and bread; to have to face a dish without bread, a stove without warmth, a pipe without smoke, and still to keep the soul to create, alive and unnumbed,—where too he had known what it was to love and have love, and see the brown eyes of his mistress shine tenderly, though in a garret; and where, through his lattice, he possessed so glorious a view over the roofs and the spires and the crowns of the trees, of the red gold of the sunsets, and the pale gold of the dawns, and all the marvelous, mystic, eternal loveliness of the ever-changing clouds.

Lélis clung to his attic; being a strange man, and a man of tenacious attachment, and a man of stubborn will; and since the world had taken the fancy to adore him, he made it toil wearily and pantingly up the hundred and twenty-two stairs to his room. Lélis had tarried long enough in his time on the threshold of great men's antechambers; it was his turn now to wait and refuse to stir, and see them labor up his crooked, unsavory, oil-lit stairway. And he would laugh grimly, standing at the top.

"I painted as well twenty years ago; why did you not see it then?" was all that he said to his patrons.

Why did they not?—and those tender brown eyes of the mistress of his youth had grown dim and tired, and closed in never-ending slumber, just because they had never seen it, and there had been no food on the naked shelf.

The world had come to him at last, because a great man, chancing to fall on a little study of his, had recognized the worth in it, and had groped his way through the darkness to the attic; and, being one whose word was powerful, and whose knowledge of art was undoubted, had in time been followed to the garret by the world.

Lélis was grateful as a dog to the man; but he was cynical to the world.

"You are bitter, Lélis," said the personage who had thus brought the world to his door.

"No; I am just," said the artist. "For you—you had not seen my pictures till you lit on that little thing, and came straight to me. But Paris—look you—Paris has seen them through a score of years, and would find no color in them, and no form, because her critics swore that there were none. If it be the truth now that I can paint, why have they lied all through these years? tell me that."

"Why? Because it is so much easier to repeat a parrot cry than to use the faculties of vision and judgment; so much easier to damn with facile unanimity than to bend the brain and the sight to the patience of investigation and appreciation!"

"That is true, whoever says it. Who is with you, Lélis?" a voice called from the doorway.

Without awaiting an answer the new-comer pushed the atelier door open, and entered. On the threshold he paused, as though inclined to draw back; but the impulse was conquered, and he came forward to where the artist and his patron stood.

"It is my Lord Estmere," said Lélis, turning with warm familiar greeting.

"So you have brought Fame to Lélis, my English lord?" said Tricotrin, without ceremony. "That was a good work of yours. She is a comet that has a strange fancy only to come forth like a corpse-candle, and dance over men's graves. It is her way. When men will have her out in the noon of their youth, she kills them; and the painter's bier is set under his Transfiguration, and the soldier's body is chained to the St. Helena rock, and the poet's grave is made at Missolonghi. It is always so."

Estmere bowed his head in assent; he was endeavoring to remember where he had once met this stranger who thus addressed him—where he had once heard these mellow, ringing, harmonious accents.

"Was it because you were afraid of dying in your prime,

that you would never woo Fame then yourself?" asked Lélis, with a smile.

"Oh-hé!" answered Tricotrin, seating himself on a deal box that served as a table, and whereat he and the artist had eaten many a meal of roast chestnuts and black coffee. "I never wanted her; she is a weather vane, never still two moments; she is a spaniel that quits the Plantagenet the moment the battle goes against him, and fawns on Bolingbroke; she is an alchemist's crucible, that has every fair and rich thing thrown into it, but will only yield in return the calcined stones of chagrin and disappointment; she is a harlot, whose kisses are to be bought, and who runs after those who brawl the loudest and swagger the finest in the world's marketplaces. No! I want nothing of her. My lord here condemned her as I came in; he said she was the offspring of echoing parrots, of imitative sheep, of fawning hounds. Who can want the creature of such progenitors?"

Estmere smiled.

"I do not think that I said anything of the kind. You accredit me with your own ironies."

"Did you not? Well—it was the deduction from your words, at any rate. How fares my Dante?"

"The Dante!" echoed Estmere in surprise, and with sudden remembrance. "Ah! I surely remember now; it was you who made me the fortunate possessor of that rare specimen of Attavante?"

"A very polite phrase; it was your own gold that made you the possessor of it. Yes; I sold it to you. I wonder you recollect it; but great men have clearer memories, I believe, than little busy-bodies. The book lives still?"

"Certainly; in my library at Villiers."

"He sold his Dante?" asked Lélis. "He and I have known what hunger and cold mean, both of us. The kingdom of Bohemia has other sides to it than the side that humorists sketch, and that poets portray. The dance, the song, the laugh; the holiday in the woods, the waltz in the cabaret, the romp in the orchard,—it has them indeed; but then no less has it also the fireless stove, the soupless platter, the winter nights of starvation, the dull stupid misery staring out of a garret window to watch the lights being lit in the palace over the river."

"Bagatelle!" cried Tricotrin, "if we are true bohemians we stamp our feet in the snow till we are warm, we read Rabelais till we forget to be hungry, and we look up at the winter planets, and think how pale they make the palace gas look. Bah, Lélis!—has fame already turned you renegade?"

"If Bohemia do indeed make such philosophers of its subjects, it must have been as deeply wronged by the world's construction as the Epicurean doctrines!" said Estmere, with that mixture of contempt and wonder, which a man of his character and of his order feels for the disciples of the religion of "*rire, et ne rien faire.*"

"Nay," said Tricotrin, "I will not profess for it as Lucretius does of Epicureanism, that in reality it consists of renunciation. But I believe, on the whole, its followers bear deprivation better than most followers of other deities,— which may be the second best thing perhaps. But you can know and tell nothing of it, Lord Estmere; it is a world you have never entered!"

"I can endure my exclusion!"

"I will warrant you can; but, nevertheless, if you had entered once in awhile, you might have learned a few things useful perhaps; and you might have unlearned the only thing that mars your character and your career, to my fancy."

"You do my character and my career much honor by making them the objects of your study."

Tricotrin smiled: the sarcasm did not sting him.

"I study most things, after my own fashion," he said, carelessly. "Though, to be sure, an English Eupatrid like you is a little too cold and costly a crystal, may be, and comes from too high a glacier to fit well into a bohemian's microscope. And, in truth, I like you better for your loyalty to your Order; it becomes you. The Optimate flattering the Populares, because he fears the deluge, is the most pitiable spectacle that the world holds. I like your exclusivism better."

"I am happy to merit and receive your approbation!" said Estmere, with his delicate contempt.

"You think a bohemian should not even venture to praise a statesman?" laughed Tricotrin. "Oh, I know that temper of yours so well;—it just does what it sees fit and deems becoming its royalty; and cares not two straws whether the nations shout exultation or execration after its acts. You would go to the guillotine as you would receive your country's stars and crosses,—with just the same indifference, with just the same conviction that neither decapitation nor decoration could add anything to, or take anything from, your dignity!"

Estmere glanced at him with some wonder, and with more distaste; and, without reply, turned to examine some sketches that leaned against the wall.

Among them was a little pinewood panel, on which was painted the head of a child of some fourteen years, with a red hood half over her curls, and her eyes gazing out, as if into the future, half smiling, half awed, with eagerness, with rapture, and with a tinge of fear.

"That is very lovely," he said, as he turned it to the light. "It is yours, Lélis, of course?"

"The thing belongs to me," interrupted Tricotrin, quickly. "And it is not for sale."

"Perhaps you can oblige me with the name of the artist?"

"No! He wants no patronage."

The answer was curt and ungracious. Estmere laid the panel down as he heard.

"Whoever painted it must have genius."

"Genius!" interrupted Tricotrin. "Pooh! What is genius? Only the power to see a little deeper and a little clearer than most other people. That is all."

"The power of vision? Of course. But that renders it none the less rare."

"Oh, yes, it is rare—rare like kingfishers, and sandpipers, and herons, and black eagles. And so men always shoot it down, as they do the birds, and stick up the dead body in glass cases, and label it, and stare at it, and bemoan it as 'so singular,' having done their best to insure its extinction!"

Estmere looked keenly at him.

"Surely genius that secretes itself as your friend's must do," he said, touching the panel afresh, "commits suicide, and desires its own extinction?"

"Pshaw!" said Tricotrin, impatiently, and with none of his habitual courtesy. "You think the kingfisher and the black eagle have no better thing to live for than to become the decorations of a great personage's glass cabinets? You think genius can find no higher end than to furnish frescoes and panelings for a nobleman's halls and ante-chambers? You mistake very much; the mistake is a general one in your Order. But believe me, the kingfisher enjoys his brown moorland stream, and his tufts of green rushes, and his water-swept bough of hawthorn; the eagle enjoys his wild rocks, and his sweep through the air, and his steady gaze at the sun that blinds all human eyes;—and neither ever imagine that the great men below pity them because they are not stuffed, and labeled, and praised by rule in their palaces! And genius is much of the birds' fashion of thinking. It lives its own life! and is not, as you connoisseurs are given to fancy, wretched unless you see fit in your graciousness to deem it worth the glass-case of your criticism, and the straw-stuffing of your gold. For it knows, as kingfisher and eagle know also, that stuffed birds nevermore use their wings, and are evermore subject to be bought and be sold."

An answering sarcasm rose to Estmere's lips—he had seen the vultures of genius, deeming themselves eagles, ofttimes so ravenous for his gold!—but he checked it, for he remembered that both these men were poor, that neither was his equal. He laid aside the panel once more in silence, and, with a farewell to the painter Lélis and a bend of his head to the stranger, passed from the room.

"You were surely rude to him, Tricotrin," said the artist, as the door closed.

"I might be so."

"But why should you be so? He is a man whom one can honor with sincerity; he is generous without ostentation, full of infinite thought for others, and has the tenderness of a lover, not the condescension of a patron, for all Art."

"I do not dispute his high qualities; but he is safe to be surfeited with sycophants, a rough word can do him no harm. As far as I know aught of him, he prefers an acid truth to a sugared lie."

"But why would you not let him learn that you painted that little study?"

"To what use? I once sold him a book. He would never have understood that I would not sell him a picture. Moreover—you know well enough I am a kingfisher, and I like my brook to be quiet. If my lord there once took it into his fancy to point me out to his world, my brook would be forever muddy with the feet of gazers, and forever choked up with the purses they would fling at me. Art is my tuft of rushes, my wild hawthorn bough, that lend me shade and sweetness. I do not want to be asked to vend them at so much a blade, at so much a blossom!"

And he threw a cloth over the panel, and put it under his arm, and crossed over to the easel.

Lélis said no more. He knew the temper of his friend; and he did not know that any memory endeared this little portrait of the child in her scarlet hood. He had been away in Egypt at the autumn season when the bright eyes of the Waif had first gazed upon Paris; and of her Tricotrin never spoke.

Estmere meantime went out to where his horse waited, and passed on to pursue his visits to various houses where painters, obscure, poor, some young, some old, but all unable to seize the world in that mood which gives fame to those who know how to strike the hot iron aright, lived in that misery of the physical life, and that supremacy of the mental life, which are at once the curse and the blessing of such men's existence.

Estmere was well known to the whole art-world for the patience with which he would seek out buried talents; for the delicacy and discrimination which tempered in him the connoisseur's ofttimes too pitiless science; for the munificence and graceful generosity wherewith his gifts and his aids were invariably given. Though cold, contemptuous, negligent, and keen of satire, with his equals, to men of genius who lived in poverty he was ever gentle, cordial, tolerant of all prejudice, and skilled at rendering his assistance in such fashion that he never made them conscious of their debt.

Some time elapsed in the visits that he paid; it was much later in the day when he rode through the quarter on his homeward way. In one of its tortuous streets his farther passage was blocked by a throng of people who had poured out from the wineshops, the masons' yards, the miserable houses near, and congregated in one narrow way before a stone-worker's little court, which in its turn was filled by a dense, close-packed, screaming mob.

It was the fashion to flock to Lélis, who was at that moment the chief theme of Paris; and two or three equipages were arrested, like himself, by this frantic and tumultuous crowd, against which outriders and equerries vainly thrust their animals, and lifted their whips.

"What is it?" he asked: his servants answered him that it was a mere nothing:—a rope had given way in a well which they were clearing, and had precipitated a workman seventy feet into the choke-damp and water:—that was all: the populace was always so excitable, so noisy about nothing. That their lord should be delayed, merely because a stonemason was drowning in a dead well, was intolerable, was ridiculous.

"It is you who make revolutions!" thought Estmere, as he heard his attendants' mockery of their own class, and strove in vain to force his horse against the press. There was a louder cry going up from the throats of the street crowd: in its uproar he could hear the words—"Tricotrin!"

"Who is it that is hurt?" he asked of an art student nearest him: the lad replied readily:

"The stone-mason has fallen—of course: but it is Tricotrin who is gone down to save him; it is Tricotrin we are anxious about."

"He will find but a corpse; and he will never come up alive himself!" cried a black-browed woman of the fishmarts: her dark, hard, coarse features working with strong emotion. "I know what that well is:—my father was killed there thirty years ago. It is full of poison."

"They wanted to lower a dog down to see if the beast could live in the air!" cried the shrill piping voice of a baker's boy. "But Tricotrin would not have it so; he said we had no business to imperil a poor brute that could not speak for itself; he called it cowardly to put a cur in a place we were afraid of ourselves!"

"Silence, silence!" shouted a score of voices. "We cannot hear what they are saying in the yard!"

What they were saying in the yard,—in broken tempestuous outcries,—was that they had left fifty yards of cord out over the windlass, and both men were still at the bottom.

"Is he dead?" shrieked the mob outside, in a frantic paroxysm of terror.

"Is he dead?" echoed a woman's voice, with a thrill in it that froze the hearts of every hearer of it. Estmere, absorbed, like the people, in listening for the answer from the little courtway and in watching the violent gesticulations and useless movements of the throng within it, started and turned his head. At his side stood an open equipage, glittering in all the panoply of rank; in it its owner had risen, and the haughty beauty of her face was rigid and colorless and strained with horror. He recognized the face of the Duchess de Lirà.

"She has a soul in her,—for she has pity," he thought,

touched by that terror on a countenance commonly so dazzling and so chill—a terror for the physical hazard of an unknown man, for the beating hearts of a plebeian crowd, for simple tragedies of daily life, as he believed it.

At that moment a loud moan came from the throng within the little court.

"Do ye hear?" cried the fishwoman, mad with emotion, and struggling upward till she had set her bare feet upon the motionless carriage-wheel in such fashion as gave her nearer sight. "That was how they moaned when they dragged my father up dead! Hark what they say,—all the rope is run out, and it is as dark as pitch in the pit,—the choke-damp has killed the light that he carried!"

The cry shuddered through the people.

The light was out! Was all hope over?

The slender fair hand of the patrician woman clinched the brown, brawny arm of the fishgirl in an unconscious gesture: in the instinctive sympathy of the same fear, the same love, the same anguish.

An awful hush fell upon the crowd,—alone, and raised above the others, the two women stood side by side, with scarcely one touch of common sex or common humanity betwixt them in their vast divergence, yet made as one in that brief moment by the unison of dread, by the leveler of grief.

Then from the press within the yard a shout of wild joy echoed: joy hysterical, triumphant, adoring. The rope had curled a hundred times back again over the windlass; they had drawn him upward to the fairness of the day; he was living,—he was unhurt,—he had spoken to them,—his light was out indeed, but it had only fallen in the water, because he had loosed his hold on it to seize the lost man's body, and bear it up to the living world. He was safe!—and even the mason whom he had rescued might still live also. The crowd went mad with ecstasy, and all the infectious strength of heroism; as it had gone mad a moment earlier with pity and with fear.

Thus ardently will the high daring of one man work on,

and fuse, and melt, and set alight the sluggish, apathetic, selfish mass of human lives.

The aristocrat in her carriage sank silently downward among her cushions, her face was white to the lips; and she trembled violently.

The fishwoman flushed a deep red over her tawny skin, and muttered a curse in the jargon of her tirade, and bent over her creel that had got shaken and half emptied in the crush.

Estmere had never withdrawn his gaze from the face of the woman whom he had condemned as so cold an egotist, so heartless a coquette; and whom he now beheld thus moved by what he deemed were sympathy and compassion for unknown and imperiled lives. Some wonder touched him at the strength of the emotion that he saw in her: but it was outweighed by the attraction which this pain, and pity, and infinite fear, softening that dazzling countenance, possessed for him; imagining them as he did to be born from that mere human sorrow for human suffering which gentle-natured women feel for the calamity of a stranger, for the pang of the lowest creature upon earth. He bent to her, and addressed her with a more tender accent in his voice than she had ever heard: she started as his words fell on her ear, and answered him hurriedly,—

"Ill? No, I ail nothing. I thank you much. This scene has shocked me: that is all. Can you learn for me,—how it is really with him?——"

"With the man who fell?"

"No! With the man who saved him! Is heroism so common in this self-absorbed and brutalized age of ours that we shall do it no homage, show it no interest?"

"I honor it as greatly as you can do," he answered her gently, and with some surprise. "I will go at once, and see him myself, if possible."

He went, and as quickly as he could, having dismounted, forced his way into the court. She sat breathless and motionless; her mouth was parched, her brain throbbed, her limbs quivered,—in that hour all the long-buried, long-forgotten memories of her childhood, and all the love she had once borne the savior of her life, awoke in passionate remorse. She was so base, so low, so cowardly in her own sight:—these people, these creatures of the cellar, and the wineshop, and the fish-mart, and the timber-yard were true to him, were loyal to him, dared show their fealty to him and their fears for him. But she!—she who scorned dastards, and loathed liars with all the force of a proud and fearless temper, sat silent, and motionless, and stirred not to welcome him from out the jaws of death!

The fishwoman, shouldering afresh her huge creel, looked curiously at this "aristocrat," who had been joined with her for one instant in the communion of terror.

"She must care for him,—in some fashion," she mused. "Her great eyes looked all blind and mad. They say these cold, dainty things in their palaces, sometimes,—well! she is the first of them I have not hated."

The subject of her thoughts, with a sudden impulse, leant to her with a score of gold pieces in her hand.

"Your merchandise is half lost," she said hurriedly. "Let me put these in your basket in their stead."

The fishwoman fastened her black ruthless eyes on her as the eyes of her ancestress might have fastened on the white, haughty loveliness of Marie Antoinette.

"I have not earned your money. I do not want it," she said, curtly. "But I like you, though you are one of *them;*—you care for Tricotrin."

She shouldered her creel and went.

The Duchess de Lira leaned back in her carriage very pale still, and with a quiver in her curling, haughty mouth. The words struck to her heart like a blow of steel.

"That woman is nobler than I!" she thought, bitterly. "She is not ashamed of what she feels for him,—she can dare to have sincerity!"

Estmere returning, approached her again through the swiftly-dispersing crowd.

"You have seen him?" she asked, feverishly, with a curious apprehension of what evil she scarcely could have told.

"No: I regret to say I found it impossible to obey your wishes and my own," he answered her. "This hero of the populace must be of a strange temper, and of a very noble one. He was no sooner safe above ground, they say, than he dived into a house, and disappeared through its back ways into some adjoining lane, to escape the eulogy and the adoration of the people. The mason whom he went down to save is breathing and can speak; there is no doubt of his recovery. It was a noble rescue: I regret more than I can say, not to have been in time to arrest the actor in it."

"If he be gone so swiftly he can have no hurt?" she asked with a deep quick breath.

"None. It seems that he is of a singular strength and agility: such men escape where weaklings or fools would perish. And now, shall we move from this throng? Where is it that you desire to go?"

She endeavored to smile as she answered him:

"I was about to visit your wonderful Lélis. But the noise of this crowd has made me disinclined for anything save quietude. I will return to my hotel if you please."

He assented, and rode beside her carriage through the long and various roads that led from that poor and obscure neighborhood to her gates.

The color was still blanched from her face, and she was both graver and gentler than her wont; but to him she had never been so seductive.

"She has feeling in her. I did her wrong," he mused; and his nature was one which ever led him, in view of an injustice done, to make even too full and too generous an amends.

As he left her at her own residence, and went homeward himself, his thoughts lingered over the scene which had touched her thus deeply.

"Tricotrin?—Tricotrin?" he murmured. "Tricotrin? I

have heard that word somewhere. Surely it is the name or the pseudonym of that man whom I spoke with to-day; of that man who once sold me my Dante!"

And he felt a certain regret; for, toward the hero who had gone down into the foul air and poisonous perils of the well in the stone-yard, he felt the attraction of one courageous temper to another; but toward the bohemian who had treated him with such unceremonious familiarity on that morning, he felt the aversion of a haughty and exclusive Order for a class in which all that it deems most perilous and most lawless are embodied.

"They are strange men—these Ishmaels of social life," he thought. "They will plunge into all the chances of a horrible death to rescue some fellow-creature from a tomb, or share it with him if his delivery be impossible; and yet they will beguile, and lead, and drag, and goad hundreds of those poor, ignorant, blind wild-beasts of the populace to be mowed down at barricades and in street riots, on the mere impulse of a rabid hatred of Class, on the mere chimera of that 'Universal Equality' which every law of nature and of science proves an impossibility—a monstrosity that would be found utterly untenable if it ever could even be reached and essayed!"

As he thus mused of a theme so different, there drifted back into his thoughts, by some untraceable connection, the memory of the little portrait he had seen of the child in the scarlet hood.

He recollected what fugitive intangible likeness it had been which had attracted him in the golden, bright, tender-hued picture—it was a likeness to the woman from whom he had that hour parted.

Though the face of a gipsy child, yet surely it had a look like this scornful court beauty, this omnipotent Duchess de Lira.

"That man must have, himself, been the artist," mused Estmere. "I will ask Lélis of him."

But when he asked Lélis he found that the painter could tell him but little.

"Tricotrin?" said Lélis, "Tricotrin? Yes: it is surely his name, my Lord Estmere. And why should it not be? We have odd names among us; odder than that. Of Tricotrin I know nothing: except the one thing—that I have loved him for far over twenty years. We are not given to the asking of credentials, to the taking of passports, we of Bohemia. He may spring from sovereigns; he may come from cobblers; I cannot tell you. Of a surety I never asked him.

"We met first of all at a Wirthshaus in Bavaria. I forget where exactly; but in one of those pretty quaint villages toward the Tyrol. There was a big brawny man with a box of fantoccini, and there was a slender dark girl, with a tambourine, whose duty it was to play while the puppets danced. There was a little black monkey, starved, frightened, miserable; ordered to dance also, and shivering and moaning piteously, instead of dancing.

"The big man thrashed the little monkey till it shrieked; the girl wept, and then the man beat her. Tricotrin and I were sitting in the wooden gallery over the door, taking our wine. He saw all this, and down he leapt from the porch, right over the rails and the vine; got the stick from the man, and collared him, and belabored him till he swore and screamed as only a Roman could do. Then he flung the wretch into the river; a brawling, foaming, shallow stream, that wetted him to the skin. Then he lifted the monkey up in his arms, caressed it, talked to it, took off its little dress, and came up again to the gallery, and sat down to his walnuts and wine.

"The Roman made a horrible outcry below; Tricotrin looked over the wooden rail and threw him a doubloon.

"'Brute,' said he, 'I will come down and give you another beating, if you desire it; also another ducking, with readiness. But have your monkey again you never will. There is its value as a marketable thing; of any other value you know naught. If you have wisdom you will betake yourself to some other hostelry.'

"The man slunk off, pocketing his doubloon, and Tricotrin kept his monkey. That is how I came to know him first. I thought that scene better warranty of his character than a banker's certificate. But then we bohemians have queer notions."

## CHAPTER XIV.

THE stone-mason, lying in the narrow hospital bed, with broken limbs and bruised body, unhappy in his thoughts, and fast fretting himself to fever over the coming destitution of his wife and children through the many weeks wherein he would be unfit for labor, was made happy by news which came to him. News that a great lady, who had chanced to witness the accident from her carriage, had sent her people to say that she would charge herself with all the needs of his family during such time as he should be incapable of labor, and after also if they needed it.

The man was a tough republican, a communist to the core, one who had been in troubles of the barricades, and who had tasted prison fare more than once for the too frank and sturdy utterance of his opinions over the black coffee and the domino-table of his evening haunt. But he swore a great oath, with the tears falling like rain down his cheeks, and muttered:

"I will never say one word against the aristocrats again! They will have bread, do you hear? my little ones will have bread!"

For the great revolutionist of Hunger, who preaches with a force so frightful and an illogical eloquence that the dullest can comprehend, had been his chief political teacher; and had bade him take a pike because he could not lay his hand on a loaf.

The servants of Estmere, sent to inquire what could be done for the family of this injured workman, brought him word that they had been forestalled by a few minutes only; all that the poor people wanted would be supplied to them by the Duchess de Lira—a support much needed, for the wife was infirm of health, and lame, and there were more children than generally crowd around a French laborer's table, to share its sour bread and meager onion soup.

"She must have a noble temper; I may have done her wrong," he thought once again.

Was it possible that behind this woman's dazzling extravagance, and egotism, and vanities, and vagaries, and semblance of utter heedlessness and heartlessness, there were hidden such gracious and generous things of mercy, and of pity as was this?

It seemed only just to think so. He was willing to believe it; he did believe. And a danger that had never been in her before for him, gave her peril for him now.

She might be callous only because none had known how to awaken her heart. She had been wedded so young to an unloved lord: this in itself was so dire a temptation. She was flattered by fools, who weakened her reason, while they heated and strengthened her errors and her foibles. She was surrounded by an atmosphere so artificial, by a homage so deteriorating, by influences so dangerous both morally and mentally.

There was so much excuse for her faults and follies, for her cruelties and egotisms; who could tell how fair and sweet a nature might not wake into life, if—she loved?

So he mused, with fanciful conjectures; fancies wholly unlike his grave, sarcastic, and sceptical intelligence, but characteristic of every man attracted by a woman, whose sorceries charm him while his reason condemns her.

He commenced a study that was the most hazardous tribute to her power he could have rendered; he commenced the study of her temperament, of her actions, of her heart. Oftentimes when she resented the neglect he was guilty of toward her, the silence he preserved in her presence, the indifference with which he remained apart while others crowded around her, she, and she alone, occupied his thoughts that were intent on analyzing her ironies, scanning her coquetries, and weighing the changeful indices of her anomalous vagaries.

He saw much that repelled, much that offended, much that alienated him, in her: but he also saw much that irresistibly beguiled him, and much that seemed to him to tell of a dormant soul, which only slumbered because none had known aright how to stir it from its indolent sleep.

"There should be a fine nature there; with such eyes as those no woman, surely, can be soulless," he mused, as he glanced at her one night, at one of the many houses where they were in the habitude of meeting.

"Of what were you thinking, Lord Estmere, when you looked at me so keenly an hour ago?" she asked of him, later on, when he took for a moment a seat beside her.

"It would be to risk your anger to answer frankly."

"And any other than a frank reply you would not give? Of how few of the men that I know could I say the same! Well,—answer me candidly then: hazard my anger."

He leaned slightly nearer to her: a cantata that was being sung by the most famous singers of Paris prevented their words reaching the ears of any around them.

"My thoughts then were——could a woman with so much poetry in her face as Madame de Lirà carries in hers, be as utterly given over to the vanities, the artifices, and the egotism of her world, as the whole tenor of her life, acts, and words, would lead one to infer?"

"You but wonder what I wonder, also!" she said with an accent in the answer which left no doubt of its sincerity. "We women, I think, have poetry on our lips, poetry sometimes in our faces; but we have hard, bitter, bad prose in our hearts—the passionless calculating prose of avarice, of self-love, of insatiable ambition!"

"Nay—you at least must have something higher than this, or you would not lay blame to yourself!"

"Why? May not one see one's own sin, even when one

is saturated through and through with it? A man murders; but I do not believe he ever ceases to see bloodshed as hateful. So we murder our higher natures, but, if we have anything of conscience left in us, we know that the slaughter is criminal."

"You have not killed yours if you still regret it?"

"How can you tell? I can scarcely tell myself. I have not killed it? No! By such a subtle euphuism as that by which Byzantine sovereigns swore they had not killed their predecessors, when they had only smote their eyes to blindness, and sealed their lives down in dungeons!"

He regarded her earnestly.

"You have not killed it. With you the prison-bars will be loosed, and the blinded eyes will see the light, when——"

"When what?"

"When you shall love."

The graveness and the sadness of his voice made the words far more impressive than if they had been uttered in the accent of a lover. They were passionless and melancholy, strangely contrasting with the gayety, the brilliancy, and the levity of the palace-scene around them.

She heard, with a sense of proud joy, that she had thus compelled even from him the homage of interest and warning; also with a vague sense of wonder why the speech of this man—who in all things was most utterly dissimilar to him—brought back on her thoughts, and carried with them the same influence as the utterances of Tricotrin.

"Pardon me the freedom of speech," pursued Estmere, with a slight weary smile. "By the years which are between us, I may use a latitude of phrase that would be denied to others younger and more fortunate, although less privileged. You asked for my candor; I have given it. I believe that much softness, which you now abjure, will awaken in you when love shall have been taught to you."

Her eyes clouded, and gleamed impatiently under their languid lids and curling lashes. She was incensed at the care with which he had hastened to disclaim for his words the look of any amorous meaning, and to indicate that he left the sweet task of teaching such lessons of love to all others who might choose to take it.

"Love!" she echoed, with a light laugh. "I have said often before,—I am tired of only hearing the word! I have no want of it, no belief in it!"

"That was my conclusion."

"And you tell me so in a tone that is in itself a rebuke! Love?—the gipsies of Hugo, the sentimentalists of Goethe, the rhapsodists of Shelley, may make it the god of their being; but we—we who have the world—can look on it at most as only a toy, a distraction, a thing to blow with each breeze like the child's paper windmill!"

His eyes never changed from their grave study of her. He answered her calmly:

"I imagined you held those views. What I said was that, when you think differently, then, and then only, will that higher and gentler nature I spoke of arise in you; if—you possess it. But since you look thus upon love, is it well or merciful on your part to do your very uttermost, as you habitually do, to awaken it everywhere, and everywhere inflame it to its greatest strength, and devotion, and folly?"

She tossed her golden head backward with a magnificent audacity of consciousness.

"Would you have me veil my face, then, in pity to mankind?"

He smiled at the arrogance of this vanity: a smile that she could not translate.

"Perhaps, you save some as effectually as though you veiled it, when you succeed in proving to them that with that beauty there goes no heart! If I be discourteous, pardon me; you desired candor."

"And your candor, like most other candor, appears to be only—Condemnation!"

She spoke with bitterness; she was so deeply galled by this second sentence, in which he had conveyed to her that, however perilous to others, she was free of peril to him.

Estmere smiled again.

"Poor candor! It is never right. If agreeable, it is denounced as flattery; if distasteful, it is slighted as censure!"

He left her side soon afterward at the conclusion of the cantata; left her to a vivid, heartsick, impatient sense of powerlessness to move, or touch, or win him, such as never before had been known among her countless and effortless victories: a restless, angered, despairing knowledge that he held her in doubt, in condemnation, almost in contempt, and that he had told her, almost openly, that for him she possessed no allurement.

He had humiliated her, and deeply angered her; but he had attained more influence over her, more attraction for her, than he had exercised before; and, despite the limitless faith she felt in her own omnipotence, she did not divine that Estmere himself had thought—

"She is right perhaps! To have love withheld from her, even by the coldest and the wisest, her face had need to remain unseen!"

Nevertheless, although he acknowledged this, he lingered in the place where that face met his sight or was recalled to his memory, with every day which brought the sea of carriages rolling through the sunlight of the streets, with every night which filled the chambers of the palaces with banquet, or ceremonial, or festivity.

And he saw her beauty at its height, her nature at its worst.

Unguarded now by the care of her lost husband's tenderness, which had in other years so sedulously sheltered her from any peril, she was free to follow to their wildest extravagance her own caprices and desires.

She had been left at perfect freedom; no rein remained on her will or her fancy.

Those who had the trust of her properties were two aged men of high rank and courtly breed, who were speedily content to see all things through her eyes. There was no sort of check upon the indulgence of that intense passion for gorgeous display, sensuous pomp, and ever-varying distraction, which she—with the soul in her of the Waif and Stray—never wearied of enjoying to its uttermost abandonment. They told her, in some alarm, that with ten years of such expenditure of hers even the massive fortunes, on which she had entered, would be dissipated by the ceaseless strain. She laughed. To a woman, who knew that she could select another lord from princes if she chose upon the morrow, the threat of future ruin was only a gay grotesque jest.

All that she did was done in an exquisite harmony, refinement, and elegance of taste; because there was in her that innate sense of fitness, and of beauty, which had in her childhood made every coarse tone, or motley hue, irritating and painful to her; and which had led her, unconsciously, to arrange her very wild flowers in blending colors that would have charmed a painter's love of pure and sympathetic tones.

Though reared in poverty, she had been reared in such a manner as cultured and fostered all this delicacy of artistic feeling, and instinct for symmetrical form, to its full development. Where this sense once lives, it is imperishable; and makes the mind which it pervades incapable of doing it an outrage. It forces the Roman beggar to fling his rags around him with the dignity of a toga; it impels the Campagna model to fold her nude limbs into the sublime repose of a Phydian statue.

But for all that, she loosed herself to the sweet exercise of her power in every imaginable form of extravagance and of display. The exaggerated luxuries, the inordinate splendor, the wanton waste that are characteristic of the age, of the world, of the city, in which she lived, reached in her their greatest height. The old half-barbaric passion for the visible witnesses of wealth and sovereignty, native to her, evinced itself now that she possessed the license to indulge it.

She had the oriental love of glow, and glitter, and pomp, and sound; she had all that temper of the present century which inclines it to scenic effects in the lieu of poetic beauty, to lustrous color in the lieu of accurate proportion, to intoxicating choruses in the lieu of classic cadence. And she launched herself into such extremity of magnificence as gives to such an instinct as this an ever-changing and perpetual delight.

Unconsciously to herself, through all her chillness of pride and arrogance of scorn, there shone out in her mode of life the impulse and evidence of one who has not from birth upward inherited power: and to whom its possession is therefore as a sorcerer's wand, whose magic is unceasingly wondrous to the one brought within its mystic circle.

None noted this; for her artistic taste was so unerring that no false note, or coarse color, in the pageantry of her existence ever betrayed it. But it was there.

The born-empress is very weary of those hours in which she must wear her state-robes, and receive the formality of homage. The woman, raised from privacy, into the blaze of a monarch's glory deems no hours so exquisite as those in which the people kneel, submissive, at her feet, and the crown rests on her brow.

Viva disclosed that she was not an hereditary sovereign by this one trait alone—that she was never willing to lay her scepter aside, never desirous of being quit of her purples, never so perfectly content as when the full luster and luxury of her royalty attested to its power.

Were some rare jewel on sale, at whose cost even princes hesitated, she purchased it; were some picture in the market at a fabulous price, she made it hers; were there some tropical flower rare beyond all others, she would spend thousands to add it to her conservatories; were some entertainment spoken of, which had been signalized by some unwonted thing, she would eclipse it with some marvel a hundredfold more beautiful, eccentric, or extravagant, furnished converse for the world.

The jewel might be utterly superfluous, the picture one which did not please her taste, the flower might have no special loveliness, and the festival no special charm, to her own thinking. But merely to possess them, to display them, to furnish food for the world's speech by them, was an unfailing delight which never palled on her, because it gratified her sense of empire, her consciousness of being without rival.

In no manner could she attain this delight more easily, more constantly, or with more publicity, than by the pleasures with which she filled her own time and that of the society she gathered about her. Her inventive wit found field, and interest, in the conception and execution of countless fresh fashions of distraction and of excitement.

The graceful fantastic fancy that had once made her dance like an almàh among the scarlet beans of the cottage garden, and believe herself a queen when she sat in the old beech-tree with a tall sword-lily for her scepter, now made her devise a thousand ways of adding brilliancy, and variety, and surprise, and cost—that great modern gauge of every merit,—to her amusements and entertainments. Exclusive with all the haughty exclusivism of an earlier nobility, lavish with all the profuse prodigality of present imperialism, reckless with the levity of the age, and dazzling with a seduction all her own, her fêtes and her banquets were the theme of the world of pleasure, the paradise of her associates, the despair of all outside her chosen pale. She ruled pleasure, and was ruled by it: and no other thing was the object, or the idol, of her days.

Generous, indeed, she was; whoever asked her for money had it. In moments of remorse she would strive to still her conscience by some such large charity as that with which she succored the stone-mason's desolate family. But these were fitful, unguided, the offspring of impulse always, never of principle.

She had delivered herself wholly over to the worship of egotism, and extravagance, and the joyous religion of pleasure; and she abandoned herself all the more completely, and violently, to the pursuit of these when the sting of one man's neglect pierced through the velvet folds of her exultant vanity, when one thorn amid all her innumerable roses thrust itself into her bosom, and reminded her that she was mortal.

Thus he saw her empire at its height—her character at its worst; and still, despite these, he lingered near her, and still doubted if, in this woman, there were not something higher and nobler latent, that her sycophants never roused and her lovers never wakened.

And one night when he chanced to be in her presence, an incident again arose which again made him ask himself: "Since she has the emotion of pity, will she not have also one day in her heart its twin-divinity of love?"


## CHAPTER XV.

THERE was a new piece at one of the most famous and most sparkling of the theaters of Paris—one of those gay minglings of music, travesty, beauty, burlesque, and wit, which are half opera, half comedy, wholly spectacle, to which the world will run, leaving the grave decorums of legitimate art as the Romans would run to the gladiators and the rope-dancers, leaving the stage of Terence.

"Let me be but amused! Let me only laugh if I die!" cries the world in every age. It has so much of grief and tragedy in its own realities, it has so many bitter tears to shed in its solitude, it has such weariness of labor without end, it has such infinitude of woe to regard in its prisons, in its homes, in its battle-fields, in its harlotries, in its avarices, in its famines; it is so heart-sick of them all, that it would fain be lulled to forgetfulness of its own terrors; it asks only to laugh for awhile, even if it laugh but at shadows.

"The world is vain, frivolous, reckless of that which is earnest; it is a courtesan who thinks only of pleasure, of adornment, of gewgaws, of the toys of the hour!" is the reproach which its satirists in every age hoot at it.

Alas! it is a courtesan who, having sold herself to evil, strives to forget her vile bargain; who, having washed her cheeks white with saltest tears, strives to believe that the paint calls the true color back; who, having been face to face for so long with blackest guilt, keenest hunger, dreadest woe, strives to loose their ghosts, that incessantly follow her, in the tumult of her own thoughtless laughter.

"Let me be but amused!"—the cry is the aching cry of a world that is overborne with pain, and with longing for the golden years of its youth; that cry is never louder than when the world is most conscious of its own infamy.

In the Roman Empire, in the Byzantine Empire, in the Second Empire of Napoleonic France, the world, reeking with corruption, staggering under the burden of tyrannies, and delivered over to the dominion of lust, has shrieked loudest in its blindness of suffering—"Let me only laugh if I die!"

The piece commenced with gay, airy, mirthful music; extravagant, sparkling, indecent, ironical, spectacular, voluptuous, as suits the temper of this modern age; suits its fatigue, its languor, its fever of discontent, its exhaustion of speculation, suits it because, being full of despair, it desires distraction, and, all its thoughts being doubts, it strives so hard not to think.

As the first silvery notes of the chief actress rang on the air, the audience welcomed them with tumultuous delight.

She was a great artist in her fashion; in the by-play, the trivialities, the amorous glances, the sensual graces, the union of elegance and lasciviousness, the eloquence of smile, of word, of gesture, which are needed far more, on the modern stage, than is tragic passion or scholarly comprehension. She was a great artist; she seemed to have the gift of eternal youth and of everlasting fame; her public had never wearied of Coriolis.

The night was a new triumph, many as had been the nights of triumph which she had numbered.

But there had come a certain weariness to her in this public festival; a certain toilsomeness had stolen into the perpetual play of the mime; a certain impatience of this endless robing, and singing, and laughing, and dancing, and wearing of smiles, had entered into her, well as she had long loved her life.

There came hours now in which she wanted rest; hours in which she felt her head ache and her limbs grow tired; hours of satiety, of exhaustion, of fretful fever; hours, inevitable, that come to the empress as to the actress, to the statesman as to the stage-clown. And now, as she frolicked on the boards, and moved like a sylph, and caroled like a bird, her eyes, wandering over the great semicircle of the house, rested on one woman who sat regarding her,—a woman young, of exceeding beauty, appareled like a sovereign, and with her courtiers surrounding her in a group that was inattentive to the spectacle, and only attentive to her face and to her words.

"Who is that piece of splendor yonder?" had asked Coriolis once, first seeing this woman.

"It is the Duchess de Lirà," they had answered.

Coriolis ever looked at her closely when she herself passed to the front of the stage.

"You are a Duchess—a great lady of France,—you are in the flower of your youth and the flush of your beauty,—you can have all I have had without taking thought for it or toil for it,—you are an aristocrat;—and I hate you!" she said in her soul, this night, watching this spectator, whom she envied, as she played on in her new extravaganza, and heard the thunders of the theater hail it as the greatest of all her successes.

She herself had enjoyed, indeed; but time was stealing the elasticity from her limbs, the buoyancy from her spirit, the bloom from her skin, the gloss from her hair, the spontaneity from her laughter; and from such women as she Time robs all, and to them brings nothing. She had her scepter, indeed; but the passage of the years had loaded its ivory and gold with lead, and she began to grow tired of the incessant exertion which was needed to hold it in her own grasp, and prevent it from passing to the outstretched hands of her rivals.

Meanwhile, the one whom she envied watched her in turn with a curious emotion.

Viva never heard the actress's name without a thrill of horror. She never saw it lettered on the walls of a city without a throb at her heart, as though she saw a snake's eyes watching her. It was ever an agony to her to recall that night of her madness. As she had grown to know the ways and the wisdom of the world, and had beheld the danger through which she had passed by the light of that world's knowledge, she knew what the precipice had been on which she then had stood in such laughing and trustful security. At times when its memory rushed over her, she felt the hot blood flush over her brow and bosom at the mere thought that such a peril had ever touched her, such an ignominy ever approached her.

Who her boy-wooer had been she never knew; she wondered often. And when she mused on him, and on her temptress, a deadly hatred, alien to all the negligent gayety of her temper, woke in her; a scorching shame consumed her.

All the fair, sweet, harmless things of her early life were well-nigh forgotten; all that sunny, serene, innocent existence, while yet she had taken no more thought than the lilies of the field, or sinned more sin than the birds of the air, had faded into one soft haze of dim, pure, confused color. That perfect peace in which she had not known that she was happy,—because she had not then known what sorrow meant, and thus had found no measure of her joy,— was all far distant to her, scarce remembered more than is the sunlight of some tranquil unmemorable summer-day of long ago. But that one night's memories were branded forever as with fire on her brain.

That men should still live who, if they only knew what she once had been, could point at her as one whom they had beheld at the house of a courtesan!

If she were alone when this remembrance came on her she would pace her chamber like a magnificent leopardess, and set her teeth in wrath that a woman, who could command the world, could not yet purchase the oblivion of a few brief hours!

It maddened her the more because she knew that, but for the guardian hand which had seized her from the flower-hidden abyss, she would have entered this kingdom of evil to which she had been tempted, in all her supreme faith and ignorance and guileless vanity. She knew that—but for him—she would have fled to the pollution of the stage, which had looked to her such immortal glory.

She knew that now she would have been even as Coriolis:—even as all those women who concealed the leprosy of sin with the satin domino of the masked ball; who avenged their own outlawry by pitiless plunder, by merciless dupery, of the world which had proscribed them; who dressed, and danced, and feasted, and had no future; and secure of a banquet to-day, might be left to starvation to-morrow. The women of whom she thought with all the horror of a haughty and untempted soul, with all the scorn of an imperial and lofty life.

She would have been of them,—must have been of them, she knew,—unless, indeed, in the first moment of despair, when the truth of her fate should have broken on her, she should have hurled her young form into the depths of the river. And the sound of the name of her temptress ever smote on her ear with a throb of shame, with a pang of guilt, with the stealing hiss, as of a serpent whose fangs had once been to her flesh, and whose wound, though it had left no scar, might even yet prove mortal.

Still—she had often gone to see Coriolis. Gone, on that indefinable impulse which sometimes draws men and women to the presence of their foes; on that mysterious attraction which deadly injuries, or deadly rivalries, will make more potent still than the attractions of love or of sympathy. Though it wounded her so poignantly to remember that night of her wicked folly, yet she went where that remembrance was most vividly forced on her.

Such anomalies are strong in all human-nature; they are especially strong in woman-nature.

"Could *I* ever have been that little fool who was allured by her specious promises, who saw heaven itself in the tinsel of her stage!" she thought as she gazed at Coriolis.

It seemed incredible to her that the same soul should live in both, that the same personality should exist in both,—in the little bohemian with the scarlet hood over her fair curls, who had listened to a lie as to a voice from heaven; and in the superb duchess whom her mirror portrayed, who had so indolent and ironic a disdain for all words that were breathed to her, and who had all her world beneath her foot.

"She is not changed!" she murmured unconsciously aloud.

"Changed!" echoed the one nearest to her in her box, "from what?"

"From the time that I saw her first,—and I was very young then."

Her eyes never left Coriolis as she spoke. Now, in the supremacy of her power and possessions, in the fullness of her knowledge and experience, in the security of her rank, it filled her with a strange wondering pity to think of the foolish, trustful, credulous child that she had been, and of the pathetic senseless love that she had once borne this sovereign of the stage. A fierce hate thrilled in her also as she watched her temptress. Through this woman that one ineffaceable memory was burned into her haughty life; that one intolerable shame had been drawn down on her proud head; that one loathsome hour had been lived through to pollute her past!

"Actresses never change,—till we see them by daylight!" Estmere answered her, ignorant where her thoughts wandered. "Look through your glass ere you judge."

She did so:—looked long, then dropped it with a shudder.

"It is a death's-head under a mask of roses and lilies! And yet how lovely that woman still is!"

"She seems to move you?"

"She does; for,—when I saw her first I longed to be an actress too!"

"*You!*—an actress! Is it possible?"

"Yes, I. Perhaps I am one, as it is. How can you tell?"

He did not know the spring of the half-remorseful words; he thought she implied some consciousness that her coquetry was but a cruel acting, since her heart was never touched to feeling.

"Let your higher nature speak, and follow what it says. You will never be one then," he murmured in her ear.

She was silent; unwittingly he had rebuked her.

"If he knew!" she thought, meeting the clear, grave eyes of the man whose one idol was inexorable Truth, whose one unpardonable sin was specious Falsehood; and she drove the thought from her as fast as it arose. She had had no need to think all through the years of her fortunate life: she left that travail to the weary, the unlovely, the wretched, the solitary. Thought was their sentence, their solace: with her it had naught to do.

Outside the theater it was a cold, dark, ghastly night. Although late in the spring, it was very cheerless and rained heavily.

About the end of the second act, while from within the bursts of music came, now faintly, now fully, out into the street, a wanderer, who had moved restlessly all day and night to and fro the labyrinth of the lighted town, strayed near to the play-house and paused;—he could not have told why, except that others paused with him;—opposite the building and its glittering arc and stars of gas-jets.

The wanderer was Bruno.

He stood, without knowing what he did, looking up at the crescent of lights; and hearing, without knowing what he heard, the distant cadence of the joyous and airy music.

Close at his elbow pressed a sailor of his own southern seaboard, a great, fierce, black-browed barbarian, half smuggler and half pirate, who yet had softness sufficient in him,—because that day he had met his whilom comrade, and had been scared by the haggard face which he had once known so bright and brown under the shadow of their tawny sails,—to stay staunchly by the side of the stricken man, though in the eyes that turned on him there was no recognition, but only the mute dull suffering of an animal spent by the hunters unto death.

"What would you do, Bruno?" he asked hastily, as the fisherman seeing persons enter through the glittering doorway, moved forward with them to enter also.

He paused, and looked for the first time with a gleam of consciousness on the features of his ancient sea-mate.

"It is you, Royallé?" he murmured wearily. "Are the boats ready? You must go without me;—she is not come home."

The streets, the gas-lights, the throng, the music, were naught to him; he thought he was on the yellow sands of his old home with the fishing-smacks standing out to sea in a fair wind, and his little cabin high up upon the rocks above the silvery plumes of olive.

"There are no boats," muttered Royallé. "We are in Paris, and this is no place for you."

"Paris? Paris?" the other echoed, the dulled brain playing with the word. "Is it Paris? She used to wish for Paris. May be she is here,—I have sought everywhere."

And he forced his way nearer to the open door.

Royallé seized him and sought to force him back.

"Not there, not there, Bruno!" he murmured. "What avail to seek her in scenes of pleasure?"

The sailor shook him off, and went forward with the dogged resolve of the insane.

"Losing gold ye seek hither and thither," he muttered. "Shall I do less by my treasure?"

Ere he could be stayed, he had flung down a coin as he saw others doing, and had thrust himself into the throng that was forcing itself through the mouth of the pit. They were separated; Royallé could do nothing except follow him.

The glare of light, the din of music, the blaze of gold and of color seemed to blind and to stupefy him. He stood wedged in by the crowd into whose center he had thrust himself; his gaunt, tall form towering above theirs; his wild pathetic eyes glancing from side to side like a hunted dog's; his blue canvas shirt flung back from his chest; his long dark hair streaming backward from the bronzed southern grandeur of his hardened features. He was like a desert animal suddenly strayed in among a laughing human crowd.

There was a scene of fairy-land on the stage which the audience were applauding till the roof rang again; a scene of wood and water, and silver cascades, and aisles of roses, and white-winged sylphs that fluttered on the branches, and troops of girls, arrayed like every flower that bloomed beneath the sun, who danced in airiest measures to the music sounding through the house.

To the fisherman of the Riviera it was all real; his great brown eyes gazed on it with wondering awe; through his dimmed brain there wandered weird tales, heard in his childhood, of enchanted lands where no mortal foot might wander. He stood erect, amazed, motionless; dizzy with the riot of sound and the modulations of motion, and the radiance of color that had broken on his vision as he came out from the darkness of the night.

And all the while his eyes were seeking out each separate face in the massed loveliness of that myriad of dancing girls; —seeking out hers which he could not find.

From the back of the flowering glades there came the graceful, swaying, floating form of a woman arrayed like a lotus-lily. Her form was scarce clothed in the white and green that fashioned the leaves of the lily; her sunny hair, chaplet-crowned, streamed behind her; her azure eyes laughed with arch gayety;—Coriolis looked in the spring of her earliest youth as she bounded into the circle of girl-flowers, and poured out her song with the easy sweet mirth of the lark.

Across her song a wild cry rang:

"*It is she!*"

He stood erect a moment, his eyes blazing with light, his arm stretched out, his chest heaving with deep-drawn breaths; then with a leap like a deer's he sprang from seat to seat over the heads of the people on to the stage where she stood.

The music on her lips was stricken mute; the band of living flowers fell from around her and left her alone. Criminal fear came into her radiant eyes. She stood powerless, motionless, gazing on the man she had dishonored, while on the players and their public a horrified silence fell.

He stretched his arms out to her, while his voice thrilled through the stillness.

"Madelon! Madelon! Thou art in paradise, and hast forgot me!—is it so?"

His whole frame drooped, his limbs lost their strength, he shuddered, and stood gazing at her:—the rising tumult of the house, the confused clamor of the amazed multitude had no power to reach his ear; he only saw the woman whom he had sought through the desolation of the world;—the woman who, found, shrank from him, and was afraid.

That guilty fear which he met in her look pierced him like a dagger's thrust; reason seemed to come back to him with the shuddering horror that ran through his senses. He lifted his head, as the lion mortally wounded will raise it to look once more at his foes, and gazed on that heated, breathless, motley multitude below, then gazed again on her;—on the snowy bare limbs, on the bosom that panted above its vesture of gold, on the painted loveliness which, near, had no youth and no bloom.

Then he knew that this was not heaven, but hell; and the blindness of half a lifetime was pierced in twain by that terrible light. He seized her, and gazed into her eyes, and crushed her soft frame against him, and flung her from him with a cry that smote the listening people as though they had but one ear and one soul.

"You are not *mine*, though you live in her form! Ah! vile thing, cruel devil, that mocks me! What have you done with the creature I loved? You give her limbs to the eyes of the lewd; and her loveliness to the lust of the mob; and the lips that I kissed to the crowds that devour her!—but where is the soul that I worshiped? where is the life that was mine? They were God's; *you* could not take them! They lie in His hand: you could not steal *them* with her body!"

He stood erect one moment, as men will stand when a death-shot has struck them; his eyes gazed out over the risen throngs, burning and blind; on his face was the majesty of an unutterable despair. Then, with one great cry from a broken heart, he flung his arms above his head and fell— his forehead striking on the fallen limbs of his wife, the lifeblood welling from his mouth, and staining purple the white lilies on her breast. When they raised him he was dead:— he had been dying more than twenty years.

And on the silence of the horror-stricken throngs the voice of the sailor Royallé rang as he turned and faced them, lifting up the lifeless body in his arms.

"She was his wife, look you. Yet God made women,— God made women and gave them to men!"

A shudder ran through all the listening multitude. For once the people of Paris saw no mirth in the tragedy of a man's dishonor.

And in the tumult, and the terror, and the stupefaction of the great crowded house, the proudest and coldest woman there staggered to her feet, and, blind and faint, stretched out her hands to the one nearest her.

"Take me away!" she murmured. "Oh, take me away. I heard their story once, and saw no sin in *her!*"

## CHAPTER XVI.

UNTIL the latest hours of that night Estmere sat in the loneliness of his great apartments, with his hound's head lying on his knee, and his thoughts sunk far into the past.

The scene which he had witnessed had opened afresh a long-closed wound. The wound had pierced too deeply for the jarred nerves ever to close again impervious to pain; and the tragedy of the theater had brought back on his memory, with all the freshness of a recent blow, the time when he had himself surprised the sin of the wife whom his roof had sheltered and his honor crowned.

On the autumnal day when Tricotrin had gazed upon him in his solitude at Villiers, that wound had been soothed only by the passage of a few years. Betwixt then and now there had stretched a long interval of public life, filled with a long succession of public honor, public services, public ambitions, public dignities and labors. The early treachery lay far away, folded under the sealed pages of his lost youth.

The throb of its horror had been soothed by the anodynes of great attainments; the ache of its shame had been stilled by the balm of a nation's trust. Many seasons would now pass by, and leave its memory unawakened. But there were times when that memory was still roused in all its suffering; and this was one of them.

All that passage of his life was stamped into his mind with letters of fire.

The idolatry with which he had loved the woman who had betrayed him; the intoxication of their first hours of union; the slow-dawning consciousness, so long thrust back from sight, that this creature, so exquisite in form, was mindless and soulless as any beautiful cheetah gamboling under Indian suns. The loyalty to her, strong in him as a religion, which, because she was *his*, forbade him to insult her with so much even as suspicion; the proud chivalry which withheld from him by its noble blindness a thousand signs that to meaner natures would have sufficed as warning. The unutterable horror which overwhelmed him, when chance revealed his own dishonor to him, and he found his spoiler in his household hireling, in the creature of his bounty, in the pampered, trusted, caressed debtor of his race and of his purse—all these seemed to him as things of yesterday, as their memories arose with the death scene of Bruno.

That treachery had colored all his life. It had killed happiness in him with one blow. It had left him without aught of the colors of joy upon his life, though he had in their stead wide command and passionless peace. Suspicion it could not teach to a temper too generous, too fearless, and too proud for suspicion's timid meanness. But it made the fair faces of women without beauty in his sight; and it left him in his lofty loneliness without companionship and without sympathy.

The passion which to other men was so fair, was only to him as the deadly poison which counterfeited the bread of life.

The law had freed him; his betrayer, for aught he knew, was dead; the world never paused to recall that early tale of a life whose maturity it honored; but he could never forget—he could never live as though this thing had never been.

And its remembrance was sharp as iron in his soul this night; for he knew that he loved again.

"Love, love! What have I to do with love?" he mused. "It betrayed me in my youth; it can only fool me more fatally still, now that my youth is gone!"

Yet, while his reason spoke thus, his impulse thirsted for that old, sweet, wild folly of his forgotten years; his heart ached for all the long-lost joys so free to every common fate; his passions wakened from their sleep, and longed for the sunlight that lies in a woman's eyes, for the paradise that lies in a woman's lips; his solitude grew cold, cheerless, unutterably desolate.

"Am I mad, that after all these years I dream thus!" he asked.

But the madness was upon him; and ambition, and renown, and honor, and the tribute of men, and the peace of the past, all grew worthless and bitter, and even as empty mockeries of his pain; for in his loneliness he knew that he would give them all, only once more to lose himself in the delirious sweetness of his youth, only once more to murmur in a woman's ear—

"I love!"

## CHAPTER XVII.

WITH dawn the next day vast throngs poured to a small house beside the theater, in the pearly light of the spring morning.

There was only a dead sailor lying there: with the look upon his face of one who had died seeking what he could never find on earth; and with a little knot of dried sea-grasses, tied around by a woman's azure ribbon, lying on his broad, brown, emaciated breast, where the coarse blue linen of his shirt fell asunder. But they came all the day through, throng upon throng, ever succeeding each other into the chamber where he lay:—then at nightfall they flocked to the theater.

"She acts?" they asked; and they were answered, "Yes, she acts."

And they poured in faster and faster, till there was no standing-place in the building, and the waiting crowds stretched far down the street.

She, herself, sat in her chamber, with the diamonds in her bosom, and the white wings on her shoulders. Her face was ashen-hued, and her eyes, so blue and laughing, had a startled horror in them as of one who sees some ghastly shape:—but she would act. She was thinking, with her cheek resting on a jeweled fan that had been an emperor's gift. She was thinking,- -this thing that had no thought.

She saw the yellow level shore down by the south; the sea glancing in the sun; the rocks covered with olive and myrtle and aloe; the blue distance severed here and there by the tall slender shafts of a palm. She saw a child of fifteen, with the fairest of faces, rosy and pearly as the gumcistus blossoms; idling away all her days under the brown shadow of a boat, or dappling her pretty feet in the play of the surf; listening to the love words of a handsome black-browed sailor, half seaman, half-fisherman, and laughing as she took with graceful greed his corals, his shells, his pieces of silk, his little golden crucifix, his earrings of silver.

She saw a cabin high up among the luxuriance of Riviera vegetation on the sunlit slope of a rocky shore, where, when the sails of the lateeners grew smaller and smaller as they went coasting westward, a young girl, full of petulant discontent, would bite her scarlet lips, and ruffle her hands among her yellow hair; and wonder what life away from these endless seas was like; and break the coral necklet of her husband's gift because she was so weary of the giver; and throw the beads away, one by one, into the water-spring bubbling from the rock, counting, "Je reste—je m'en vais! —je reste—je m'en vais!" in a Gretchen-like fashion of forecasting fate.

She saw a young child sleeping in a cradle shaped like a boat, and a seventeen-year-old mother who stooped over it, and kissed it once upon the mouth, and then went from it slowly, looking her last farewell, and thinking, "Gérant will have it cared for—the child will not be harmed;" and so passed swiftly across the threshold never to return; fleeing faster and faster as she heard that the lateen craft, returning, were in sight.

She saw all these things, pictures of dead years; where she sat with the diamonds glittering in her bosom, and the music of the overture floating dreamily into her chamber from the theater beyond.

The years since had been mirthful and glittering: remorse had never touched this light mercurial nature, sin had never weighed upon this volatile sceptical temper. She had done well for herself, she thought; she had gained riches, and fame, and lovers, and pleasures; she had had thousands of days of delight, thousands of nights of triumph. She had worn the jewels kings gave, and she had heard the tumult of nations' applause. She had feasted her sight and her senses; she had reigned in her way as queens reign. She had laughed on all her life through; and had drunk the secret joys of the passions. She had roved as the butterflies rove; and the flowers had all borne her honey. She had been glad,—glad,—glad ever; as things soulless and sensuous are. And only to-night did she hear the hush of the seas in the south; only to-night did she hear the sound of the voice of the dead.

The man sinned against, had suffered, dying hard, through a score of years; but the woman who had sinned had rejoiced through a score of years of light, and of laughter, and of life. Yet men say that remorse strikes the balance between the lives that endure and the lives that offend! Remorse!—that steals in for one hour out of a million, and thrusts one thorn amid a long season of roses, and furls one leaf beneath the bed of pleasure, and cries "Lo! I am Compensation!"

There was a deafening shout without; she did not hear it. She heard only the music of the Mediterranean as its waves washed upon the strand.

They came to her; the public clamored for her; the stage waited.

She rose, with the startled glazing look in her eyes as of one who beholds a horror not of the visible world.

Some, more merciful than the rest, bade her wait; the penalty could be but forfeit. As they spoke, from the body of the house there ran a loud hoarse roar, as of a lion savage for its prey; the Public knows no pity.

The old familiar sound aroused her; she laughed, tossing some more gold dust upon her sunny hair:

"Do you hear it? It is a beast that must be fed, or it will tear. I sold myself to it long ago. Besides—half a million francs!—I cannot lose them, though I have spent them in a day!"

Then with an airy antelope-like spring she bounded on the stage.

The theater was closely filled from pit to roof. They welcomed her with a tempest of applause.

Its director smiled content.

"The piece will hold the stage a year," he said; for he knew that the Public is as the dragons of old legends, and asks not what perishes, so that only its greed for new food be appeased.

And she played on:—her gay feet gliding, her rich song rising, her airy laugh echoing, over the place where Jean Bruno had died.

## CHAPTER XVIII.

IN the late spring-tide, verging upon summer, Paris was once more rejoicing:—rejoicing as her fashion is, with laughter on her lips, and war within her heart; with gold eagles gleaming on her arches, and wealth stagnating in her coffers; with flowers blossoming in all her corners, and exiles barred from her shores for the dread crime of uttering truth; with the word of Peace blazoned on her pyrotechnic showers, and half a million of her soldiers armed to the teeth, and waiting for their work. Rejoicing with infinite gayety, and wit, and song, and color; rejoicing with cartridges hidden in her soldiers' accoutrements, that the hail of the shot might sweep clear her boulevards, if amid all her festivities she once dared to remember that Liberty was missing.

Foreign sovereigns had traveled thither; there were feasting, and singing, and marshaling of troops by day, and illuminating of streets by night, and all the various beguilements and intoxications by which France is persuaded to forget that she is in fetters.

Under the green aisles and avenues of her pleasant

places, there were the glitter of arms, the bright hues of flags, the flutter of banners, the sounds of ceaseless music, the constant roll of drums and challenge of cannon, and an ever-flowing sea of dainty equipages rolled from noon till sunset through the streets and squares, and under the rich foliage of the woods of Boulogne.

Among those thousands of carriages there was one which, for its mingled pomp and elegance, its ermine, and its velvet, and its gold, its fiery fury of speed, and its outriders like a guard of honor, drew all eyes upon it; and the mistress thereof, lying back with her little dog beside her, was so marvelously fair, that the beauty-loving senses of the inflammable crowds made them rush, and press, and tear headlong to gaze at her; and uncover their heads to her, as though she were a sovereign, and hail her with a sudden spontaneous acclamation. She,—accustomed to that homage of the *monstrari digito*, and amused by its unwonted manifestation from the echoing shouts of the throngs—smiled, and bowed to the people, as though she were in truth their empress, and looked and laughed at the two persons who were seated opposite her.

"I am dangerous to the peace of France," she said, with light amusement. "They will want to crown me next!"

As she spoke her horses were perforce detained by the passage of cavalry, going at full speed, with their lances gleaming in the sun, to their place in the field of manœuvre; and her glance, idly straying around, over the heads of the closely-packed multitude, met the eyes of Tricotrin.

He alone of all the men in that crowd had not uncovered his head to her in homage; his gaze was fastened on her with a look in which, for the first time in her whole existence, she saw gloom, and rebuke, and passionate scorn.

Her gay laugh died on her lips; her face was shadowed; over her there stole a certain fear.

She remembered her first entry into Paris;—she remembered the hour when he had led her to look upon the miseries and agonies that hid beneath the brightness of the city's surface life;—she remembered the night when she had returned from the dwelling of her temptress, a trembling, tired, heart-sick child, who, but for him, had perished in that death of honor and of conscience which the world for lack of a better word calls sin.

Then the petulance of her stung pride rose and ruled in her.

"Must I ever be pursued by his memory, like some murderer by a ghost!" she thought, with cruel merciless impatience; and she turned her eyes from him, and laughed in all her airiest and most negligent levity, and tossed her little jeweled sweetmeat-box to a pifferaro's monkey, in the wantonness of waste.

Above, in one of the white spacious mansions fringing the broad road, were spectators, filling every balcony and casement to watch the court, and the troops, and the equipages of fashion and of rank sweep by in the summer afternoon.

In the window immediately above her, a window, velvet-hung, veiled with lace, filled with flowers, there was a gilded balcony, with exotics, and china vases, and stands for parrots; a balcony hung and cushioned on such days as these with crimson satin, powdered over by golden butterflies.

With her arms sunk in the cushions' ruby depths, and her cherubic face leaning on them, laughing as she watched the pageantry go by, and turning now and then to tease a parroquet, was the woman to whom that gilded balcony belonged, of whom those gilded butterflies were the self-chosen emblem.

The throngs as they moved below looked up often-times; and laughed also; and called out to each other, "There is Coriolis!"

For that night when they had asked breathlessly, "Does she act?" and had seen her act as gayly as ever on the stage, where the fisherman of the Riviera had dropped dead, had endeared her afresh to the people of Paris:—had made some touch of that seduction of assassination, which so strangely beguiles the modern mind, lie for them in those serene azure eyes, those rosy childlike lips, of their play-idol.

Coriolis, leaning there, with her arms on her cushions, and her hand toying with a knot of bright roses, looked down, and noted that equipage, checked by the passage of the squadrons.

"Those horses are more perfect than mine," thought the actress, whose glory it had ever been to excel the aristocrats.

As her hand hung over the balcony it accidentally let fall one of the roses. It was caught by a puff of wind, and wafted into the carriage. Its occupant looked up: perceived whence it came—then with a gesture of shuddering aversion, threw the rose out, to fall where it would among the multitude.

Coriolis, leaning above, saw the action, and saw the gesture of loathing which accompanied it.

"It is that Duchess de Lirà!" she thought, while her teeth set in that bitter rage which is ever the wrath of such mindless and soulless things as she, if hate once break through the sunny placidity of their profound egotism. "She flings my rose away as though the plague were in its petals. She is as beautiful as I was a score of years ago. She has youth, she has rank, she has splendor, and love, and pleasure, and triumph, all in their prime. Ah! how sweet it would be if the days of the revolution came again, and we could make her come down from that princely chariot to ascend the tumbril of the guillotine!"

So she mused, gazing into the street beneath, with her arms imbedded in the soft rose satin. A vague yet acrid hatred of the women who lived in honor had ever moved her, although she had ever affected to hold them in light and insolent contempt.

The cavalry left the street free; the carriage dashed away with speed, and glitter, and noise.

Coriolis quitted her balcony, and went into the luxurious chamber it adjoined, and pushed her hair off her temples, and stared fixedly at herself in a hand-mirror.

"I hate her! I hate her! She has youth; and I——"

She flung the mirror aside, with a violence that shivered to atoms its glass and its ivory frame.

The only vengeance which ever overtakes such women as she stole, with slow sure steps, upon her.

## CHAPTER XIX.

IN the house where Mère Rose once lived with her linnet, there was now a young carver of ivory. In that little ancient, unfrequented lane, few buyers of his pretty toys ever wandered. He managed to live by letting all his rooms to other people, and by keeping only the small shop, and the dusky den behind it, for his fair fond wife, and for his white Liliputian wares.

The former carried grace and beauty even into the cobweb-hung, pent-up place, where, in another time, the greengrocer had sold his herbs and vegetables, and picked out his largest chestnuts to do pleasure to the Waif and Stray in the attic. The latter gave the brightness of her own youth, and of her own still unfaded hopes to the dark prison-like room, where she sang all day long like a bird.

The day after the great military fête, Léon Clérot, the carver, having taken down his shutters, was flecking the dust from his ivory treasures with a feather-brush, and talking meanwhile to his wife within. She, having brightened and lightened her chamber with the old happy grace of Gaulois blood—with a ribbon here, an atom of gilding there, a pot of common flowers, a bough of blossoming lime,—answered him gayly, sewing all the while at one of his coarse gray shirts.

It was the early forenoon; and both started as they heard the roll of a carriage, and saw one stay at their door. In that out-of-the-world by-way, there was scarce anything upon wheels seen, save the baker's cart, or the hot-chestnut seller's barrow.

Léon stood stupefied as a great lady entered his little

domicile; and asked the cost of his crucifixes, his prayer books, and his miniature cabinets.

He confused the prices sadly in his answers, so bewildered was he at the presence of such a patroness; but she seemed scarcely to attend. She chose some dozen ivory works, of the highest value in his collection; paid for them with two big rolls of gold, which dazzled his sight, and made his hand shake as he took them; bade him give the purchases to her footman waiting without; and then lingered—looking at a cross.

"My carving must be very wonderful then, it seems!" thought the poor Dieppois, who had never had the vanity to think so before.

"You live here with your wife?" asked his visitant, suddenly.

"We do, madam."

"You have a good trade?"

"A very bad one, madam."

"You must be very wretched?"

"No, madam; we are happy."

"Happy!"

She threw her glance into the dusky little den where the Picardy girl was sewing, with the little pot of common flowers, marygolds, and lavender, and mignonette at her elbow.

"Happy!" she thought. "He must speak in derision of his own misery!"

She swept up to the girl with her soft languid grace of movement.

"It is impossible; your husband mocks you. You cannot be happy here?"

"Oh yes, madam: we are!"

The aristocrat stood and gazed at her with supreme, incredulous, musing wonder.

Happy? But how?—why?—on what?"

The girl smiled softly, with a flush on her cheek.

"Ah, madam! We love one another."

Her visitant moved away, with an impatient shadow on her face. Love! Must this word meet her at every turn? must men and women ever have the audacity and insincerity to pretend that it could do for them all that her rank, and riches, and celebrity, and conquest, did for her?

"You have in your house one who calls himself Tricotrin?" she asked quickly of the young bride, whose face beamed brightly as she answered that they had.

"Is he within now?"

"I cannot tell, madam. He is scarce ever at home. But I will see."

"Do so. Tell him that I—Ask him to have the goodness to come hither."

The girl went.

The great lady sat alone in the little room, indifferent how strange her visit might appear to these poor people.

Clérot remained in his outer shop, gazing at his gold, and dreaming of all possible and impossible glories that would arrive for him from the patronage of this stranger, in whom he believed he saw, at the least, some foreign empress.

He had been but a brief while in Paris; he was incessantly occupied on his carving; and he knew few of the celebrities of the city either by sight or name.

His visitor sat gazing, through the little, dusty, cheerless place, out on to the threshold of the door; where, so many years ago, she had once sat under the green-grocer's canopy of thyme, and marjory, and lemons, and grapes, and had listened to the messenger of Coriolis.

Ere long the little Dieppoise, picturesque in the sea-side dress she still retained, returned and approached her with shy deference.

"He is within, madam, for a miracle; he stayed awhile with old Bénoit, the cobbler, who is ailing. He will be here at once;"—then, with the quick tact of her nation, she glided away to her husband's side, and left her little den to her guest's sole use.

11*

At that moment Tricotrin entered; with gladness and anxiety at once in his eagerness of regard.

"Is there aught ill with you?" he asked, hurriedly, in a low murmur, as he greeted her. "Speak some foreign tongue; they know no language save their own."

"You think some ill must befall me ere I can remember you!" she said, bitterly, in Italian. "Ah! I merit the satire! Nothing has happened; but I—I was near you the other day in that fearful danger. I have never been at ease since then. And—yesterday you looked so sternly on me; I felt afresh the whole guilt of my life to you. I come to you to say—forgive me!"

All the uncertain impulses, the unregulated instincts, the variable emotions of her better nature were uttered in the words.

She would live again as if this repentance had never touched her: but despite this, the repentance was sincere and ardent while it lasted.

His voice was unsteady as he answered her:

"You have no need to use that word to me. You had my promise long ago to pardon any sin that you might sin against me. But—is this visit prudent? Is it not an error against your usual codes and caution?"

"Such prudence is shameful selfishness, and as cowardly as it is shameful!" she murmured, passionately. "But, here, there is little fear. The shop is an artistic one, such as I often visit. My servants will suspect nothing. 'Suspect!' Good Heavens!—I dare speak thus to you, in this house where I lived upon your charity—as though the boundless goodness of your past to me were some dark crime which needed to be screened and hushed!"

She covered her eyes with her hand where she sat leaning her arms on the table. In such moments as these all the arrogance and chillness of her pride vanished, and all the greatness of her debt was alone remembered.

Yet—to the woman who through long years had only known the sweetness and the omnipotence of riches, rank,

and power, it was unutterably galling to recall that she had
once dwelt under this lowly roof a child of the people,
happy in the gifts of chestnuts from the fruit-seller below,
happy in the mirth of a charlatan with his noisy drum,
happy in wandering out, to gaze at the gas-lighted shops,
and listen to the bands of the streets!

If there had only been some means whereby she could
have repaid her debt—some gift and grace such as sovereigns
bestow upon those who loyally have served them,—she
could better have borne the memory of her obligation. She
could have succeeded in banishing the past, or in retaining
but such remembrance of it as that with which such
sovereigns, when seated on their thrones, recall the season
when they were discrowned wanderers and exiles. But this
was not possible.

With all her longing to give some magnificent quittance
of her debts, with all her warmer and holier desire to pour
some of her golden treasure into the hands which had lifted
her from the grave in her infancy, she had never ventured to
offer gifts to him; she had never ventured to tender to him a
portion of those things for which she had abandoned him.

Unconsciously, she felt that it would be as vile an outrage
as for the faithless wife to tender to her forsaken lord, the
gold, and the lands, of the lover for whom she had deserted
him.

"I spoke to you the last day you were with me as I had
no right to speak," she murmured, her eyes shaded by her
hand. "I should have remembered that you had a title to
address me with what severity you would. Sometimes—I
wonder that you do not denounce me, before all the world,
as the basest and weakest thing that ever lived."

"Why?" he said, gently. "I should have no justification, even if I had desire, to do so. When we toss a bird up
in the light, free to come or to go, we are foolish and unjust,
indeed, if, because it sail away from us on high, we cast a
stone after it to bring it earthward in punishment for its
abandonment of us. You were just such a bird—you chose

the sunlight. Well—so best—you would never have borne storms."

"You think, then, that in the lack of riches I should have been delivered over to evil!"

"I have said: I think you—a woman, nothing less, nothing more."

"I am unlike most women!"—involuntarily she turned and glanced at the little broken piece of mirror that hung above the stove.

"In your beauty you excel them—yes. But in all else you are most essentially feminine."

She played impatiently with an ivory chain that she retained in her hand. She had conceded his right to say to her what he would; but none the less did she resent the total absence of that homage which was as the very daily bread of her existence, and the relegation of her to the vast community of that sex which, in her soul, she disdained with all the glad contempt of a woman whose friends are men, and who is independent of all female sympathies.

"Were you not hurt that fearful day in the stoneworker's court?" she asked him quickly. "Oh Heavens! I can never tell you what I felt——"

He smiled: if she heard of his death on the morrow, would it hold her back from a state-ball at night?

"Hurt? No. I am never hurt. I bear a charmed life, I think, for I come safely out of strange perils."

"But you may rely on that once too often?"

"Well—if I do? A quick death, a death while one is of use, is a thing to be desired. The only thing I ever dread is slow sickness that might keep me long in dying. But how could you come amid so rough a crowd, and in so poor a quarter?"

"I was about to visit Lélis."

"Lélis! My Lord of Estmere's new-found Velasquez!"

A slight flush came on her face; his eyes watched her with earnest, keen scrutiny.

"He is a great artist!" she said, hurriedly.

"Oh yes! He has been a great artist for twenty years; only, for want of great nobles saying so the world has never seen it!"

"There is a use, then, at least, for the great nobles!"

"You fancy I deny their use? You are wrong. To do so is to sink to the demagogue's class-hatred. I am well aware of how much art, and manners, and learning, the grace, and the scholarship, and the refinement of life, all owe to the aristocracies of all ages! It is as illiberal to hate a nobility as it is to despise a people."

"In a democracy they would call you an aristocrat then?"

"Perhaps; as in aristocracy they call me a democrat. A man who is universally tolerant is sure to be antagonistic to whatever is absolute and in the majority. As politics stand, we dream of the idealic isonomy of the Greek vision; and—find no better reality than a military despotism or a mob-anarchy! You see much of Lord Estmere?"

The question was irrelevant and abrupt. She answered it coldly:

"We move in the same world; I meet him continually."

"And have you solved the questions that interested you —whether attained ambitions and public honors content him? —whether there is any place in the eminence of his life for the weakness of passion?—whether there is any chance of his strength and his peace falling earthward to be the toys of a woman?"

Despite all her self-command, her face flushed, her hands played hurriedly with the ivory chain. His words pierced to a secret which she had striven to hide even from herself.

"I am not aware that such questions ever occurred to me," she made answer, negligently. "I scarcely suppose their investigation would repay me."

"What! You admit that you cannot alter his indifference?"

The words stung all her arrogant vanity into being.

"Do you suppose any indifference could endure one hour longer than *I* chose to grant it lease of life!" she interrupted him, with all her most superb scorn and self-consciousness in arms.

"You have conquered his, then?"

She was silent; her eyes clouded with anger, her hand beat impatiently on the low deal table. She was truthful by nature; and she knew that the one victory alone lacking to her was victory over the man of whom they spoke.

"You are uncertain?" he said, abruptly. "And in that uncertainty lies his chief interest for you! Whether his indifference to you will endure I cannot tell; he is mortal, and you have more than mortal seduction in you! But watch your own heart, ere you attempt to play with his. If you have, indeed, the soul in you to feel the force and truth of his nature, it will be well for you that you have ever known him. But if, in the mere wantonness of vanity, or the mere impulse of irritation because he has not fallen before you, you seek to change his coldness only that you many triumph in his weakness, you will do an accursed work, an unpardonable sin."

Her delicate teeth set, her breath came quickly, as she heard; she looked up suddenly in his eyes.

"Why have you this compassion for him? I have dealt cruelly and inconstantly enough with many; you never interfered to avert *their* fate?"

He paused a moment; then he answered her with an effort,

"There are not many such men as he. Moreover,—he has been once forsaken and betrayed; this should be sufficient to make him sacred to the most wanton coquette that ever found her playthings in the ruin of men's lives."

"You are right," she said gently—and asked no more.

"You will leave him untempted, then?"—there were vivid eagerness, imperious authority, in the demand.

A soft smile, half cruel, half tender, played about her mouth; her glance stole away once more to the mirror.

"Is that wholly in my power to promise?" she said, as she rose.

He knew all the conscious power which was uttered in the vain-glorious question; and he knew that it was as idle to ask her to forego its exercise as it were to ask a brilliant gerfalcon to forego her quarry. An impulse woke in him to tell her of what race her first young lover had come; to tell her that it had been the son of Estmere for whom she had been tempted into the house of Coriolis. But he held his peace; it could avail nothing save to disquiet her and to alarm her; it could only serve to make her more likely to betray herself whenever the time should come that she should meet again the "Prince Fainéant" of her childish fancies.

"Wholly in your power?" he answered her. "May be it is not so. You have the charms that befool men. But all that I say is, spend your seductions elsewhere, sate your passion for triumph otherwise than in misleading, and mocking, and wounding a noble nature that has already been branded, through too frank a faith in the honor of women. He has stung your pride by his neglect—I know!—deadlier crime no man can have against such a trifler as you. But, if there exist in you one lingering touch of the nature that once lived in the child that I cherished, you will have mercy enough, purity enough, generous strength enough, in you to renounce one effort for triumph, to abstain from one indulgence of vanity, to hold back your hand from thrusting fresh thorns into the old, deep, cruel wounds of a husband's dishonor. I have asked nothing of you since the years that we parted. I ask this now. Do with others as you will. But spare him."

Ere she could answer, he had turned away and gone from her, and passed up the dim, narrow stairway, without farewell.

She stood, moved, silent, wondering, with a mist of unshed tears gathering over her haughty eyes. All the latent tenderness in her had awakened at his words; for—she loved the man for whom he had pleaded thus.

"He and Estmere are strangers!" she mused. "Strangers—and yet the one can feel, and can sue, for the other like this! A time there must have been when their lives touched, and were the lives of friends! And yet——"

And yet he had said this was not so; and she knew well that no lie ever tainted his lips.

She went to her carriage, giving orders to the carver, Clérot, that in twelvemonths' time he could scarce have space to execute; and, as she drove through the streets in the bright noonday, her face was pale, and grave, and troubled.

Tricotrin went to the little dull chamber, high in the roof, where the old cobbler lay, slowly dying; and he read aloud the gayest wit of the journals of irony and of caricature, till the cobbler, with the Gaulois temper still in him, laughed again and again where he was stretched on his bed, and half forgot his suffering, and never dreamed that his friend, who thus brought the mercy of mirth and oblivion to his couch of torture, had a bitterness in his own soul surpassing that of death.

## CHAPTER XX.

A FEW weeks later, one sweet moonlit night in the month of roses, a man and woman wandered through the orange aisles of the Palace of the Abdication. They were alike guests of the court, and had strayed somewhat away from the torchlight curée, and the illumined waters, and the gardens and galleries filled with the pomp of imperial festivity.

"You will come to Villiers?" he asked, bending low his stately head; he had spoken of her approaching departure, and had entreated for her presence at the summer gathering which was about to fill his own château.

She looked at him with a startled, wistful, doubting look, and hesitated some moments ere she answered.

"To Villiers?" she said, at length, with a strange softness and sadness in her voice. "To Villiers? Yes—I will come to Villiers."

And he, noting that strange intonation, that unusual emotion, thought, in a dreaming wonder, that made his pulses beat with the fever-heat of youth—
"Is it possible that my love would ever be welcome to her?"

## CHAPTER XXI.

THE park-gates of Villiers were opened wide in a mellow summer evening; carriage after carriage passed through them, bearing guests to the great château. Torches flared, though the sun was scarce set, the silken standard flowed broad upon the breeze, the wide courts were filled with princely pomp, its lord, long absent, had of late returned.

At the lodge a brown-eyed woman stood, smiling to see the equipages sweep by, and holding back the too eager delight of her youngest born—a ruddy boy of but a few years old. They were people of a sunny, loyal temper in the little gate-house, and had no grudging envy of the "aristocrats." They liked the pageantry and the vivacious life that came with these gatherings of the "noblesse."

"Look, look, mère!—quick!" whispered an elder daughter of some fifteen years. "Paulin told me I should know her, because he would put the ermine rug in her carriage and sables in all the others. Look!—that must be the Duchess de Lirà!"

The mother looked, shading her eyes from the glare of the sunset and torchlight.

The horses slackened their pace as they came through; the great lady, of whose advent there had been much converse among the household of Villiers, for the fame of her beauty had spread even through the provinces, leaned slightly forward, and stretched her hand with a coin to the little boy, looking into his parent's face.

"You are well here, and happy?" she asked.

There was a great sweetness in her voice as she asked the simple question.

"Ah, yes, madam—thank God!" the mother answered to the unlooked-for mark of interest, as the carriage dashed on through the avenue.

"What has thou, Raoul?" she said to the child. "Holy Mary! what a great gold piece. She must have a tender soul —that proud duchess."

"And how beautiful she is!" sighed her daughter. "Paulin was right." (Paulin was an equerry, who had been in Paris with his lord.) "Paulin says," the girl murmured on, "that she will be châtelaine here ere long. Think you, mère, it is likely?"

"How can we tell?" rejoined her mother absently.

Awhile later, as she moved to and fro, getting his evening meal for her husband, who had come from his labor in the gardens, he asked her what made her so grave and so silent.

"I do not know," she said, with a smile. "Dost thou remember at all, Valentin, that pretty child that lived with the old Virelois, and died, they say, far away?"

"Tricotrin's Waif? Ay—what of her?"

"Naught of her. But that great lady had a look of her in her face, and set me thinking of her—the pretty, nameless thing—that is all."

Valentin laughed, a man's good-natured contemptuous laugh at a woman's imaginations.

"The Duchess de Lirà like that little foundling! Ah, wife, what a woman thou art for fancies! Do not tell them aloud, for they say that our lord will wed with her."

"I have no fancies to tell," said Ninette, giving him his salad. "She made me remember the child—that is all. It is the dark eyes and the light hair, I dare say. The child had them."

Meantime, in the great vaulted hall of the château, the Duchess de Lirà was welcomed by her host beneath his roof.

She answered him with her accustomed grace and ease; she smiled on him with her accustomed witchery and eloquence; she conversed lightly of the trifles of her travel; she looked in his face without a fear in her eyes or a flush on her cheek for that bygone time, so ever present to her sight, and so deeply buried from his; but when she reached her own chamber she bade her attendants, with imperious haste, leave her alone—she was fatigued—she desired rest. And, locked in her solitude, she flung herself upon her couch, and sobbed bitterly.

The place moved her with strange passion. The dead days thronged like ghosts around her. She felt guilty and ashamed, and filled with a vague terror.

If the pictured walls, the storied chambers, the dumb statues could find voices, they could tell their lord that the woman whom he welcomed as nobles receive their monarchs, had once been a nameless, penniless, alms-fed child, wandering with his peasants in his halls!

"But I have greatness; *that* is no lie!" she thought, as she rose and gazed at herself in those mirrors, whose solace never failed with stormy longing and disquiet at her heart. "I have fulfilled my dream; I have borne out my ambitions; I return with riches and honors, and triumphs in my hands. I have won my empire, and I am crowned. Men wear their diadems forgetful of their pasts: why may not I? I am his equal; what need to remember that any other time has ever been? My kingdom is real: as real as his!"

Then she smote the tears from her eyes, and smiled at her own loveliness, and called her tire-woman, and burnished to threefold brilliancy the weapons of her charms; and descended the great staircase—proud, radiant, imperial, conscious that she was beyond all rivalry.

His hand shook slightly, and his grave weary eyes softened with a new light—the light of his lost youth—as he bowed before her, and led her to the banqueting-chamber, where, in the autumnal day of a long-forgotten time, the song of the Diogene had echoed from the forests on his ear, and the great man in his solitude had envied the careless singer.

## CHAPTER XXII.

"It is you! Ah! how glad we shall all be!" cried the wife of Valentin, in her lodge-house, dropping to the ground in her joy a kirtle full of purple plums which she had just gathered from her sunny south wall. Her welcome was given to Tricotrin, as he came across her threshold in the fresh hour of earliest day.

"It is like a summer rain after drought to see you here again. You come so seldom now, and the people all hunger for you, ever," she pursued, laying her hands on his knapsack, and sending her children in all directions to get eggs from the hen-house, fresh honey, fresh fruits, and fresh salad, to do honor to his breakfast, with many lamentations that her husband should be already gone off to his work in the gardens, and should thus miss the pleasure of seeing the man he most loved and revered.

In the later years, Tricotrin had returned at intervals to his once-cherished vine country; but still he came far more rarely, and for far briefer sojourn than of old.

The old familiar places had a cruelty in their beauty, a sting in their peace. And there was little save pain to be found at the river-home which he kept for grand'mère and the swallows. She derived no solace from his presence, she understood naught that he said, she would only grasp his arm with a hard nervous grip, and look straight in his eyes, with a look that made his heart ache, and mutter in his ear, "Will she never come back? will she never come back?"

Of the lost child, the people never spoke to him. Most believed her dead; some believed that worse than death had befallen her; all understood, that of her they must not question him.

He accepted the eager hospitalities of Ninette, and took a seat in the deep embrasure of the wide oak-lined window; and listened to her rapid babble of things that had chanced in the country-side since last he had been seen there; and glanced, ever and again, as he drank his coffee, at the blazoned arms and the gilded coronet without on the great gateways.

"How is it with grand'mère?" he asked her, in one of the pauses betwixt her gossipries.

Ninette shook her still comely head.

"Ah, you see it is so far, I can rarely go myself,—never, indeed, unless I have something to take down the river. When one has children!—But, indeed, one can do her no good, and she knows no one now. Manon Rixe saw her last week—so she stopped her mule to tell me,—and Manon thinks she is breaking fast. You see,—" she hesitated, she was about to add that grand'mère had never recovered the loss of the child; but she changed her phrase,—"you see she is wonderfully old; and when people have been so strong up to that age, they break all at once—so!"

And she cracked a rotten stick sharply across her knee. He was silent.

"She has everything she can wish for," pursued the wife of Valentin, in whose eyes creature-comforts made a paradise upon earth. "She is well off,—you are so good to her. It has been a brave, tough, tender soul,—hers. Those people that were children in that old revolutionary time, have something in them greater than we have, I think."

"They may well have. The Marseillaise was their cradle-song."

"I sing that to my children, when the doors are shut at night," whispered Ninette.

She had something of republican blood in her, and her great-grandfather had been slain by a Black Brunswicker in Champagne-Pouilleuse.

"Aye! Hymns forbad at noonday, are ever so sung at night; and oftentimes, what at noon would have been a lark's chant of liberty, grows at night to a vampire's screech for blood!" he murmured. "They are gay at your château up yonder?"

"Gay, indeed," assented Ninette, who,—with all her touch of republicanism, liked her own aristocrats. "The English lord always has kept a splendid house whenever he has been here: though he looks so grave, and so tired, I do not think it can pleasure him much."

"He is well loved by all your people?"

"He is so. He is of few words, and proud; but he is generous and just."

"His son is not here?"

"No. The young lord is never here. Of Estmere himself they do say——"

"Say what?"

"Well—have you ever seen a wonderful creature whom they call the Duchess de Lira?"

"I have seen her. Why?"

"She is staying up at the château. She is a very great lady, is she not?"

"She is of high station. What is it they say?"

"Oh, it may be nonsense. I do not see how we can tell. But they do say that my lord will wed with her. Paulin, the equerry, told us first; and now every one is repeating it. It may well be: she is most lovely, and his horse is always beside hers as they ride through the gates."

Tricotrin put out his hand, and thrust the half-shutter against the window.

"The light is strong," he muttered; and he continued his meal, sitting backward in the shadow, in silence.

"It may be folly," continued Ninette. "I know nothing of her, of course; she spoke gently to me, and she gave little Raoul a great gold piece. But they do say that she will only break his heart if ever she gets it. She loves to see men mad for her, they tell me. But it may be only gossip, very likely. I remember in the old time, when my lord was so much here, before he went to that kingship in the east, they were always saying he would marry this princess or the other when the great ladies visited at the château. People must talk. Do you like that shutter shut? You were always so fond of the sun."

She was absent awhile, busied in rescuing a pumpkin from the too vigorous play of her four-year-old son, on the strip of turf outside her door. When she came back she stood silent, with her hands in her sides a little while, surveying her guest; then she spoke very softly:

"Tricotrin—I wonder if you would be angered if I asked you something?"

"I am not likely to be. Try."

"Well—did you ever see in that great duchess a look of that pretty dead thing you were so good to,—of the child Viva?"

"There is a look—yes."

"Ah! I am glad to hear you say that. Valentin mocked at me. There is an enormous difference, of course; but there is a look——"

"Valentin is the wiser of the two," said Tricotrin, as he rose from the table, with a smile. "A great lady would be ill pleased to be likened to a foundling. And now, farewell. I will come back at evening to see your husband. For the present I must go visit grand'mère, since you have heard it is worse with her."

And he went, dropping into Raoul's hands, as he passed, a toy he had taken out of his knapsack—a clock-work cuirassier, who went through wondrous evolutions, and completely eclipsed the pumpkin.

An ingenious toyseller and mechanist had pressed it upon him a few days earlier, as the sole return it was in his power to render for services done, on a hot summer night, to him in a fire that had broken out on his premises.

"Take it, I pray you," had urged the toymaker. "It is a clever puppet, and you can bestow it on some child;—you always like to give pleasure."

And Tricotrin had put it in his knapsack, knowing that to refuse were to deal pain.

Ninette stood thoughtfully regarding his shadow as he

lengthened on the sunlit road. It was the first time he had ever spoken of his lost Waif.

"If the child should not be dead after all!" she mused; and she remembered that the belief in this death had gone abroad alone from what the old grand'mère had said, and that Tricotrin himself had never once spoken of her fate.

## CHAPTER XXIII.

IN the indolent summer day, some hour or more ere the fall of evening, a riding party paced slowly through one of the wooded valleys beyond Villiers.

They were above, on a steep rocky road that wound down toward the deeply-scooped dell, where a little hamlet lay; unseen under its dense chestnut and sycamore cover, and only betrayed by its roofs thrust up here and there, gray and soft in hue with the lichens, or red with their tiles that glowed under the leaves, bright as poppies underneath ferns.

The horses were somewhat tired; the dogs paused to drink thirstily from the hillside brooks; the riders went downward over the dangerous picturesque way, with that pleasant sense of languor, and content, which comes from such slight fatigue as only makes the ear more grateful for the soothing sound of falling water, and the eye more grateful for the perfect rest of dark cool green.

Their voices sank; their laughter was hushed; through the odorous scent of the dying day, heavy with the opening buds of night-blossoming flowers, and the crushed heart of wild fruits, fallen overripe, they rode on silently.

As they went, from the valley far down below there rose the faint echoes of music, as a song rises up from the leafy hedge-sheltered nest of a bullfinch. Aerial, subdued, exquisitely delicate, it mingled, as its notes ascended, with all the sweet sounds of the earth; the brook's bubble, the leaves' murmur, the chime of sheep's bells, the singing of grasshoppers; blending with all, broken by none.

Involuntarily they checked their horses; and listened, midway down the descent.

"A French Rubezahl!" said one.

"An Orpheus of the Loire," added another.

"Hush, hush!" said the foremost of them. "It must be the Straduarius!"

"Whose?" they asked.

She struck her whip with a gesture of annoyance against the bole of the tree she passed.

"A Straduarius, or,—some other perfect violin. One can tell that even here."

"But you said *the* Straduarius, madam? Who is the marvelous player?"

"I have no telescope to ascertain! We shall see in the valley."

Her host riding by her side, looked at her in a certain perplexity.

"It is Tricotrin, I will wager," said the Marquis de Valdanha farther behind. "Who else would play so to those villagers at our feet?"

"Tricotrin?" murmured Estmere, "Tricotrin? I have heard that word of late——"

"Who has not?" laughed the other.

"Tricotrin?" repeated Estmere, thoughtfully. "That is not a real name?"

"Is it not? It is one the people love as they love the Marseillaise. He is well known hereabouts; you must have met with him."

"I have done so. He is an ally of Lélis. A man of peculiar life, if I were told aright."

"A man with the wit of a Piron, the politics of a Jean Jacques, the eloquence of a Mirabeau, the utopia of a Vergniaud!—a man with the head of a god and the blouse of a workman, the brain of a scholar and the life of a scamp, the soul of a poet and the schemes of a socialist."

"I see!"

"A cosmopolitan——"

"That is—speaks the tongues of all nations, and keeps the laws of none!"

"A character——"

"Who has lost the fact ere he gains the title!"

"An universal genius——"

"Who is of equally universal inutility!"

"A republican——"

"Who finding labor distasteful preaches the community of goods, and the equalization of riches! Thanks: you have sketched me the man in four phrases."

"And you have slandered him, my lord, in four epigrams!" said the Duchess de Lirà beside him, interrupting their converse.

He glanced at her with increasing surprise.

"I would slander no one, even in jest," he said gravely. "You know this—musician?"

"I know something of him,—all France does," she answered him; and the woman of the world felt her cheek redden and her conscience smite her, at the first evasion of truth made to the first man she loved. Such semi-falsehoods she and all her kind used by the score every day, dainty masks in the masked ball of life; but—to lie, to touch the shadow of a lie, with *him?* She felt as though she had sinned against him.

"I must know something also, since he has interest for you," he said, with a certain wonder still on him as to what this interest could be. "I confess to have no special regard in usual for enthusiasts and eccentrics; the brass slipper, abandoned on the brink of the volcano of originality, is commonly typical of the forsaken common sense that is left behind in the plunge of your Empedocles of Fanaticism! And the man who turns his back on the world, has generally seen the world's back ere he does so!"

"You are unjust," she said, curtly. "It is precisely these men who free the world!"

"What! Must one have rent the decencies of moral order ere one can cut the withes of illiberal thought?"

"That is a satire; not an argument. Does he of necessity violate moral order, because he breaks through social conventionalities? Yours is an assumption, not a deduction."

"Possibly: but I confess that I fail to see the inevitable relationship of a coat out at elbows with a mind out of the common; and I do not admire emancipators, whose first emancipated captives are their own passions and fancies from the limbo of law."

"There spoke all the prejudices of your Order!"

"Prejudices in favor of social decencies?—they are like prejudices in favor of cleanliness;—beggars marvel that we care for our baths, but is that an argument against ablution?"

"Prejudices!—because you assume that a man who is eccentric must needs be likewise immoral; as you would assume, I suppose, that a man who is poor in purse must of necessity be also filthy in person. I do not perceive the inevitable connection."

The path had suddenly narrowed so that but one rider could pass at a time; her horse preceded his, and the discussion was broken.

"She betrays an almost personal interest in this vagabond," meditated Estmere, restlessly. "What can she know of him?—what link can they possibly have in common?"

It was this wonder which, unknown to him, had lent an unaccustomed acerbity to the enunciation of his patrician distaste for the levities and laxities of eccentric genius.

For the first time she had differed with him: for the first time she had flung at his Order a phrase that spoke of it as kindred to him, but as alien to her.

"It must be but a woman's caprice," he mused, as he followed her. "What tie can that brilliant creature have with the vagaries of bohemianism?"

She, herself, went onward with a strange emotion at her heart: she felt as though she were, in some sort, traitress to them both; she recognized even at that distance, with unerring instinct, the silvery melodies of the violin; she thought of the time when that music had preceded the grape-laden wagons of the vintage-feast, and the great noble who was now her host had cried, "She cannot be of the People!"

The music still stole up from the valley, toward which they drew nearer with every step that their animals set into the deep wet moss of the hillside.

On her face an unusual softness, an unwonted regret deepened as she heard. She knew that she had two sins upon her, sins of the coward and of the traitor:—false shame and long ingratitude. Sins low, and dastardly, and unworthy of her!—sins for which her conscience smote her heavily.

Since the eyes of Estmere had met hers, new thoughts had stirred in her: the ice of the world's frost had melted in great part from her; she had been moved to deeper thought, quickened to warmer feeling, than she would have imagined it possible she could stoop to from the elevation of her superb disdain.

Because she herself had learned the meaning of love, she had felt wherein to love she had been traitress. Because she herself had learned to desire a tenderness withheld, she had seen where to tenderness she had been false and full of cruelty.

All things had fallen to her hands in lavish gifts, save this one thing she craved; in its denial it taught her a mercy that her life had been without from the earliest days, when she had torn down with childish hands a score of summer lilies that she might triumph in the mock wealth of gold their broken stamens yielded her.

Yet the nobler feeling was not without its baser to alloy it. There was shame—of which in turn she was ashamed—that this bitter past she loathed could never be effaced. There was the intolerable dread lest when she passed—as pass she must—through the valley where he played, one look upon her face should show old memories of the player. And in her own wayward fashion she had deep attachment to him still: his voice could move her, his regard could touch her still, as those of a deserted husband stir the half-dormant soul of a woman who has long forsaken, and forgotten him, in the dazzling oblivion of a far-distant life.

As the wife loves no more, yet still half vaguely regrets; would abhor to return, yet half wistfully repents of desertion; so did she, whenever she met the gaze of the savior whom she had denied.

She shuddered as their cavalcade wound down into the hollow of the valley, and the little hamlet lying in it came into their full view.

"Ah-ha! There is King Tricotrin!" cried the rider who had spoken of him. "I thought so; with all his Court about him—look well, Estmere, you will see the happiest man on earth."

Estmere glanced at the Duchess de Lirà as he answered:

"Then I shall see the man who has fewest responsibilities. Possibly your hero recognizes none? It is the way of his fraternity."

"You forget the dead well in the stone-mason's court, my lord; and what you were pleased then to grant was 'heroism.'"

She spoke quickly, and with bitterness, stung by his tone into recalling the scene, whose recollection had escaped him at the moment.

He started, and bowed his head.

"I had indeed forgot it. I thank you for the reminder. The man who could so imperil his life for a fellow-creature must have courage, and therefore nobility, in him."

"But it cannot be allowed, I suppose, for all that, to counterbalance the misdemeanor of being a bohemian! A decorous citizen would have probably stood on the brink, and not have presumed to interfere so rashly with the designs of 'Providence!'"

"You are pleased to be sarcastic," he replied to her, with some tinge of impatience. "I trust that I should be the last to depreciate so generous, so grand an action; but, at the same time, I admit that I have known very high deeds of courage, even of self-devotion, done by men who had very little sterling worth in them. Are all the private soldiers of an army heroes, with martyrs' souls, think you? Indeed, we know them as the dregs of the worst part of a nation; yet, is there a battle-field or a campaign that does not yield us hundreds of examples of splendid daring, and even of infinite self-sacrifice? It seems, then, that the deliverer of the stonemason was known to you at the time of that accident? I was unaware of that, or I should still better have comprehended your fears for him."

She understood the surprise, the bewilderment, the vague sense of suspicion and of wonder which spoke in his words. She could have bitten her lips through for having recalled this incident to him.

"Better have comprehended them?" she repeated, with an effort that was successful to answer him with no trace of embarrassment. "What! Is it so unintelligible, then, that one can have some feeling in our world for those in peril, some sympathy in our own empty egotism, with honor, energy, and endurance?"

He regarded her earnestly.

"If the Duchess de Lirà," he replied, at length, "have too well succeeded in persuading the world that she is heartless and pitiless, she cannot complain. She has striven studiously to misrepresent herself. I, for one at the least, shall rejoice to believe her self-slandered."

She made no response.

At that moment another sharp bend in the path brought them in full view of the village, and the young nobleman, who had called him "King Tricotrin," challenged their attention afresh, and pointed out, with his riding-whip, the high red roof and the brown wooden gallery of the village tavern, half-buried in hollyhocks, and cherry-trees, and climbing gourds, where Tricotrin was playing to the crowd.

A small hushed crowd of villagers, old men and old women, maidens and mothers, strong men and little children; all the dwellers of the valley, who, at the first notes of the violin, had left their spinning-wheels, their house-work, their seat in the sun, their play with the dogs, their love-whispers under the boughs, and had gathered about him hushed and entranced.

The valley was full of loveliness, of poetry, of pastoral peace; it was as a Theocritan idyl, as a Cuyp's conception, in the full luscious light of the declining day. But, there were in the lives that peopled it, exceeding labor, infinite pain, pressure of hunger oftentimes, continual toil that dulled the senses to the beauty around, fatigue that had no haven of rest to which to look.

Therefore they needed him, therefore they needed his music to raise their hearts from the earth that they tilled, to give them ears for the voices of winds and of waters, to translate to them the unknown tongues of the flowers, to pierce the deadened heaviness of souls slumbering from the stupor of overconstant travail. Therefore they needed him; and he gave them what they needed, as he had given to the people who loved him through so many seasons of so many years.

Vainly had kings, and those who served kings, sought to win him to bring that melody to palaces. He would not take it thither. He kept it for those in whose gray, hard, aching lives the pulse of joy was still, the sense of beauty numb; till, beneath its spells, those pulses quickened once again, that long-dulled sense revived.

The thyrsus of Dionysus was not wanted where the roses, and the lilies, and the myrtles blossomed; where the young goat browsed off sweet thyme shoots, and the earth was purple with trailing vines. It was the black sea-circled rock, the salt-marsh, where the water-bird moaned in loneliness, the parched plain, on whose sands the slave sank dead, that the wand of the Wine-God touched, and made laugh out in loveliness.

The only road through the valley homeward to Villiers led directly past the doorway where the player stood. She would have given years of her life not to have passed him there and thus; but she was a woman of the world, she was a graceful actress; she chose rather to trust to her own power of self-control, than to risk exciting comment and surprise—perchance suspicion—by any evidence of the reluctance that she felt.

"Let us see this marvelous musician; let us hear him nearer still," urged one of the great ladies of the party to the young Marquis de Valdanha: and with one consent the band of riders reined up as they passed the sign of the Silver Stag, swinging above its gourds, and fruit-trees, and blossoming syringa.

Tricotrin played on as though he saw none of them, with his head bent over his bow, and his face shaded by the broad leaf of his hat. He had recognized them even while they had been far distant on the hillside path.

"Good day, Tricotrin!" cried Valdanha, with careless good humor. "You have played for the villagers. Now play for their seigneur."

The music ceased. Tricotrin lifted his head with a smile.

"Good day, Valdanha! I play for the millions—not for the units!"

And he laid his fiddle down behind him, on the oak settle of the porch. The people fell aside; the horses grouped around the doorway; he uncovered his head to the women, where he stood with the careless grace that was as natural to him as it is to a noble untamed forest beast.

"Nonsense!" cried the young noble, pressing forward, not knowing with whom he had to deal. "Your music is worthy of Paganini, of Bamboche; do not deny it to us!"

And he cast his purse at the feet of the violin player.

"You have dropped something," said Tricotrin, quietly, lifting the purse up to its owner on the end of his bow.

Valdanha laughed, a little discomfited.

"Pooh! Keep it," he said, with a certain embarrassment. "We give a hundred times what is in it every week to an opera-singer, who has not a hundredth part of your genius."

Tricotrin laughed in answer—a scornful amusement in the laughter.

"You of the imperial court think everything is to be bought and sold?—even your own wives! Well, my music is out of the fashion; it is not to be had for coin. Take your purse up, my young sir."

"Not I!" said the marquis, pettishly, as he reined his horse back, angered to be made absurd in the eyes of his companions.

"Very well, then; take it, old Yetta," said Tricotrin, tossing it to the oldest woman in the village group, an octogenarian, whose sons had all been slaughtered in Africa. "It is not the first time alms-giving has been born out of pique. I suppose one need not quarrel with the root in face of the result. The edelweiss springs out of Alpine ice——"

They were silent; regarding him with the languid wonder, the serene curiosity, of men and women ill used to any failure in deference shown to them, yet attracted by the promise of some new and singular thing.

The Duchess de Lirà alone kept aloof, letting her horse nibble at the shoots of the drooping lime-boughs, and looking herself upward to their pyramids of starry blossom.

"But will you only play for the peasantry or for the populace?" asked Estmere, drawing nearer, remembering his latest interview with the man whom he mistrusted as a character, and regarded as a vagabond, yet who interested him despite himself.

Tricotrin, at length, met his eyes;—in his own laughed his brilliant enigmatical smile.

"Will you tell me who want to be played to more? Music is education."

"Certainly. But—no ignorant mind, no untrained ear, can appreciate melodies as perfect as yours seem to be?"

"Can an ignorant, or an untrained brain follow the theory of light, or the metamorphosis of plants?—yet it may rejoice in the rays of a summer sun, in the scent of a nest of wild flowers! So may it do in my music. Shall I ask higher payment than the God of the sun and the violets asks for himself?"

Estmere looked at him with an increasing interest.

"A noble answer," he said, with a bend of his haughty head. "But still, despite this, you must sometimes desire a more appreciative audience?"

"Appreciative! Oh-hè! how shall we call that? There are many kinds of appreciation. The man of science appreciates when he marvels before the exquisite structure of the sea-shell, the perfect organism of the flower; but the young girl appreciates, too, when she holds the shell to her ear for its music, when she kisses the flower for its fragrance. Appreciation! It is an affair of the reason, indeed; but it is an affair of the emotions also."

"And you prefer what is born of the latter?"

"Not always; but for my music I do. It speaks in an unknown tongue. Science may have its alphabet, but it is feeling that translates its poems. Delaroche, who leaves off his work to listen; Descamps, in whose eyes I see tears; Ingres, who dreams idyls while I play; a young poet whose face reflects my thoughts, an old man whose youth I bring back, an hour of pain that I soothe, an hour of laughter that I give;—these are my recompense. Think you I would exchange them for the gold showers and the diamond boxes of a Farinelli?"

"Surely not. All I meant was that you might gain a world-wide celebrity did you choose——"

"Gain a honey-coating that every fly may eat me and every gnat may sting? I thank you. I have a taste to be at peace, and not to become food to sate the public famine for a thing to tear."

Estmere smiled; he did not understand the man who thus addressed him, but he was attracted despite all his strongest prejudices.

"You are right! Under the coat of honey is a shirt of turpentine. Still—to see so great a gift as yours wasted——-"

"Wasted? Because the multitudes have it, such as it is, instead of the units? Droll arithmetic! I am with you in thinking that minorities should have a good share of power, for all that is wisest and purest is ever in a minority, as we know; but I do not see, as you see, that minorities should command a monopoly—of sweet sounds or of anything else."

"I spoke to the musician, not to the politician," said Estmere, with the calm, chill contempt of his colder manner:— the cold side of his character was touched, and his sympathies were alienated at once.

Tricotrin, indifferent to the hint as to the rebuff, looked at him amusedly.

"Oh, I know you well, Lord Estmere; I told you so not long ago, to your great disgust. You and your Order think no man should ever presume to touch politics unless his coat be velvet, and his rent-roll large, like yours. But, you see, we of the *école buissonnière* generally do as we like; and we get pecking at public questions for the same reason as our brother birds peck at the hips and the haws—because we have no granaries as you have. You do not like Socialism? Ah! And yet affect to follow it."

"I!" Estmere looked at this wayside wit, this wine-house philosopher, with a regard that asked plainly, "are you fool or knave?"

"To be sure," answered Tricotrin. "You have chapel and chaplain yonder at your château, I believe? The Book of the Christians is the very manual of Socialism: '*You* read the gospel, Marat?' they cried. 'To be sure,' said Marat. 'It is the most republican book in the world, and sends all the rich people to hell.' If you do not like my politics, *beau sire*, do not listen to the Revolutionist of Galilee."

What Estmere would have answered was never heard. At that moment the Duchess de Lirà turned her horse's head quickly, and glanced at Tricotrin with a swift flashing regard, that conveyed all to him, naught to others.

"Have you no word for me?"

She spoke on an impulse, half of remorseful shame for her own silence, half of unreasonable feminine impatience at the absence of all recognition from him. She knew that his abstinence from it was out of noble delicacy toward her, generous submission to her will and to her welfare; she would have been incensed had he claimed intimacy with her, yet she was irritated that he could thus ignore her presence.

With the remorseless vanity of a beautiful wayward woman, she could not bear to see indifference even in one to whose peace it was indispensable, and in whom her pride refused to acknowledge before the world a friend. This alienation between them had been from her own wish, by her own work: yet his acceptance of it always stung her with a vivid sense of humiliation.

Therefore, though to pass him as a stranger was what she had desired, her self-love and her remorse forced her to break through the barrier she had herself imposed: she voluntarily drew all eyes upon her, as with something of the enchanting petulance of her early years she asked:

"Have you no word for me?"

He uncovered his head to her again, and smiled.

"Many words, madam, if you wish for them; but my phrases are not the chocolate-almonds palatable to great ladies. Besides! are you so unaristocratic as to remember an old debt? What will these noblemen think of you?"

Estmere's regard was fastened on them both with a surprise he did not attempt to veil; what she did, what she said, had an interest for him no other living being's acts and words possessed, and he beheld with no less disquietude than amazement this address, to a lawless bohemian, from a woman whom even her own society found so languidly cold, so mercilessly scornful.

She, a patrician, as proud as himself, far aloof from all weakness of her sex or derogation to her dignity, yet had some close bond in common with a strolling musician, a roaming eccentricity, a scamp in a linen blouse, with a monkey in his pocket, and the salt of a lawless wit on his tongue!

Tricotrin divined the thought in his mind, and turned toward him.

"I said so! Madam, you will lose my lord's esteem forever if you do not take care. Earl Eustace, see here; long years ago, when this fair empress, whom you know now, was childish enough to object to a premature death, I chanced to save her life one summer's day; by mere accident and without risk, so that she has nothing to thank me for,—still, she remembers it. She errs to her Order in harboring such a plebeianism as gratitude; but in consideration that her life has turned out worth having, you may perhaps be brought in time to understand and to pardon it!"

The light sarcasm, the easy disowning of all his vast claims, the swift desire to save her even from the passing suspicion of her companions, touched all her latent conscience, stung all her latent generosity, touched and stung them as no assertion of his rights and of her debt could ever have done.

Her higher nature flashed out in the reply she gave, as she glanced from the one to the other:

"Were it possible that I could incur my Lord Estmere's censure for a sentiment that the very beasts and birds can feel toward their benefactors, I could not lose his esteem so utterly as he would assuredly lose mine!"

She paused suddenly, her face hot with shame; she felt the poverty, the futility of any acknowledgment to him, while still actually she denied him, like the apostle who was ashamed of his Master,—while still, untold, unguessed, the width and the depth of his benefits to her lay buried for sake of her pride.

Estmere bowed to her,—in his heart dissatisfied and perplexed.

"The duchess is right; I should indeed merit her disdain were I capable of such baseness. In her childhood you saved her life! The world is greatly your debtor. May I ask how it chanced?"

"Ouf! nothing to speak of; she was lost in a wood, and would have made a choice meal for a wolf; that is all. Mistigri here had more to do with the rescue than I. The world my debtor! A pretty phrase from a great lord's lips; but was it the debtor of Antiochus for Cleopatra? These beautiful women are no good to the world, they are what the peasants here think comets are:—dazzling messengers of evil, that bring fire, and war, and pestilence in their train. The beauty of woman,—it is the passion-flower of our lives; but it has poison in one leaf of it, and healing in another. Madame de Lirà is your guest?"

In the quick transition there was a sequence of thought which Estmere caught, though it was unuttered; his own impulse to let himself be beguiled by this beauty, whether it brought him the poisoned or the healing touch, spurred his comprehension.

He gave a cold assent to the question, wondering still what manner of man this could be who talked thus at the door of a peasant's ale-house, and who presumed to convey to himself a veiled warning against a passion whose existence no sign even had ever betrayed to its object.

"You stay in the valley yourself, Tricotrin?" asked Valdanha, at the same moment.

"Pardieu! I never stay anywhere!" laughed Tricotrin. "The *pérégrinomanie*, as sturdy Guy Patin styled it, is the only salt of life; always on the wing, like a swallow—it is to keep perpetual youth, perpetual spring. You flee from the winter, and follow where the sun goes. Do you know, to my thinking, the Peruvian's notion of paradise eclipses every other;—endless, buoyant movement, through never-ending fields of light! There is a grand conception!—how vulgar beside it is the Christian, how unpoetic even the Hellenic, picture of immortality!"

"You are always a wanderer?" asked Estmere, impelled,

against his own will, to interest himself in one who half offended, half pleased, half alienated, half attracted him.

"To be sure I am. Why not?"

"There would be scant obedience to the duties of citizenship if all men were like you," said the other with a smile.

"And no opportunity for an Oligarchy, which you would resent still more! Well—see you here, my Lord Earl. You are born in the purple, you have the scepter of power, the Aaron's rod of wealth, you can summon all fair things about you, you can have all the delights of the soul and the senses; and if Satiety curse them all for you, it is only because you begin them too early, and ask more of them than it is reasonable to ask of any things of earth. You possess all you desire; and have no foe to rob from you: save the devil of disgust, that hides underneath all possession. But if you were a poor man, with your soul and your senses all quickened, but no incantation rod of gold in your hand, it would be different with you; you might like then to find your kingdom in your liberty, your treasure-house in the light of the sun, your artists in the colors of the sky, your empire in the stretch of forest, sea, or desert; your poem in a flower, your music in a torrent, your temple in a palm grove. Have you ever thought of that? Have you ever thought how dear, to men who have not wealth, are color, sound, and sense and dreams?—the miraged cities that only those who travel in long drought behold as compensation. You need them not—you live in palaces."

Estmere listened, in a grave wondering courtesy: the poetic nature scarcely belonged to him; he had led the life which kills it, his temperament was that of the statesman, not of the speculator, of the lawgiver, not of the visionary. He could not wholly comprehend the tenor of the fantastic, vivid, half-metaphorical answer given him; yet there was too much sympathy in his mind—from which no noble thought was alien—for him to ridicule or slight it.

"You are happy," he said, with a sigh that was almost of envy. "There is no wand of gold that summons such fair shapes as can the poet's power of fancy. Only—I incline to think you live twenty centuries too late, or—twenty centuries too early."

Viva turned on him a swift and eager glance.

"Of course!" she said, with a certain emotion, whose meaning he could not analyze. "Was there ever yet a man of genius who was not either the relic of some great dead age, or the precursor of some noble future one, in which he alone has faith?"

"Chut!" said Tricotrin, rapidly; he could not trust himself to hear her speak in his own defence. "Fine genius mine! To fiddle to a few villagers, and dash color on an alehouse shutter! I have the genius of indolence, if you like; as to my belonging to a by-gone age,—well! I am not sure that I have not got the soul in me of some barefooted friar of Moyen Age, who went about where he listed, praying here, laughing there, painting a missal with a Pagan love-god, and saying a verse of Horace instead of a chant of the Church. Or, maybe, I am more like some Greek gossiper, who loitered away his days in the sun, and ate his dates in the market-place, and listened here and there to a philosopher, and—just by taking no thought—hit on a truer philosophy than came out of Porch or Garden. Ah! my Lord of Estmere, you have two hundred servants over there at Villiers, I have been told; do you not think I am better served here by one little brown-eyed, brown-cheeked maiden, who sings her Béranger like a lark, while she brings me her dish of wild strawberries? There is fame too for you,—his—the King of the Chansons! When a girl washes her linen in the brook,—when a herdsman drives his flock through the lanes,—when a boy throws his line in a fishing-stream,—when a grisette sits and works at her attic lattice,—when a student dreams under the linden leaves,—he is on their lips, in their hearts, in their fancies and joys. What a power! What a dominion! Wider than any that emperors boast!"

"And," added Estmere, with a smile, "if you were not Tricotrin you would be Béranger?"

"Assuredly. A lyric poet, if he have art, or rather nature enough in him, to wind himself into the lives and the souls of the people, reigns as no Alexander, no Cæsar, no Sulla ever did yet. A statesman rules,—ay, for a lifetime; but it is only the poet whose scepter stretches over generations unborn. But good day to you—or rather good night. I have no business to weary you with words, if I do not give you music."

"But will you not give us both?"

"No," he answered abruptly, and, lifting his hat to the women of the group, he turned with a rapid movement and went within. The memory was keen in him of the day when he had played to the little child that had dropped her lilies and forget-me-nots to listen.

She who once—so long ago!—had been that child, happy in her floral wealth, let him go from her in silence, with only a courteous gesture of farewell. Conscience was not dead in her; but it was numb, vacillating, bewildered; it allowed her passively to accept the tacit sacrifice made to her. It allowed her to acquiesce in his acceptance of her abandonment, in his self-negation for her sake.

Yet she felt debased, unworthy, a coward to the core; she started like a guilty creature when her host addressed her as they rode away from the tavern porch, whose golden sunflowers the evening sun was just commencing to redden into stars of fire.

"A strange character,—this man!" he said to her. "A genius, no doubt; but a genius wasted."

"No doubt," she answered, with a certain comtemptuous satire, in which her own emotions found alike mask and refuge. "He makes no money by it!"

"That was not my meaning," replied Estmere, annoyed at the misconstruction. "It is not for gold that the highest intelligences labor in any age. But talents thrown away upon a wineshop audience are still less profitably employed than wrapped in the napkin of the parable."

"The wineshop audience feels!" she answered, with that occasional ironic scoff at the patrician order which would now and then break out in her, and seem to show some latent though repelled sympathy with the bohemianism of another class. "Can we say so much for the vapid circle of a palace drawing-room, murmuring scientific jargon, and tapping faint applause with fans and gloves!"

"I think we may,—sometimes," said Estmere, coldly. "I cannot myself perceive why educated faculties in the admirer make discriminative admiration less honorable to its object than a clown's grin, or a milkmaid's tears. It is the cant of the age to presuppose the monopoly of all sympathies by the uncultured classes; now, I believe that there are no classes more utterly unsympathetic on the earth. Sympathy has its birth in the mind yet more than in the heart;— the sympathy of the boor is restricted to his own hearth; it is only the sympathy of the scholar that extends to things totally opposed, and persons entirely alien, to him."

"Yet there are scholars who, if they climb the ice-mountain of their own ambition, care not whom the avalanches slay in the villages below."

"Well,—that is not a worse, it is to an extent a higher, form of egotism than the peasant's, who, if his own hayrick be not in flames, cares not what torch of war desolates the neighboring plain. But can you tell me no more of this man—Tricotrin? Tricotrin! it is not a name."

"I have never known him go by any other. No,—I can tell you very little of him. He is a logogriph, whose leading word I have never guessed."

"Yet he saved your life, it appears?"

"That is a sarcasm! He saved my life certainly; but I was an infant, I have no recollection of the circumstance; I have merely heard of it——"

"And you know nothing of him?—I mean of his antecedents, his modes of life, his pursuits, of what first made him the bohemian and the eccentricity that he is now?"

"I have no idea. I have never had any means of ascertaining. I know that the Duke de Lirà held him in high esteem for some great service rendered in an insurrection; I know that he is a man of infinite wit, infinite resources, infinite nobility of feeling,—that is the extent of my knowledge. I greatly doubt, also, if any one's influence is greater. He is 'Tricotrin,' the people say. Both he and they seem to consider all uttered in that word which you find so singular."

"I find it singular because it is so evidently but a pseudonym——"

"I never thought of it as such. There are strange names among the French *bas peuple.*"

"But that man does not belong to the '*bas peuple*' of any nation."

"By his look—no. Yet—I never heard anything that suggested his belonging to any other grade than that which he assumes; although——"

"Although what?"

"Although,—is not his tenderness for the people rather that of one who has voluntarily associated himself with them than that of one who naturally belongs to them?"

"This was my own thought. Would it not be possible to learn something of him?"

"I do not think so; I imagine no one would more acutely resent any attempt to penetrate his past."

She spoke hurriedly, for the first time losing the easy and negligent self-possession she had preserved throughout the conversation. She felt an intense anxiety to divert his thoughts from the subject, and his inquiries from the fortunes, of Tricotrin; and she allowed her anxiety to overcome the tact and facility of her assumed indifference. To penetrate his past was to penetrate hers!

He perceived that restless fear; but he said nothing of it. He accepted her words in their surface-meaning, and assented to them.

"Those men," he added, "who fling away great gifts in gipsy-camps, and dash their Castalian water with pot-house drinks, are usually the heroes of adventures as amusing as, but not more reputable than, those of Gil Blas; and, though they censure the world and laugh at mankind, they have generally first been shown a jail by the one and the door by the other. 'A great Character!' says Society: when it means —'a great Scamp!'"

A hot flush of color passed over the fairness of her face; her teeth set.

"You love to turn an epigram, Lord Estmere!—and care little what you sacrifice to its points. Look in the face of that man we have left, and say—you who pride yourself on your knowledge of men—whether any single thing of shame, or of crime, or of dishonor, could go with the features you see, with the bearing that defies you, with the lion's regard that meets your own!"

He bowed his head.

"This person is fortunate in his interest for you—proud in his defender."

Then silence ensued between them; and lasted until they rode up to the doors of Villiers.

## CHAPTER XXIV.

"I HAVE lied to him!" she thought, dropping her head on her hands when she reached her own chambers. She had been ashamed of the sin of ingratitude, of the sin of cowardice, but she was far more bitterly ashamed of the sin of falsehood,—because this last sin was against the man in whose sight she desired not to have only the semblance, but the reality, of perfect truth, and purity, and honor.

She had said no absolute word of untruth to him, perhaps; it was true that she knew nothing of the whence and the whither of the one of whom they had spoken. While protected by Tricotrin she had been too young to question the life that seemed almost divine in her eyes; since she had quitted him the memory of it had been blotted out by a thousand more vivid interests and more selfish pursuits. It was true she knew nothing—never had asked aught—of this fate which from her childhood upward had been too familiar in her eyes to have any aspect of strangeness or of mystery.

She had adhered to the letter of the truth; but that was all;—in spirit, in effect, in purpose, she had lied to Estmere; lied to the man whose regard pierced the coldness and the vanity of her life, as the sun's rays of the mature year pierce the snows and the ice of the mountain-peaks, and who called the long-buried beauties of her gentler nature into fresh existence, as those rays recall to blossom the crocus, and the gentian, and the edelweiss.

Her sin against him, as weighed with her sin against the other, was as a grain of wheat beside a millstone; yet the life-long guilt had left her without remorse, without regret, almost without moral consciousness of it: the guilt of the evasion, the concealment, made her feel covered with shame, and forever without fitness for him.

He had no right to her confidence; she owed him no allegiance; he had no title to search out her past;—but these sophisms availed nothing to reconcile her with herself.

In that moment she was utterly base in her own judgment; she had lost dignity, and purity, and truth, and even courage; she had been a coward! There was nothing viler or lower in her esteem; and in that one hour she saw down into the depths of her own heart, and saw there weakness and worthlessness, that made the haughty duchess, who exercised so superb a power over the souls of men, immeasurably beneath the child that had learned her simple lessons of loyalty and justice from the lips of an old peasant woman.

"I cannot deceive *him!*" she thought, "and yet, he must never—he shall never—know!"

A more poignant shame than even that of falsehood smote her as she mused thus; a shame that made her ready to tear her very heart out of her living body,—the shame that she gave her love to a man who had never uttered to her one word of passion or of tenderness.

"I fascinate him,—I perplex him,—I gain his censure,—

I excite his scorn,—I force his admiration;—but are any of *those* love?" she thought, in the bitterness of her soul.

And her head sank, and her eyes grew blind with tears, and her life ached with vain vague longing.

Then the imperious coquetry in her rose, and she looked at her own face; and her eyes flashed, her mouth laughed in proud resolve and consciousness of power.

"He *shall* love me!" she said half aloud, in her closed teeth: it was as much a menace as a vow. She had said it often, when but vanity alone had been involved in its realization; she said it now with all her soul set upon its fruition. She drove aside her repentance, her self-condemnation, her sickening sense of danger and of error: and summoned her women about her, and gave herself into their hands, and had the gold powder scattered over tresses brighter than itself, and gossamer laces cast over beauties which they half veiled only wholly to enhance, and the diamonds girdle a form fit for the cestus of Venus, and a single scarlet flower set to glow against the whiteness of her bosom.

"He *shall* love me!" she thought, as she glanced at the mirrors ere she swept from her chambers, voluptuously lovely as any goddess that ever passed through the Ivory Gate to haunt the dreams of poet or of painter.

But—Estmere never had feared her as he feared her sensuous grace, her intoxicating charm, that night.

It was the scarlet flower of passion, of pride, of victory, of delirium, that glowed within her breast:—not the white flower of purity and of truth.

The one had already betrayed him; the other he had sought as the knight sought Yolande with the Yellow Hair— in vain.

Still he loved her, though he withheld the knowledge of his subjection from her; though he resisted, and scorned, and feared the emotion that possessed him. He concealed it jealously, because he mistrusted her; mistrusted that she might fool him as she fooled all men; that she had danger, and evil, and cruelty in her, as have all things dominated by vanity.

Also, he mistrusted himself; he was no longer young: with this boy's play of love he had had naught to do, since it had dealt him back the gray ashes of a desolated honor, in return for his fair gold of faith. It seemed to him as a madman's folly to suppose that he alone could succeed, where all others had failed, in awakening tenderness and fealty from such a woman as this. He had distrust of her; distrust of himself.

The proud noble could not sue to be rejected; the grave statesman could not bend his neck in an unvalued homage; the superb gentleman could not stoop in vain, and give himself to the gay languid disdain of a successful and sated coquette.

He loved her with a passion only stronger and deeper for its suppression; but still stronger than itself were his fears of hers, and his own self-respect. He would not give up his honor for her wanton play, his dignity for her captious triumph.

Moreover, a certain vague but painful suspicion had arisen in him with the reticence that he had noted in her on the subject of that tavern-musician whom she defended, yet ignored. No single trace of embarrassment and of reluctance that she had displayed had been lost upon him. He perceived that there was here some memory, or some circumstance, that she desired to thrust away; some bond between her and this wanderer that she wished unrevealed, undivined. His own mind was too lofty, his own thoughts too noble, for any coarse or base suggestion to present itself to him as the reason of this; still the fancy—for it was scarcely more—haunted and troubled him.

He loved her:—hence he would have had her life stainless as the driven snow, and open before him as the leaves of a book. And he felt instinctively that it never would be thus.

Ere he had met her, she had lived through many seasons of victory, of brilliancy, of luxury, of celebrity; in them how many dead passions, dead joys, dead pleasures, dead pains, might lie of which he could never know? They said that she had never loved: but who could tell?—who could be certain that her scorn for all her facile conquests might not be born from some secret and silent emotion of which she was ashamed? some impulse that could not be indulged without derogation from her code, degradation to her rank! This well might be, without shame to her:—this stranger might hold the clew to whatsoever the secret was; might, even, have been the object of such an attachment. Thus he mused in the self-torture with which the wisest torments himself when once the love of woman has entered into him.

He was riding slowly through the outlying woods of his estate, in the freshness of the very early day. Some forest question had needed his presence there, and he had been glad of the stillness, the loneliness, the freedom from his duties as a host.

"What he would have given for youth!" he thought, "for the years of his son's youth!"

That futile desire had never touched his life before; it was spent in grave ambitions, high pursuits, fair fame; it was too lofty for envy, too serene for regret:—it was only now when the weakness of passion undermined it, that he felt, with a restless weariness, sorrow for the many years that had slipped by and never brought him a joy; desire for the glow and glory of the hopes which, with him, had died out so long ago, crushed like bruised asphodels in the white false hand of a woman.

A sigh escaped him: a quick, low, impatient sigh of pain:—had he dwelt in peace through all these many seasons only to fall before this sorceress at the last!

He started, as in answer to that sigh a voice challenged him in what he had believed to be so perfect and profound a solitude.

"You are weary, Earl Eustace, and on a midsummer morning, too! For shame! Ah! the grass-wreaths of the Scipiones and the Julii were searer in all their honor than the fresh

Campagna grasses that boy poets wove for Nævia's or for Flora's hair; it is so to this day, is it not?"

Estmere checked his horse, and glanced around in the sun-lightened woods.

Beside him, knee-deep in flowers and ferns, with a wounded quail in his right hand, stood Tricotrin, under a group of pines, from whose boughs Mistigri was swinging.

"I have been bathing in one of your pools," pursued his trespasser, whose hair and beard still glistened with waterdrops. "A little man-forgotten lake there, under the trees, that no creature ever sees save the water-fowl. You bathe in a dainty marble bath, with a fresco of Leda on the walls, I believe;—bah! my teals' and widgeons' and wild swans' Jordan is far better."

Estmere did not answer him at once; surprise at his presence there, annoyance at the audacious freedom of the address, and the latent attraction that this man possessed for him, all holding him silent. He had desired to meet with Tricotrin again; but he was scarcely prepared for so unceremonious a greeting.

"Good day to you," he said at length, with that cold and gentle courtesy which marked, far more definitely than other men's insolence, the differences of rank. "You have a bird there?—is it dead?"

Tricotrin looked up and laughed in his eyes, touching the little quail softly.

"You think I look like a poacher? No—the thing is living; but I found it with its wing broken—by a blow from a stick or a stone, most likely; and I shall keep it with me and cure it. '*Fratres mei*,' said François d'Assises to the birds: he was a bold man to claim brotherhood with the innocents! And he talked to them—the fool!—instead of listening. What presumption!"

"You are fond of birds and animals? you are a naturalist?"

"God be praised, no! I am fond of them, yes. How honest they are, how tender, how grateful! They do not take your benefits as so many reasons why they should cut your throat lest you should ever claim a debt against them, which men are apt to do. But a naturalist! A man who thinks himself justified in making all creation groan, if he can tickle his own vanity with one straw of knowledge; who will give the tortures of hell to the dumb meek brutes, if so be that thereby he may gain some scrap of false science, which the future will laugh at as the present now laughs at Aristotle! No! For what do you take me?"

"For what do you bid me to take you?"

He asked the question on an impulse: he ardently desired to learn something, were it ever so little, of this wandering life, that was the entire antithesis of his own.

Tricotrin's eyes laughed again at him with their amused and sunny irony.

"Rather tell me what you select for me; I am three abominations in your sight, I fancy: a cosmopolitan, a democrat, and a vagabond—eh?"

"Surely, the cosmopolitan is a man of too high powers and gifts to be fitly associated in designation with the other two appellatives?"

"Pooh! What is there to object to in the other two, pray? David, Mithridates, Artaxerxes, Nezahualcoytl, Viriathus, scores of great kings, were vagabonds and wanderers in their novitiates; and as for democrats! well, one may have worse company, I fancy, than Buzot, Vergniaud, Milton, Hampden, and all their like, stretching up to Caius Gracchus. Not that I altogether hold with *him* for his bribes, his rancor, his corn proletariat, and other such matters——"

"You cite honorable names," answered Estmere, with a smile, unconsciously falling into his companion's vein of speech. "You forget that, for the few kings errant, there are a million of thieves and gipsies; and that for one Gracchus we get a Cinna, a Critolaüs, a Glaucius, more or less miserably repeated a thousand times in every nation."

"Ay,—as for one Drusus, one Scipio, one Sempronius, and one Estmere, to whom 'nobility is obligation,' there are a million petty patricians who play at a paper-tyrannis, and disgrace the order, while they ape the ways of the great Eupatrids. But I do not see, myself, that the dignity of the original type is harmed because it is unworthily imitated. For the real *patina* of a true Correggio, you get the false glaze of ten thousand copies from the schools; but that does not change the true Correggio's value."

Estmere bent his head in acknowledgment of the tribute to himself, which he saw was no lip service, but the offspring of a cordial sincerity; while increased surprise came on him: this man, with a democrat's codes, had none of the democrat's blind class-hatred.

"You have a silver tongue," he said, resting his eyes on his companion in grave speculation. "You, yourself, I believe, with all your professions of lawlessness, admit that 'humanity is obligation,' a law still more stringent, and far more wide-spreading. I was present when the Paris crowd worshiped you for your noble rescue of the stone-mason from the dead well."

Tricotrin gave an impatient gesture, and almost an embarrassed laugh. He hated such things as these in his life to be known or be quoted.

"Pshaw! What was that?" he cried lightly. "I did not get even a sprain. To those poor, sickly, effeminate, city-mewed Parisians, who scarce ever stir outside their barrier-walls, it might look a great feat; but to any one who knows anything of mountaineering, to any one who has hung by a rope over an alpine precipice, the mere going down into a well was a nothing at all."

Estmere smiled.

"You may undervalue the action; no one else is likely to do so. It was a very splendid result of such a union of courage and coolness as we do not very often find; and it was a great self-devotion also."

"Self-devotion? Pa!! Not a bit of it. Is death such a terrible thing that we are such wonderful heroes for risking it? I am Pagan enough to deem it no such awful visitant. By-the-way, it is a sufficiently droll affair, that Christianity, which professes itself so sure of the justice of Divine judgments and of the possession of an eternal Hereafter, should be the one religion whose followers have most assiduously dressed up Death as a King of Terrors? Anomalous, assuredly."

Estmere still regarded him with earnest interest, paying little heed to what he uttered, so intent was he himself in speculation as to what this wanderer could possibly be.

"It was certainly you," he said, at length, "whom I met, not very long since, in Lélis' atelier, and who reminded me of my having once purchased the Attavante?"

"Yes; it was I."

"Lélis spoke of you to me with the deepest attachment, and told me the tale of that little black familiar which swings yonder. Yours is a peculiar name."

Tricotrin's eyes laughed a little.

"Is it? It is a simple one enough."

"Of what part of the country, may I ask?"

"A cosmopolitan has no country."

"But even a cosmopolitan must have parentage—race—birthplace?"

"Must he? Well, a bohemian need have none of the three. He is a great deal freer than his prototypes, the gipsies; for they are the slaves of tribe-law and blood-influence. Like Micha Hall, of Mam Tor, he can write on his tombstone, if, indeed, he care for one:

> 'Quid eram, nescitis;
> Quid sum, nescitis;
> Ubi abii, nescitis.
> Valete!'"

Estmere smiled at the epitaph; and felt himself compelled to admit the hint to discontinue his inquiries. He turned to another subject.

"The Dante had been long yours?"

"Yes. Why do you ask?"

"Only to know if you have regretted its loss."

"I never regret anything. What is the use?"

"I merely meant, that—it would give me pleasure to restore it to you if you would permit me?"

"I never take gifts. I thank you for your intention, all the same."

"Well—will you purchase it, then, by allowing the château to hear that music which you bestow so lavishly on the tavern?"

"No," said Tricotrin, more briefly still. "I do not play for any wage, nor in any châteaux. I play when the spirit moves me; not when men dictate."

"That is the waywardness of all genius," thought Estmere, as he answered aloud:

"It is our misfortune that you are so antagonistic to the châteaux; and—you surely find no debtor such an ingrate, no master such a tyrant, as the People?"

"Perhaps. But, rather I find it a dog, that bullies and tears where it is feared, but may be made faithful by genuine courage and strict justice shown to it."

"The experience of the musician, then, must be much more fortunate than the experience of the statesman."

"Why, yes. It is ungrateful to great men, I grant; but it has the irritation of its own vague sense that it is but their tool, their ladder, their grappling-iron, to excuse it. Still—I know well what you mean; the man who works for mankind works for a task-master, who makes bitter every hour of his life only to forget him with the instant of his death;—he is ever rolling the stone of human nature upward toward purer heights, to see it recoil and rush down into darkness and bloodshed. I know——"

Estmere's eyes still dwelt on him with keen, grave study. The desire he had to become acquainted with this man's past and present, overcame the reluctance in him to betray what might seem curiosity or intrusion.

"I wish that you would tell me," he said, with a certain hesitation, "tell me without epigram or argument, simply how it arrives that a man of your talents and culture—as they appear to me—occupies with content a position where the world can so little perceive those powers, or offer them their due honors and awards?"

"You wish to know *that*?"

The question was rapid and stern: a look of impatience, of anger, of contempt, swept stormily over his features; but its duration was brief, his careless serenity returned again, as he answered with a laugh:

"Is there aught so wonderful that a man likes his liberty, likes to wander at his ease, likes to get riddance of the trammels of a civilization which, in multiplying wants and desires, has multiplied envy and greed?"

"That is the vagrant's excuse for preferring licence to law, and theft to honest labor," said Estmere coldly. His inherent distrust of a "Character" began to revive.

Tricotrin shrugged his shoulders.

"Pardie! so it is, poor simpleton. If he do not know that he who enters into crime subscribes subservience to the weightiest bondage on earth, it is because his ignorance is as strong as his lusts. And who teaches him otherwise? He beholds so many successful sins throned on high and rolling in their chariots!"

"To accuse the world of dishonesty is always the outlaw's defence of his own stolen goods," answered Estmere, in his chillest tones. "But I started no general proposition. I asked you a personal—perhaps a too curious—question. I may seem rude, I have no title to ask an answer; nevertheless, I must repeat, it is impossible for me to reconcile the great gifts you undoubtedly possess with the career you are content to pursue."

Tricotrin's eloquent eyes changed their expression many times through the few sentences. As they were concluded, his regard grew graver, though in it there still laughed the delicate, fine irony of his careless scorn.

"Well,—I will answer you, though I would not any one else. Tell me first, though, what it is you find so reprehensible in my career? Is it my consorting with a little animal who bears too close token of his relationship to us to be an agreeable object of contemplation to man?—is it because there is only virtue in your velvet, and gross guilt in my linen blouse?—is it the telling of plain truths, the calling of things simply by their names, a sin that blackened Sulla's name far more than the blood that he shed?—is it because I play to those who want amusement instead of to those who can pay for it? It is all these, I suppose; but what else?"

"Simply—that having genius you do not care to be worthy of it, and to worthily bestow it. An insolent answer, you will say; but you have demanded my opinion."

"Certainly. Well—let us see. What is bestowing it worthily? I will tell you a story.

"Once there were three handmaidens of Krishna's; invisible, of course, to the world of men. They begged of Krishna, one day, to test their wisdom, and Krishna gave them three drops of dew. It was in the season of drought, —and he bade them go and bestow them where each deemed best in the world.

"Now one flew earthward, and saw a kings's fountain leaping and shining in the sun; the people died of thirst, and the fields and the plains were cracked with heat, but the king's fountain was still fed and played on. So she thought, 'Surely my dew will best fall where such glorious water dances!'— and she shook the drop into the torrent.

"The second hovered over the sea, and saw the Indian oysters lying under the waves, among the sea-weed and the coral. Then she thought, 'A rain-drop that falls in an oyster's shell becomes a pearl; it may bring riches untold to man, and shine in the diadem of a monarch. Surely it is best bestowed where it will change to a jewel!'—and she shook the dew into the open mouth of a shell.

"The third had scarcely hovered a moment over the parched white lands, ere she beheld a little, helpless, brown bird dying of thirst upon the sand, its bright eyes glazed, its life going out in torture. Then she thought, 'Surely my gift will be best given in succor to the first and lowliest thing I see in pain!'—and she shook the dew-drop down into the silent throat of the bird, that fluttered, and arose, and was strengthened.

"Then Krishna said that she alone had bestowed her power wisely; and he bade her take the tidings of rain to the aching earth, and the earth rejoiced exceedingly. Genius is the morning dew that keeps the world from perishing in drought. Can you read my parable?"

Estmere bowed his head; touched and rebuked by the poetic reproach.

"I do; forgive me that I ventured to pass judgment on you."

"I forgive!" answered Tricotrin, simply; then, with the light and rapid movement that was common with him, he sprang like a deer across the freshet of water by which he stood, and, plunging into the depth of wood that lay on its farther side, was lost from sight before the other could arrest him.

Estmere sat and gazed at the green dense wall of foliage that the young and old oaks of the forest placed between them. He was astonished, attracted, perplexed; a feeling he could not account for moved him, and filled him with a vexed impatience at his own failure, and a deepened interest in the one who had vanquished him.

There was that about this fearless grace, this poetic eloquence, this mingled pride and carelessness, the one as of a king, the other as of a gipsy, that fascinated him, were it only by sheer force of contrast; and wrung from him a reverence that he was almost tempted to ridicule, yet which he could not resist despite his own resentment of it. He was accustomed to control, to command, to dominate, to criticise men, as he who is born to rule them must ever do if he would hold a leader's place; but here was one man with whom he could do none of these,—one man who excited all his strongest prejudices, who called up all his haughtiest creeds, but who won on him, and who challenged his attention as none of his own order ever had done.

Yet he was impatient with himself for having yielded to such an influence.

"Because he has the gift of a fair tongue, and evades a direct inquiry by a poetic and fanciful allegory, is he any the truer and safer? is he any the worthier of credence?" he thought, as he rode slowly homeward through the only road intersecting the oak glades.

But, although he argued with his impulse of faith as a weakness, although he repeated to himself that the charm which had lulled his suspicions had been but the charm of an adventurer's facile and valueless eloquence, an instinct stirred in his heart—the instinct of one truthful nature's loyalty unto another—which told him still that the doubt was dishonor to the one whom it attaindered with suspicion.

"A clever actor—what more? A scholarly outlaw, cunning of fence, and with a winning tongue—that is all," he mused, and strove to believe.

But the memory of the heroism in the stone-cutter's court rebuked him; and the scepticism engendered by the world was conquered by the native generosity within him. Instinct trusted where reason had condemned. But whether reason or instinct were the truer guide, both alike impelled him to know far more of this wanderer: both alike made him think, with the old Homeric line:

"He only is a living man; the rest are gliding shades."

## CHAPTER XXV.

IN the balmy rose-gardens of Villiers a group like one from the Decameron strolled, and sat, and loitered, in the warmth of a summer day.

Among those highborn, languid, amorous idlers, slaying their hours with lightest love and lightest wit, a little rabbit, white, and with fleecy hair, ran rapidly, half frightened at the novelty of its intrusion, half enchanted with the lowhanging roses, at which it nibbled hurriedly, to flee, as hurriedly, with its mouth full of rose-leaves. No one noticed it; it had its way among the buds; and ventured at last to sit demurely still, a ball of snow among the crimson blossoms.

Suddenly, and with clumsy vehemence, there rushed to chase it a large-limbed, brawny, bronzed woman of the farms, breaking in where none of her class had ever dared to stray. She caught the terrified thing, and shook it angrily; and turned her eyes, as though she also were stupefied at her own temerity, on the face of the great lady nearest her.

"Pardon, madam," she stammered, with uncouth, embarrassed eagerness. "I should lose my place if it were known I dared come in here:—but this little beast skipped from my arms as I passed the gates, and I thought it would damage the roses, and so I ran—and ran,—and I never saw where it was I came. Will you say something for me if they threaten me?"

The Duchess de Lirà smiled.

"Oh, yes; meanwhile I would say—do not swing that poor rabbit by its ears."

The woman shifted the rabbit at once to an easier mode of detention.

"It is very good of madam to think of the dumb brute!" she muttered, with awkward courtesy. "I should be loth to lose it; it belongs to old Virelois, and she is lonely, and makes friends of these things—but I forget, I have no business here—forgive my rudeness, madam."

And she thrust her huge coarse form through the delicate loveliness of the rose aisles; her wooden shoes clattering over the velvet sward, the white rabbit trembling in the hard grasp of her hand. She went over park, and meadow, and the stepping-stones of a brook; and threw her rabbit aside in a hutch; and entered the cool dairy-house, and sat herself down on a stool.

There was a sullen savage pleasure, and a coarse cynicism, on her face; and her wide mouth laughed with a broad hoarse laugh.

"I thought so—I thought so, when she swept past me in that carriage!" she muttered, in a brutish glee, with which envy mingled. "I said I should know that dainty face out of a million,—there was a look that *knew*, in her eyes, when I said the old granddam's name. God's mercy! that bastard a duchess!—how can it have come to pass? They said she was dead,—and we thought her in shame,—and all this while she has lived among princes. Well—I will keep my tongue till the young lord comes; but it shall go hard if I do not hurt her somehow. She to be an aristocrat—that nameless, useless, wanton, insolent thing!—it kills one with laughter only to think on it!"

And she laughed again, her hard, rough, riotous laugh, sitting there in her solitude; and she thrust over, with a savage turn of her foot, the wooden stool on which, one summer evening, the child whom she had hated had sat, and counted her magic grapes, and crowned herself with her magic jasmine.

While she thus mused, the Duchess de Lirà had gone within, for the heat grew oppressive even in those cool, shadowy, fountain-filled rose-gardens, and was moving slowly up and down the picture-galleries, accompanied by her host.

His galleries were of great extent and value; year by year he had added to his collections, until their excellence was scarce to be surpassed; and since the early dishonor of his wedded life had made his old hereditary home distasteful to him, he had gathered together all that was richest and rarest of his possessions in this, his favorite, dwelling-place of Villiers.

As she swept to and fro them, she conversed of art, and of many things beside art, with the airy subtleties of wit that a woman of the world gains from society, as a flower gains its hues from the bees which lend it brilliancy while they steal its sweetness. With her, indeed, it was rather inborn than acquired. Without any touch of genius,—which could not arise from a temperament so volatile, so self-centered, so full of gay levity, and so devoid of impersonal sympathies as was hers,—she yet had talents of the brightest and most facile kind.

Unconsciously to herself, and unknown to others, there was sufficient of the instinct of the bohemian in her to make her quick-sighted to the weak points of the order to which she now belonged, and to supply her with delicate barbed shafts of satire to aim at them. The influence that had been so long upon her childhood had not wholly lost its effect upon her womanhood. Though all her tastes and attachments were with the rank to which she had attained, there remained sufficient in her of the temper she had caught from her earliest teacher, to lead her into wayward rebellion against some of its codes and exactions. Something of the salt of the gay trenchant sarcasms she had been fed on in her early years remained upon her lips, and not seldom seasoned what they spoke.

The diversity, the contradiction, lent a special charm to her speech, whenever her hauteur and her coquetry were both in abeyance; as they both were with Estmere.

"What golden wit she possesses!" he thought: and he was ignorant that it was but the reflex of the wit that he had once encountered in a bohemian working among the vintagers of France.

Minds like Tricotrin's scatter their gold broadcast, careless who gleans it: minds like Viva's catch it up as it falls, and wear it gracefully, as a beautiful woman her diamonds, making more brilliant still what was brilliant already.

She was moreover of a temper like that of many who attain to an eminence not theirs from birth; she had only contempt for the class from which she had come, but she had none the less contempt for the class of which a victorious chance had made her one. And, although her mature reason rejected in ridicule the folly of her childish credulity, still something of the beliefs instilled into her in her infancy as to her fairy origin, lingered with her; and when she allowed herself to deal in a touch of Beaumarchais-like epigram on those who "had taken the trouble to be born," it was half with the latent conviction that she had never been born of mortals at all!

She was at no time more seductive than in one of these moods of fantastic rebellion and satire; and her companion allowed himself to be beguiled. If in her absence, analyzing her words, he often wondered wherein the seduction of them had lain, none the less when he entered her presence would their charm become irresistible to him again.

As their converse at length ceased, he bade her seat herself where he pointed, to note the effect of light on the heads of a Liberi opposite.

She obeyed; and as her eyes went to the Liberi they rested also on the picture hanging next it,—the portrait of the boy with the dead water-fowl. She saw that they were now on the same spot where once the old custodian of the galleries had told her the story of that painting.

"You regretted him so much in your childhood—did you not?" she said softly, forgetful for the moment that she ought not, in wisdom, to show any prior knowledge of these galleries; and that the narrative was one never heard in the world of her own present station.

Estmere started.

"Regretted whom?" he asked.

She colored with annoyance at her own unconsidered impulse and unthinking folly, but it was now too late to recede.

"Your young brother—that boy there with the water-bird in his hand," she made answer. "I heard his story once: long, very long, ago."

"His story! Who could tell it you?"

"An old servant of yours; when I was a mere child. But the tale and the portrait impressed themselves on me; as such things will upon children's malleable minds."

"I never knew that your presence ever before now honored Villiers!"

"Oh—it was but for a few hours. I was brought to see the château: you must have been absent, of course. I was quite a child; but that picture's story stamped itself on my memory."

"I wonder you heard it. I had hoped my servants had known my wishes too well for them to have gossiped of my family histories."

"It was an old white-haired man who narrated it. I dare say because I pressed eager unscrupulous questions upon him—it is so long since then; I have forgotten."

"I can divine whom you mean. He is dead. Blame is useless."

"Yet you are angered?"

"Well—it is always cause for annoyance to find that those who held a trust could not keep it; and I am, perhaps, inclined to be as severe on those who speak blabbing words as on those who speak false ones."

The color left her cheek a little where she leaned it on her hand, as she sat in the Louis Quinze chair that he had wheeled for her use.

"But the history is a noble one for any to tell or to hear!" she said at length.

"It is so indeed; of a most noble madness. But can you not well conceive that the pain of having inherited my lands and title at the cost of my brother's death—a death self-sought—has never wholly passed away from me, has never wholly ceased to taint them with a certain sense of wrong and usurpation?"

"Yes. I can comprehend that."

Her eyes answered him better than her words; he had the power which only one other possessed, of awakening thoughtfulness, emotion, and sympathy, in this careless and vivacious nature.

"And there was yet more than this," pursued Estmere, the ice of reserve unbroken for so many years melting at her touch. "There was the sense of my father's brutal injustice, his inordinate favoritism to myself, his most culpable cruelty to his first wife, and to her son, all of which drove the boy to his abandonment of his just heritage. It was a great crime—a crime that in my sight still stains my race. If the boy had given any ground for the hate borne to him, it might have been more pardonable; but he gave none. He was of exceeding comeliness and grace, as you see there; full of high courage, of high genius, of high promise; such an heir as the proudest and most fastidious might have regarded with pride and pleasure. He was almost perpetually neglected; when remembered, remembered only to be taunted, goaded, driven wild with bitter ironies cast at his dead mother. I was many years younger than he; but I can still recall the scenes that I witnessed in infancy, and the terror I felt at seeing my father's fury fall on the head of my beloved companion; for I loved him well indeed. To me he was always gentle, generous, most infinitely patient, as youths of his age are very rarely with children. My early life was literally made desolate by his loss—"

He paused, and shaded his eyes with his hand as he gazed at the portrait.

"I grieve that I awakened a memory so painful," she murmured. "Is it certain that he perished?"

"As certain as any death can be where the body cannot be found for burial. There was no doubt left, indeed. The words he murmured over my bed, and which I, half asleep, thought the words of a dream, proved what his intention had been. It would never be possible to recover anything from the ring of water around Beaumanoir. It has deep clefts and bottomless holes, and sweeps out away to the western seas. Moreover, an old woman-servant bore witness to having seen him by twilight plunge in; but she missed him from sight, and thought nothing of it, as he was accustomed to swim, and dive, and almost live in the waters, like any bittern or gull. Immediate search was made in every direction for him; inquiries were everywhere instituted; but it was considered as conclusively proved that he must have been drowned in the moat. A mausoleum, inscribed to that effect, was erected by my father. His remorse, though utterly unavailing, was sincere. Remembering what I do of Chanrellon's nature, I can well imagine how insult and false accusation hurled him headlong to that insane self-sacrifice."

"He was accused of taking jewels, was he not?"

"Yes! such a senseless, coarse, frantic suspicion!—as if a boy who came of our race, and of his mother's bold, sea-born, free people, could have turned thief!"

"Were the diamonds ever found?"

"Never. Their loss was heavy, for they had historical as well as an enormous pecuniary value."

"Did you ever suspect any one?"

He gave a quick, broken sigh.

"In later years I have thought that the criminal was most likely a Greek youth in the household; a penniless Athenian, pampered by my father's caprices; a scorpion who stung the hands that fed and befouled the hearth that warmed him! But I might be in error—it was but conjecture."

He spoke with effort. She was silent, knowing how deeply and in how cruel a wound this scorpion had thrust its sting.

"Your son bears that title of Chanrellon now?" she asked, seeking refuge in a commonplace.

"It is the second title of the house."

"Does he resemble your brother in the least? There is no portrait of him here?"

"None. There are some at Beaumanoir. He has a womanish beauty."

"I have heard that he is not all that you desire; is it true?"

"He is nothing that I desire! But—we live almost as strangers."

"That seems terrible?"

"It is terrible. It is terrible to me that his mother's son should bear my name."

His voice had passion and emotion in it; and his head was turned from her as he spoke. She was the only living creature to whom he had ever spoken of his dishonored wife. She—the woman whom he loved.

"And there ever lived one who could forsake *you!*" she thought, as for one moment she beheld all the secret torture which his pride and his dignity had so long kept veiled from the gaze of any human eyes. Ere she could answer him, others approached them from the western end of the gallery. He took his hand from the back of her chair and moved slightly away.

"I am not sure, madam, now, that I have placed you right for the St. Catherine," he said, with his habitual tone. "Liberi is a favorite with me; there is so exquisite a softness about his female heads."

They were no more alone that day, and he sought no other opportunity to be in solitude with her; but the words that had been uttered had formed a link between them. She felt nearer to him than she had ever done. She felt that he had said to her what he would have uttered to no other.

A few days later, a young man, in his favorite summer-villa, among the Austrian woods of a fashionable mountain-side resort, whither he had brought all the levities, the extravagances, the vices, and the *ennui* of his life, received a coarse, ill-spelt missive, of a few lines only. It looked the clumsy scrawl of a cowherd, or a charcoal-burner; yet he read it with an attention which he did not concede to many elegant, perfumed, neglected letters that came with it; for the writer had been a panderer to his worst sins; a she-wolf, who would bring him any lamb within her range; a brute, who served his crimes faithfully for sheer greed of gold; and she wrote in the patois of her province:

"MY LORD,—If you have not forgot that fair fool that escaped you here years ago,—that thing they called Viva,— come hither, and let me have speech with you. There is up at the house a grand aristocrat, who they say will wed with the Earl, your father; and if ever that bastard whom you fancied lived, she still lives of a surety in this duchess. She carries herself like an empress; and it seems a mad freak for me to be bold to write this of her; but I found her out by a look in the eyes, and I dare swear I am not mistaken.

"I am at my lord's service ever,
  "ANNETTE VEUILLOT.
"Writ at this dairy of Villiers, on the 10th day of June."

## CHAPTER XXVI.

THE afternoon sun was hot and cloudless over all the country by the Loire. The barges and the rafts dropped lazily down the stream, with loads of fruit, of vegetables, or of fresh-mown hay. The women were washing their linen in places where the rocky shore made a shallow creek, or the grass grew lush and long, sloping to the water's edge. The laborers were at work among the vines, whose blossoms were just set, and changing into grape-buds. The horses of the towing-boats plodded lazily on in the warmth, while the drowsy hum of insects filled the air.

There was nothing changed in the out-door life, since the time that a child of fifteen years had sat dreaming among the swallow-swarming ivy, and weaving fancies of an unknown world, while she watched the old boatman mend his striped tanned sail.

The boatman was dead, and the sail, by his will, had enwrapped him as his shroud, where he lay, under the orchids and the vervain that blossomed over his grave: but the song of the birds, and the laugh of the raftsmen, and the noise of the water-wheel, and the voices of the washing-women, bubbled on unaltered, through the length of the dreamy, sultry, fragrant, summer day.

Above one curve of the river, where the old dead boatman had used to sit and mend the rents of his sail in the shade, a thrush was singing its little heart out upon a plume of pear-tree blossom. The house-door stood wide open, with the sun streaming in over the bare, clean, wooden floor. A cluster of pigeons was balanced on the edge of a brown earthen dish, eating its grain undisturbed. A great knot of white lilies, and moss roses, thrust in a broad pan of water, filled the house with perfume; all was still, and bright, and warm, and full of peace: and above in a little chamber an old woman was dying, the death that to age is release.

She had been born here, in these vine countries, when the tocsin was the only chime that the church-bell rang, and when the waters of the Loire were choked with the corpses they floated to the sea. She had lived here through childhood, and girlhood, and womanhood; working hardly, in field and vineyard, through the changes of the season; bronzed in the torrid noons, and bitten with the winter blasts; bearing burdens with the patience of the mule, and brightening beneath the slightest touch of mirth, like crocuses beneath the first spring sun. She had been wedded here, and here borne her three sons; and here been widowed, and of her sons bereaved; and here beheld her eldest-born's sole child die, in a weakly infancy, of the hard food that alone stood betwixt her and her starvation.

And here, also, the long, heroic, patient, unrewarded life was ended: a mystery of pain, and conflict, and courage, and endless labor, and ceaseless effort, all passed away in silence, and unrecognized of men.

She lay dying in the little darkened chamber, while the bird sang among the fruit-trees.

Each morning, in the luscious summer-time, she had made her slow way out into the porch, and sitting there had gazed with dim eyes out into the sunshine, with the expectant look of one who waits and watches ever on her face. Each day in the still cool spring-time, when the pink buds of the chestnuts were thrusting through the bark, and the violets made purple every waste space of ground, she had sat by her open casement, looking up the reach of the river, with the unrest of a baffled hope told in the nervous movement of her withered hands. Each night, when night fell at length, she had suffered herself to be led away, looking with a piteous appeal in the face of her handmaiden, as she muttered, "To-morrow!" And the little girl, ill knowing what she meant, but desiring to give comfort, had always smiled, and murmured back, "To-morrow! oh yes—to-morrow."

But the morrow had never come; and the few river-people and vine-laborers who alone knew her had said among themselves that it could never come:—would Paris give back its prey?

Grand'mère sought the sight of one whom Paris had devoured; what avail was that?

The little silvery cadence of the bell that rang before the coming of the host had sounded over the threshold, and across the breadth of the stream, until the bargemen and the rowers on the river heard the faint musical herald of a passing soul, and crossed themselves, and murmured an Ave in the hushed hot day.

The golden rod had touched with its anointed oil the breast, and brow, and feet, of the old dying woman. The blessed bread and wine had been placed to the withered lips which the religion that they symbolized had never fed during the famished hours of many bitter winters. The priest had gone once more across the threshold, with the silver bell shedding its soft cadence over the river and the vine-fields.

The ebbing and exhausted life was left in solitude once more, with no other watcher than the little peasant maiden, weeping sorely because she had no answer with which to respond to the one prayer, sounding ceaselessly upon the silence:

"Will she not come?—before I die?"

With blind wide-open eyes, that had a mute and terrible appeal within them, grand'mère, seeing no more the light through the open lattice, hearing no more the song of the thrush in the pear-blossom, but with one memory only living, still muttered this ever and ever where she lay:

"Will she not come?—before I die?"

For, through the paralysis of death, the longing of the heart still lived.

Through all the length of the years she had been patient, with the infinite hopeless patience of old age, that sinks ever deeper and deeper into the frozen desolation of its winter, and for which no spring can ever dawn, to change and beam on the eternal cold.

But now,—dying,—the long silent, uncomplaining agony broke out in one great desire, that was all the wandering senses knew: lying there, blind and confused, and stricken motionless, and chilled with the bitter frost of death, she yet retained memory for this.

Would her eyes never behold, nor her ears hear, the only life that she loved?—would she die thus, as she had been left to live, alone?

## CHAPTER XXVII.

AT the Château of Villiers, among the summer luxuriance of blossom, the snow-white statues glistened; on the rapid waters, gayly-painted boats floated under vine-hung branches; down the terraces music and laughter sounded; in the orange-aisles and the rose-gardens men and women passed their idle hours in gayety and indolence, and airy languid loves that beguiled the fancy and never roused the passions.

Among them Viva sat, playing listlessly with a gorgeous Indian bird, and casting careless words among her court, to be treasured as though they were pearls of precious wisdom.

A great fountain sent up its column of radiance near her; a mass of dates and palms screened her from the sun; the half-score of lovers round her heard her, when she chose to speak, with the charmed deference which, often denied to the sayings of sages, is ever awarded to the fair follies of a beautiful woman.

She was supreme—she was absolute sovereign here; every rival paled before her; the envy of one sex and the passion of another gave her endless assurance of her supremacy. Life was perfect to her: pleasures, glories, vanities, luxuries, votaries, all were accumulated in her path; and the new spell of a love, which she had long only laughed at, was thrown around her at last, giving fresh allurement and fresh fascination to the exercise of that sorcery which otherwise had threatened soon to pall and to satiate out of its too great facility, its too easily-acquired dominion.

Life was perfect in her hands; a scepter that the "gay

liar youth" made her credit would never be broken, never cease to have power to summon all charms from all ends of the earth to her usage and service.

Pain—calamity—poverty—age; these existed, she knew, when she paused to think of them. But they were only words; words to her soundless and bodiless. With her they had naught else to do. Certain sums, set aside from her wealth, her stewards disposed of in charity; so much done for the sake of her conscience, all else was dismissed from her mind:—she laughed here in the midst of her roses.

Down the river, which beneath the slopes of Villiers flashed in its broad silver band, a little boat glided; with it there came the ringing of a gentle bell, and in the stern knelt a white-robed chorister, bearing a glittering star aloft.

It was the Host, being borne backward reverently to the distant township whence it came.

"How prettily the bell sounds!" she said, forgetful, or careless of the fact that the little procession must have traveled to, and from, some dying-bed.

The boat passed out of sight; the tinkle of the bell passed off the air; the laughter and the languid wit resumed their reign around her.

Awhile later, a sealed paper was brought to her; a faint flush of annoyance went over her face as she saw the superscription. Her host alone noted it, and wondered what the cause could be. In that dazzling, unworn life, secure upon the heights of riches and of rank, there could be no mystery, no canker!

Some time afterward, she took an opportunity to pass into the house unobserved. There she opened the letter. It said, briefly:

"Grand'mère will not live till evening; she must see you to die in peace. I wait for you at the old ferry."

As she read, all the ice of pride, and coldness, and egotism melted from her heart. She gave a piteous cry as though death struck herself. All base and selfish thought died out from her; she only remembered the old creature she had loved through the years of her childhood, and whom she had left to live to perish in solitude.

"Grand'mère!"—with the tender homely word there came, in a rush of countless memories, a thousand ties of infancy and girlhood—ties broken by her with the gay scorn of a liberated youth,—ties ruptured, but aching forever, in the solitary heart of a forsaken age.

In that moment a tumult of remorse awoke in her; transient it might be, but violent in its truth and in its horror, with all the heat and force of her native impulses. She forgot self, pride, the peril of exposure, the difficulty of compliance; she forgot all except the debt whose payment had so long been driven off and might now be offered but too late. She forgot her station, her dominion, her distance from the peasant who was dying yonder, her cold contempt for all creatures less fair and fortune-favored than herself. She only remembered the days, so long gone by, which the brown, withered, noble face of the old Loiraise had been the first on which her eyes unclosed at dawn, and the last that bent over her as she sank to sleep.

"Grand'mère!"—the time had been when lisping out the word she had clung round the neck of the only creature who had ever filled to her in any sense a mother's place, and had loved her with all a child's careless, capricious, fond, unthinking love.

The place was three leagues off; the old ferry, long unused, was one; the way was long, the sun was burning; she dared not order horse, or carriage, or attendant, lest it should be learned whither and with whom she went. Trusting to chance for the avoidance of all notice, and acting only on the spur of inconsidered impulse, she threw a long cloak over her dress, concealed her face in a thick veil, and assured herself that none of her tire-women were in sight. Then she passed swiftly down an outer staircase which led from one of her balconies into an unfrequented portion of the grounds, and went on through the sunlit park in all the tremulous haste of one whom remorse drives and fear of detection wings.

Once, all the haughty blood in her flamed in hot revolt at this secrecy, which seemed so kin to shame. Once she was tempted to turn back and order out an equipage, and let all the world know where she went. Her errand was a righteous one; why hide it as a shame?

But the nobler impulse was beaten back by the dread lest any of her world should know that story of her past. She felt that she would rather die a thousand deaths than that those who held her now in such high honor should ever learn that she had once been found under those river-woods—a nameless foundling child.

The summons had fallen like a thunderbolt upon her, smiting her conscience from its sleep. But though she obeyed it, through all that still survived in her of the purer faiths of her earlier days, she still recoiled with loathing from the mere thought that those who knew her as she was should ever dream that she was not of their order,—should ever dream the time had been when she had owed bread to a bohemian's alms. Rather than that the truth should ever dawn upon the world where now she reigned, she took the stain of secrecy upon her, and fled on through the sunny glades, not as one who went to do a deed of mercy, but as a criminal who dreaded lest the passing of her footsteps should be tracked and followed.

Once she thought of Estmere; the soilless greatness, the integral truthfulness, of his life seemed for the moment to rebuke this falseness of base pride that screened a just act like a treacherous crime. But, with that thought, rose also the memory of his absolute and unbending pride, the pride of an Order, the pride of the Roman Optimate; and this sufficed to drive back once more the wavering impulse in her.

The large startled eyes of the grazing deer seemed to her like the eyes of the world fastened on her; the sight of a distant charcoal-burner passing down a far-off avenue made her dread recognition and pursuit. But the tract of the park through which she passed was wild and unfrequented; and the way through the vineyards and woods to the river, the instinct of early impressions made plain to her.

The winding paths down the terraced slopes, the scarce-seen roadway through vine-fields that seemed endless, the old broken hut, brown and roofless, and climbed all over with green flowering weeds, that marked the spot where a ferry, long shifted higher up the waters, once had stood,—all these things, utterly forgotten for many years, became familiar to her with that pang of remembrance, vivid almost to horror, with which the haunts of childhood startle the mind from which they have faded until they are revisited.

Against the ruined boat-house was a sailing-boat; in it a man stood erect with an oar in his hand thrust against the long grasses and reeds of the bank.

The landscape swam in mist before her sight; just thus had she seen him so many times in other years, when the hour of his coming was the golden hour in her summer, and she could have dreamt of no joy on earth or water so great as to sail with him down the long, calm, luminous reach of the river.

How near, and yet how far, that time looked to her! It seemed to kill in her all her own identity.

Which was in truth she?—that Loirais child who had basked in the sunlight, bathing her laughing face and her bright tresses in the stream; or the proud, courted, unrivaled woman, received in all the palaces of Europe?

Seeing her, he sprang on shore, and threw a rough plank betwixt the bank and boat, and held his hands out to her to aid her.

"You are come; that is well," he said, gravely, with no token of surprise, with the air of one whose command, being given, was of necessity obeyed. She, even in that moment, noticed it; and dreamily wondered whence this man, who was in social status but a wanderer, a vagabond, had gained that calm and kingly authority to which even she unresistingly succumbed.

She sank down at the bottom of the boat, worn out with the heat, the haste, the toil in the sultry day to which she was so little used.

"I am in time?" she asked him breathlessly. He spread a loose sail on a spar so that it sheltered her wholly from the sun, and from the sight of any passing on the shore or in river craft.

"I cannot tell," he answered her gently; "I trust so."

She said nothing. The old influence that he had used to possess stole over her again; she felt heart-sick, ashamed, covered with remorse. She, with all her territory, her treasures, her influence, felt humiliated and stricken with contrition in the presence of the man to whom she owed a debt that she had never paid, and that she never could pay.

He was silent also, setting the little sail to catch the faint flutter of the soft south wind, and steering down the golden gleaming brilliance of the river, running with the tide. The shore glided slowly past them; the brown sail caught colors of glory from the sun; the sweet odors of new-cut hay filled the air from grass-laden barges; the women, sitting in the rock-hewn grape-hung cabins of the banks, looked up as they drifted by, and laughed, and called across the great breadth of the stream, "Ah-ha, is it thee, Tricotrin?"

But he for once never answered where he sat at the helm. He sailed his race with death, and with every beat of the tide there went a beat of a human heart that would soon be still forever.

And thus she went back to the home of the swallows.

## CHAPTER XXVIII.

EVER and anon the old, dark, eager, noble face was lifted from its pillow, and the withered lips murmured three words:

"Is she come?"

For Tricotrin had bent over her bed, and had murmured, "I go to seek her, she is near;" and grand'mère had believed and been comforted, for she knew that no lie passed his lips. And she was very still; and only the nervous working of the hard, brown, aged hand showed the longing of her soul.

Life was going out rapidly, as the flame sinks fast in a lamp whose oil is spent. The strong and vigorous frame, the keen and cheery will, had warded off death so long and bravely; and now they bent under, all suddenly, as those hardy trees will bend after a century of wind and storm,—bend but once, and only to break forever.

The red sun in the west was in its evening glory; and through the open lattice there were seen in the deep blue of the sky, the bough of a snow-blossomed pear-tree, the network of the ivy, and the bees humming among the jasmine flowers. From the distance there came faintly the musical cries of the boatmen down the river, the voices of the vine-tenders in the fields, the singing of a throstle on a wild grape-tendril.

Only, in the little darkened chamber the old peasant lay quite still,—listening, through all the sweet and busy sounds of summer, for a step that never came.

And little by little all those sounds grew fainter on her ear: the dullness of death was stealing over all her senses; and all she heard was the song of the thrush where the bird swayed on the vine, half in, half out, of the lattice.

But the lips moved still, though no voice came, with the same words: "Is she come?" and when the lips no more could move, the dark and straining wistfulness of the eyes asked the question but more earnestly, more terribly, more ceaselessly.

The thrush sang on, and on, and on;—but to the prayer of the dying eyes no answer came.

The red sun sank into the purple mists of cloud; the song of the bird was ended; the voice of the watching girl murmured—"They will come too late!"

For, as the sun faded off from the vine in the lattice, and the singing of the bird grew silent, grand'mère raised herself with her arms outstretched, and the strength of her youth returned in the hour of dissolution.

"They never come back!" she cried. "They never come back!—nor will she! One dead in Africa,—and one crushed beneath the stone,—and one shot on the barricade. The three went forth together; but not one returned. We breed them, we nurse them, we foster them;—and the world slays them body and soul, and eats the limbs that lay in our bosoms, and burns up the souls that we knew so pure. And she went where they went:—she is dead like them."

Her head fell back; her mouth was grey and parched, her eyes had no longer sight; a shiver ran through the hardy frame that winter storms and summer droughts had bruised and scorched so long; and passionless and immeasurable grief came on the brown, weary, age-worn face.

"All dead!" she murmured in the stillness of the chamber, where the song of the bird had ceased, and the darkness of night had come.

Then through her lips the last breath quivered in a deep-drawn sigh, and the brave, patient, unrewarded life passed out forever.

A moment later, swift uneven steps sprang up the narrow stairway, and into the gloom of the little room came the glory of a woman's loveliness.

"Grand'mère! grand'mère!" she cried, as she threw herself on her knees against the couch.

The cry, for which the dying senses had been so long strained in yearning and vain desire, fell unheard on the ear which could no more be vexed with the toiling sounds of the travailing world. Calm, responseless, unutterably sad, the dead face looked upward in mute reproach.

The prayer of nine long years was answered at the last, ——and the answer came too late.

"Grand'mère! grand'mère!" she cried. "I am come! I am here! Oh, look at me once!—only once!"

But the eyes had no light, the lips had no reply. What avail was remorse?—its anguish could not reach the soul that had passed away from all earthly pain and from all mortal love.

She came too late.

## CHAPTER XXIX.

"AH! How I loathe myself!"

She spoke in agony, with the tears falling fast from her eyes, and her heart aching in vain self-reproach, where she stood in the quaint, dark kitchen-chamber that she had known so well of old. All her warmer, richer, sweeter, holier nature had awakened, and quivered under the branding iron of remorse. She looked to herself so base, so cruel, so worthless of every thought of tenderness that had been given her by the dead.

The unuttered rebuke of that colorless face, so livid, so old, so still with its own sublime peace, had pierced through all the vanities and pride and egotism of her life down to the heart of her youth, which still beat there beneath them.

Every trifle in the little room around her, every homely and familiar cottage thing of use, came back on her memory with a pang.

The place was so utterly unchanged: the burnished coppers, the clean brass utensils, the strings of drying herbs and melons, the black pot simmering over the wood embers on the hearth, the white cat sleeping in the window, the oil-lamp burning on the low oak settle, all the common things of daily life that she had known so well, were all there unaltered since the days when in her infancy her feet had danced upon the wooden chairs in glee because the hot milk foamed ready for her morning pottage.

Not one of them was changed; but she!——she burst into passionate tears as she thought of the little, gay, nameless child that once had lived and laughed amid these lonely things, and of the face, now set in death, whose brown worn features had softened to such tender grace in the light of the summer morning and at the mirth of the infant's play.

Countless memories thronged on her;—of childish pains and angers, of feverish hours of illness, of petulant outbursts of willful wrath, of April storms of passing griefs over a dead bird or a stray kitten, and, through all these, of the patient, gentle, cheerful endurance of a love that never complained and never wearied. For such a debt what payment had been great enough!—and all that she had given had been silence, neglect, oblivion,—the triple coin wherewith Love oftenest is paid.

He let her passion spend itself silently.

It was a caustic that might, perchance, burn out the cankers of the world within her soul. With her he had no bond in that instant. All his sympathy, all his pity, all his reverence, were with that aged, lonely, dauntless life that had been left to ebb out in solitude; the life lived only to see all that it cherished perish.

The first words he spoke were brief, as he raised the drooping wick of the lamp.

"Madam—it were best you went homeward. Your host and your Order must not know that you weep for a peasant!"

"Ah, hush! I merit the lash of your sarcasm and of your scorn, God knows, yet—spare me them now. I cannot bear them!"

He placed the lamp back on its settle.

"I but remind you,—would you have it known that you are here?"

She started with a throb of terror.

"No—no! Surely there may be means,—but,—I have thought of myself, alone, so long, so selfishly, so remorselessly. I can only think of *her* now! I have been so cruel, so heartless. If I could only have heard her speak to me, and only have begged once for her forgiveness!"

He smiled, very wearily, and made no answer. He knew that to himself she repeated, and would continue to repeat, the ingratitude and the neglect that, given to the dead, now caused such futile and vehement remorse. But of this his own lips never reminded her.

He stood silent, with the dusky lamplight behind him so that he could see her face, while his own was screened from her, watching her with a strange pain; wondering vaguely and incredulously if this exquisite and imperial woman, who moved slowly to and fro the narrow room, could be in truth but the developed life of the young child whose dancing naked feet had moved in such gay measure to the old peasant's crooning country-songs.

He had suffered much, and often, since the last day when she had passed out from under the low brown porch to go to the "great world" for which she pined; but he had never suffered as he did now, beholding her, for the first time, under that roof where her infancy had been sheltered by him.

Once she paused in her restless passage up and down the chamber, and turned her lustrous eyes full on him.

"Ah! Tell me the truth!—you think me base beyond redemption?"

"No," he answered her, where he stood in the deep shadow. "I think you—very human."

"To be human, then, is to be lower than the dogs that love what feeds them?"

"Perhaps! The dogs will love the hands that beat them. There is none of that love among such fair things as you."

Her head sank, with the hot blood burning in her face.

"Why did you not keep me here?" she said, with impetuous emotion. "Why did you not tell me what I should become? I should have been poor, nameless, unknown; but —I should have been innocent at least, I should have done the duty that I owed, I should have helped her in her age, and soothed her in her death-agonies!"

A breath that was almost a sob caught the words as she spoke them: she little heeded the blow which each dealt to the heart of their hearer.

The answer which sprang, hot, eloquent, upbraiding, bitter and tender at once to his lips, he restrained; he answered her briefly, gently,—

"I did not keep you against your will, because,—you would *not* have remained innocent, you would have refused to accept duty, you would have broken into perilous revolt, in such a life as the life you alone could have led here. The greatness you have gained would not now have sown evil in your nature, had none of the seeds of evil been latent there; such evil is sinless to the world's creed, in a patrician woman; it would have been evil accursed, and shameful, and wretched, in a woman nameless, and penniless, and motherless, and consumed with the corrosion of discontent. I knew you better than you knew yourself. If the Duchess de Lirà be heartless, merciless, conscienceless, what would the actress, the adventuress, have been? Once I bade you repay me what you deemed you owed, by keeping ever in you the higher things of your love, and truth, and courage. I was unwise enough to dream that my one desire would be obeyed, against all the commands of your passions, your prides, and your vanities. Once also you prayed that death might come to you if ever you forgot me: the grass would have grown through many seasons above your grave if that prayer had been granted!"

A cry of intolerable suffering broke from her.

"Say all you will!" she cried. "Your hardest words cannot scourge me so sharply as my own conscience does. I have forgotten!—more brutally, more shamelessly than the very cattle ever forget a master that has fed and tended them. And, yet, I have remembered too,—remembered more than you can ever dream. At times my thoughts of you have been an agony. At times my childhood has come back to me with such reproach that I could have found strength to kill myself. At times—in all the intoxication of the world—the sound of your voice has seemed to steal on my ear, the gaze of your eyes has seemed to haunt me as I went, till I longed for the peace of your presence with a lost child's longing for its home! This is the truth; though how shall you believe me in witness of all the false shame, the mad vanity, the infamous ingratitude of my life? You say that I should have been far worse than I am, had I remained with you; can anything be worse than such selfishness and such oblivion as mine? Besides,—you are so great, so true, of a simplicity so noble, of a justice so divine, your influence would have been too strong on me for me to have sunk to evil: you could have made of me what you would, had I but stayed by you!"

And in the remorse of the hour it did indeed seem thus to her; and in that hour she beheld, as by a vision, all that her life would have been, if never fevered by thirst for gold and rank, if never touched by the fast-lengthening shadows of falsehood, if never drawn into that furnace of ambition where all impulses and instincts are fused into one passion; if lived in peace and in contentment, purified, and strengthened, and raised high by the loftiness of truth and of self-sacrifice, beneath his love and law.

In that one hour she saw that she had forsaken the gold for the dross, the rock for the reeds, the greater for the lesser, as men do oftentimes, and women yet more surely in their headlong and blind choice.

He heard; and a great shudder shook him.

He had condemned himself to endless and unrequited martyrdom, that she might pass to the fate she desired, and never have aught wherewith to reproach him; and even out of this she wove a lash that scourged him with deeper stripes than any he had borne!

"Wait, wait! or you will kill me!" he cried. "'Stayed by me!' Oh, God! if you had done so! But your heart was disloyal, and lost to me; could I hold captive your body? You see now a worth you have missed, in that life that you would have led by my side; but then,—who could make you believe? And you forget—you forget—a creature of your sex and your loveliness could not have abode with me without a chain that you would not have taken, unless gold had gilded the fetters: you must have been my mistress, or my wife!"

She started violently; and the blood crimsoned all her face; she had spoken in the impulse of the old love and reverence she had yielded him in her girlhood; she had never dreamed of any other life with him than that of the bygone familiar communion which they had known in this lowly place when she had been a child, and he had been all the world to her.

In this hour her pride had been dead, her rank forgotten, her self-love abhorred; in this hour conscience, and memory, and the veneration she had borne him, had alone reigned with her.

Now, his indulgence of that moment's hot and unchecked utterance, recalled to her the many times that she had wept in his arms, clung to his embrace, been kissed by his lips, in that long-perished time; in this moment it seemed to her that the tie between them was nearer, stronger, more indissoluble, than the ties betwixt father and daughter, wife and husband, master and slave!

Even while these memories burned her with an abhorred sense of debt and shame, the height and depth, the might and beauty, of this life-long love that she had flung away, smote her with its greatness and its divinity as it had never done in earlier years, never done through all the self-absorption of her life. It appalled, it amazed, it affrighted her:—such a debt as this could never be paid; and, while it remained unpaid, how could any woman owing it be free!

He, divining all her thoughts, with that knowledge of her mutable nature which he had so long possessed, hastened to cover from her sight that passion which for one instant had been near its betrayal to her. She was his debtor; naught could cancel such a debt; therefore he forced himself to calmness, and hastened to repair what might have seemed a claim laid through that debt.

"You are of the world; you know its tenets now," he said, tranquilly. "You know, therefore, how idle it is to dream you could have remained with me without reproach. Unless, indeed, your whole life had been mine. But—you remember?—I asked you once if my love would suffice to you; and your answer was, that you craved greatness also. I had not greatness; how could I content you?"

"Yes! When I answered you I was vain, and worthless, and full of avarice, as I am now!"

The words were muttered low in her throat; she moved with feverish unrest to and fro the little chamber; she wondered, with that curious dreamy wonder that comes on us when, having chosen one path, we marvel whither the other would have led, how it would have been with her if she had loved and followed this redeemer of her life. And her heart told her—knowing its own passions and its own weakness—that she, with her thirst for power, and her greed for homage, and her worship of eminence and of magnificence, would have only dwelt with him in the unceasing cruelty of discontent, or have left him, to deal him the fate of Bruno.

And she was very base in her own sight; for she knew likewise that, for this very cause, she had ever been utterly beneath this great life that she had elected to desert for things, compared with it, so mean, and vain, and worthless.

She paused once and looked at him, with all the old look of her childhood back in her uplifted eyes.

"Such men as you," she murmured, "need nobler things than women to love you and to value you! We are beneath you—we know nothing of greatness such as yours!"

He smiled: the smile of such infinite sadness.

"Rather you see it not, unless it wear the purple, and bear the orb, of visible power. But I, indeed claim none; have none; unless it may be such as may grow out of freedom."

"You have the highest—the best—the only greatness!"

And in that moment she saw this truth that she had so long neglected or derided; saw that the liberty, the self-mastery, the simplicity, the courage, and the supreme scorn for the insincerity, the artifice, and the bondage of the world, which were in this man's life, had a greatness that surpassed all other the earth held, though a greatness unrecognized and unrewarded of men.

He answered her nothing.

Though she spoke thus, saw thus, felt thus, he knew well that she would make again the choice she then had made, were the election again offered her:—that now, as then, could the choice be afresh set before her, would she forsake him, and go from him to the pomps of the world.

While she owned the greatness of the truths, the liberties, and the simplicities whereon his life was founded, she would yet shrink from holding out her hands to him in her palace as her friend, from bidding her compeers and her lovers behold all that she owed to him!—and there was unuttered scorn in him, as well as unutterable sadness, as he looked on her in silence.

"It grows late," he said briefly, at length. "I must remind you once more—do you desire your absence discovered?"

She started, and glanced at the clock; with whose hands her own childish ones had so often played in mischievous fancies to retard, or to advance, some dreaded hour of study or some desired moment of playtime.

"It is late indeed! I shall be missed:—he has theatrical pieces to-night on purpose for my pleasure; my absence must not be known. How quickly can I return?"

"In two hours; scarcely sooner. You will do best to lose no time."

"I must go *there*,—once more. Then I will come," she murmured. "Stay! tell me,—there is no fear that peasant child who is with her can suspect,—can recognize me,—can speak to others?"

"No fear. That girl is from Lorraine—a grand-niece of grand'mère. She never heard of you, and she will now return east to her own people, deeming you some great princess who came out of charity to see an old peasant who once nursed you."

She shuddered a little as she heard.

"But—but, I cannot bear to think that this place may pass to strangers—that all these things of hers may be scattered,—that the animals, and the fowls, and the swallows may be ill treated or killed. Can you not purchase it for me without my name appearing, and place some one in it who will be good to all the creatures?"

She stroked the cat as she spoke; it seemed a link betwixt her and the dead.

"The place—such as it is—is mine," he made answer. "You need have no fear; care shall be had of it."

He did not remind her that to rent it, and fill it with its cottage things, and keep it for her with some sort of picturesque grace about it, he had sacrificed much, toiled hardly oftentimes, its slight costs heavily taxing his own means.

She felt what he had not uttered, and moved in silence from the chamber.

More than an hour had passed ere she returned from her last look upon the face that had been first among her earliest memories; her eyelids were swollen, and her lips white, as she came to him.

"I am ready," was all she said.

They did not speak as they left the cottage, and went down through the scarlet beans and the wild-growing gourds to the landing-place in the garden, and drifted away in the boat down the river.

Her eyes watched, as long as they could follow it, the little light burning in the chamber of the dead.

The proudest and most ambitious dreams with which she had last left that innocent home among the swallows had attained their fruition:—but remorse and repentance were with her.

No words passed between them as the boat slowly labored against the stream.

When they reached the place of the ferry, he aided her in silence to land.

"I will follow you," he said simply, "near enough to be at hand if you need me."

"That is how you have ever followed my life!"

"Well! the time may yet come when I may be wanted, wild as the thought seems of such an omnipotent life as yours. Pass onward—unless you would have your host disquieted by your absence."

"Would he care if I were dead in that river!"

The murmur was bitter and doubting. It betrayed the one victory on which she alone was uncertain, the one desire that alone was ungranted to her, the one doubt of her own power that alone had ever humiliated her.

He gave a short, sharp sigh. It had told him all.

"You still desire his love!"—the words were almost savage in their vehemence.

She was silent. She could have bitten her tongue through, that ever it should have betrayed her thus.

He let her pass on; and she went swiftly, with passionate movement, through the darkness of the forest-lands.

When the lights which illumined the terraces glistened in view, he gained her side with a few rapid steps.

"You are in safety; yonder is your entrance. The heart of your childhood has awakened in you to-night; keep it waking, or its next sleep will be death. And—if, in your cruel caprices, you set your soul on the man who lives yonder,—remember that a lie is accurst in his sight, and that he has once suffered betrayal. I forbid you to play with his peace, or to trifle with his honor."

"*You* forbid me!"—even in that moment, as she faced him in the moonlight, the chief emotion in her was her arrogant pride, that defied all dictation and authority.

"Yes—I."

His eyes met hers with a look in them that compelled and awed her, as a master's look his dog—a look which made her subject to him.

Without another word he turned away. She went onward, confused, breathless, vaguely afraid, filled with tumultuous emotions.

The lesser terror of her own discovery died away in her. It was eclipsed by a greater—the terror lest that vast granite mass of reckless and merciless ingratitude that she had piled higher and higher with every year of her life, till it had shut out the holy light of heaven, should one day fall and crush her.

She gained the terrace with swift trembling steps, passed through the entrance-door unobserved, and glided up the staircase leading to her apartments, without detection. This portion of the building was forsaken; but through its casements on the farther side, which looked out away to the great south court adjoining the stables she saw the forms of men and horses moving to and fro by torchlight. She divined the truth, that they had missed and were about to search for her.

There were none of her own attendants in her chambers; she was thankful for an absence that best befriended her. She went first to her mirrors to see how her face betrayed her; all her color was gone, and her eyelids were swollen with tears; but she was one of the few women in whom emotion increases, because it chastens and softens, beauty. She bathed her face in water; coiled up her hair which had fallen; dropped down on to a couch in all her accustomed grace and indolence of repose, and rang for her women, who entering hurriedly, could ill conceal their amaze at sight of her, and recounted breathlessly that her host, on missing her from the drawing-rooms, had found that no one had seen her for several hours, had then become alarmed as night had fallen, and was at that moment about to start in quest of her with his horsemen.

She sent him a message of graceful thanks; adding that she had wandered somewhat too far in the forest, and been belated. That was all.

Then, with haste yet especial care, she arrayed herself in her uttermost brilliancy,—in a misty cloud of black and silver, with sapphires gleaming here and there, and a knot of passion-flowers in her bosom. The slight exhaustion and loss of bloom from her loveliness only added to its charm; she looked, and was reassured that none could trace any touch of sorrow or of apprehension on her.

"He feared once that I should be an actress like the woman Coriolis. Ah, heaven! what else am I now?" she thought, as she turned from the mirrors.

When she entered the drawing-rooms, none of the many personages then gathered at Villiers looked deeper than the surface of her words, or supposed that there had been any other cause for her absence than this which she alleged—that she had strolled far in the forest, and been benighted. None —save her host, who, as he welcomed her safety, and apologized for his own needless anxieties, regarded her with a look she could ill meet, and recalled that letter which had come to her in the rose-gardens.

Yet the terror of that past hour, when he had been haunted by the thoughts of countless accidents that might have chanced to her, had told him, in the sharp eloquence of anguish, that his life were valueless without this woman.

Although he studied her keenly, he could see no trace of emotion, no sign of abstraction in her through the hours at the dinner-table, and in the bijou theater, to which, to do her pleasure, he had summoned a choice stage-troop of Paris,

She was slightly more languid, and had little of her accustomed wit—that was all.

He could not tell that all she saw, throughout that evening, was a little low bed, in a small dark chamber; and an old, storm-beaten, patient, heroic face, with the stillness and the grandeur of death set on it.

He longed to question her, but the delicacy of his high breeding, and his courtesy as a host, both sealed his lips.

"I grow a madman," he told himself. "Mystery! what mystery could there be in the life of a woman young, proud, eminent as she is? I dream; and because the strongest love of my youth betrayed me, my dreams are only suspicions!"

And suspicion was a foul and a craven thing in his sight—a spy that could have no lodgment in the frank, just, high thoughts of a gentleman.

As he mused thus, he was standing, after the dramatic representations, alone in the embrasure of a picture cabinet, that led out on to the head of the grand staircase. He had drawn the curtain back, and was gazing on to the moonlit terrace and the oak forests below, without thinking of what he beheld. He started as he heard the sweep of a woman's robes near him, and saw the object of his thoughts crossing the little chamber. She paused, with a certain hesitation. She had been ignorant of his presence there; she was leaving the reception-rooms to seek her own apartments. She was worn out with the self-command she had attained, and both fatigue and sadness were visible on her face as she passed through, deeming herself in solitude.

On a sudden impulse, she approached him.

"I have not thanked you, I fear, for your concern for my safety to-night," she said, hurriedly. "I must tell you that the reasons I gave for my absence were only partially true. The fall of evening overtook me, indeed, in your forests, but it was no accident by which I was delayed."

His eyes lightened with surprised pleasure:

"Any confidence you may place in me will be cherished and sacred, you are sure. But,—do not deem yourself called on to give it simply because I enjoy the privilege of being your host."

For the moment, a desire came over her to tell him the whole unwarped and unvarnished truth. But the desire was not strong enough to conquer the false pride within her, and the terror she felt of being lowered and humiliated in his sight.

She hastened with all her most graceful arts of speech to thank him, to assure him that this was but a slight matter: —she did not wish it spoken of, lest she should be wearied with inquiries. She had heard in the latter half of the day that a noble old woman—a peasant who had nursed her in her infancy—was lying in the extremities of death in a cottage by the river-side, and was praying earnestly and piteously to see her once again. She could not refuse such a request; she had gone thither by herself, preferring not to make her errand known. She had been unaware that her absence would be of such duration.

So the delicate polished semi-falsehoods ran, with soft successful fluency. But while she uttered them, she was degraded in her own eyes. She told him no lie, indeed: yet none the less did she deceive him.

Keen of vision though he was, and difficult to content in aught that savored of evasion, or challenged the acuteness of his judgment, he was thrown off his guard by the joy he felt at finding so much pity in the woman whom he had dreaded as an unscrupulous, heartless, and self-absorbed coquette. It seemed nothing strange to him that so sudden memory and compassion had moved her, and sent her forth on an unweighed impulse; for he had seen the sympathy and the agitation with which she had watched the perils of human life in the stone-yard. And he accepted, unanalyzed and unquestioned, a narrative which at another hour, and from other lips, he would have deemed strange, involved, and insufficient.

"I honor you for your noble charity and for your gentleness of heart," he murmured. "If you have that divine pity in you, why will you stifle it so often, and——."

"Hush, hush!" she interrupted him, passionately. "Do not *you* praise me! 'Noble charity'—mine! If you only knew the selfishness, the cruelty, the baseness of my life! When I have a touch of holier feeling, of higher thought in me, it comes too late, as it came too late to-night!"

"Too late?"

"Yes, she was dead. My words fell on ears forever deaf to the voices of earth. I reproach myself more than I could ever tell you!"

"How was it fault of yours? You knew that this old creature lived on this country side?"

"Yes, I knew; and I had promised so often—through so many years—to go and let her look upon my face once more, and yet I never went. I let summer and winter glide away again, and again, and again; and I never remembered that time brings death to the old. I had leisure for all the pomps, and the pleasures, and the frivolities, and the caprices of my life; but I never had leisure for this one simple duty. And when I reached her side, she was dead!"

The tears gushed into her eyes afresh; her lips quivered. This was real, and sincere, and unstudied. On this she could utter the truth to him.

His thoughts were not with the obscure lost life of which she spoke, but with this exquisite, wayward, changeful, imperious, incomprehensible woman, whose moods varied like the sun and shade of a spring day, and whose tenderness and remorse were as passionate as her vanity and her egotism were cold. Fear and doubt, suspicion and wisdom, all faded away in him as though they had never been; he only remembered that she beguiled him as no temptress had done since the days of his youth.

"If you have so much pity for the dead, who cherished you in your infancy, have you no pity for the living, who worship you in your womanhood?" he said, suddenly; with a sound in his voice that she had never heard, a look on his face that she had never seen, as the white moonlight fell about them where they stood by the opened casement.

"It is the common reproach against me that I have had too little," she murmured, in answer.

"A reproach you deserve only too well! But—but—will you find mercy at last? Passion has no place on my lips. It betrayed me in my youth; it has no fitness in my present years. And yet, you have won my secret from me to-night; you must hear what I thought never to tell; you must know —that I am mad enough to love you!"

He spoke, almost without hope. He spoke to a coquette who had never spared, to a sovereign who had never stooped, to a woman who had never pitied. Yet, as she listened, her face changed with a marvelous light, and flush, and tenderness that no eyes had ever beheld on it. She was silent, but she raised her head, and turned, and looked at him:—one look only, still, by it he was answered.

And as her proud head dropped down upon his breast, and his lips sought hers to find there all the lost joys of his dead youth, he felt her whole frame thrill in his embrace, and heard her broken words:

"I am not worthy of you! I am not worthy!"

## CHAPTER XXX.

"IMPERIL his peace—trifle with his honor. Ah, heaven! There will be no need to forbid me that!" she thought, in the solitude of her chamber an hour later, while the touch of his first kisses seemed still to linger on her lips, and the fervor of passion seemed still to gaze on her from the eyes which she had thought would never soften in their regard.

A joy had come to her, beside which all the joys of her victorious years looked faint of hue and poor of treasure. From its long opium-sleep of deep-drugged vanity her soul had stirred at last; and the love which she had so long derided and disdained, had awakened in her for the one who alone, amid throngs of crowding flatterers, had neglected, condemned, and distrusted her.

She loved him—with a vivid force, a reverent humility, an impassioned tenderness, that a year earlier she would have mocked at as lowest weakness, wildest madness. She loved him—with a love that set its heel upon her pride, and bent her strength beneath it. She loved him—and this one missing jewel from her triple diadem of youth, and power, and loveliness, was found and added to her crown.

Love had had cruel usage at her hands. It had watched over her from the hour when her young eyes had opened at the music of the Straduarius, to gaze at the purple butterflies dancing in the sun; it had been lavish of every richest thing to her, and had waited upon her with a slave's submission; its chaplets were wound on her brows, its blossoms strewed her path, its wings had lifted her up to loftiest heights, and its smile had ever shed sunlight upon her. But she, in answer, had only cast to it some gay scorn, some light irony, some child's cruelty, some woman's contempt.

Yet even now it was not weary; it was not driven away; it brought to her the latest and the holiest of all its countless gifts, it nestled in her bosom like a dove that bears glad tidings, it changed even the pangs of remorse into the throbs of joy. Love had been forsaken by her in a thousand careless seasons, yet it remained with her, and was faithful ever.

Even from this death-hour, when the sin of her ingratitude had dealt its deadliest stroke, there had sprung, through Love, the fullest sweetness that her life had known: and a vague fear came on her of this giver so prodigal, of this slave so patient, of this friend so constant and unwearied.

"Oh God!" she murmured in her solitude. "I have been so base, so faithless, so guilty to all love. If his, the only love I treasure, should take its vengeance and forsake me!"

She had cast one great life away from her as idly as a

child casts balls of cowslips on the air, as selfishly as a falconer casts hawks down a south wind, as cruelly as a murderer casts dead limbs upon the sea: was it just that another should become hers also?

Was no retribution near? Its terror seemed to touch her, and daunt her strength, and wither her pride, and freeze her new-born joy with its breath of ice, where she stood in her loneliness, and gazed at that beauty of her face and form which had so late been to her all she heeded upon earth, yet which now would have grown worthless and without radiance in her sight, unless fair in his eyes, and given to his arms.

For the voice of conscience spoke in her, and questioned ceaselessly—

"Will you go to his heart with a shame concealed? Will you lift your lips for his kiss, with a lie hovering on them? Will you answer his faith with your falsehood?"

A day since, an hour since, she had said to herself that he should never know; that though she should heap lie on lie upon her head, the truth should be concealed from him and from the world. An hour ago her pride had been holier to her, her eminence dearer to her than any other thing.

But with the touch of his lips, with the possession of his love, all that was still noble in her nature had sprung to life once more. Now that she knew his peace, and honor, and future all were hers, she knew that she might with less baseness strike a knife into his heart than be his wife with one treachery between them.

She knew that to take his love, leaving him in blindness, was treacherous as any assassin's thrust. She knew that by reason of that very guilt which had deceived him in his youth, to deceive him afresh was the foulest cowardice that ever stained a woman's life. Better, she knew, be forever severed from him, than glide into his life through the channels of falsehood, than live in union with him with one act in her past untold, than sleep in his bosom with a single secret to haunt the hours of the night. Better to summon all the world about her, and fling her story to the winds, and stand before him, without pride, without power, without any single thing of greatness or of dignity or of possession left, but able to look into his eyes without one fear of what they should there read; able to say to him in honesty and strength—"there is no lie on the lips that you kiss: there is no secret in the life that you make one with your own."

Her heart and her conscience had been startled from their long sleep that night. She was awakened from the deep dreams of that supreme selfishness which had drugged her like an opiate; the courage, the truthfulness, the spirit of her childhood were once more roused.

"What is it I do!" she thought in horror. "Win love, and trust, and honor, on a lie!"

She knew that it was possible,—nay, likely,—that, knowing all, he would put her from his life forever. She knew the pride of birth that was in him; the patrician contempt that shone forth so often in his slightest words; the intense dread of any shadow of dishonor that the early infidelity of his wife had left perpetually on him. She knew that with all the passion he bore her, he loved his honor, and the dignity and purity of his name, far more. She knew that if she told him the bare bitter truth, it was well-nigh a surety that she would never look upon his face again. And this—not alone from the mere impulses of pride, but from the doubt in his soul which would say—"faithless in her childhood, and a falsehood to the world, what warrant have I that she will be truer and more loyal to me!"

And yet all that ever had been nobler in her was aroused and in tumult that night. The dead face of the woman whom she had deserted; the burning rebukes of the man she had abandoned, had withered up the vanities and arrogancies of her life; and beneath them the living heart beat still—beat faster and more loudly because it throbbed in pain.

She gazed at her own loveliness with the old rapt worship of it still in her regard.

"I shall give him all this!" she thought, while a hot flush stole over her face. "It is enough!"

But in her conscience she knew that this beauty would be the most cruel, the most fatal gift that ever woman's beauty was to man, unless with it she gave also—truth.

There stole on her the memory of a day,—long, very long, ago,—when one, against whom her past had been an endless sin, had murmured to her in the words of his farewell:—"Let my memory stand between thee and thy temptations, so shall I have no gift to give thee."

And she fell on her knees, and wept in an agony of grief, and prayed in passionate, inarticulate, wild prayer, "Oh, God, make me for one hour worthy of the mighty love that I forsook!"

When she arose, her face had a weary, hopeless, rigid look, as of one who has striven and conquered, indeed, but with such strife and such conquest as leave the victor broken, exhausted, well-nigh slain.

"He shall know all," she muttered through her colorless lips. She turned, and moved through the loneliness of her chambers, and passed out in the deserted corridor.

The great building was silent; she knew that he was alone in his library, since, when they had parted, he had spoken of letters of import that would occupy him until daybreak. She went to seek him that night, that hour, dreading her own weakness of shame and of self-pity, dreading lest her strength should fail, and this martyrdom pass from her.

The two white lines of marble stairs ran parallel with each other, severed by the vastness of the hall below. All the lights still burned and glittered on them. As she stood on the head of one, up the ascent of the other there came a swift, silent step, like the light tread of a greyhound.

She glanced across,—the stranger glanced at her. It was but one instant that their eyes met. He passed onward, with his eyelids lowered, and his swift step unchanged. She stood as though rooted to the ground, her whole frame shivering like that of an antelope which sees the panther afar off.

"Chanrellon! Are you coming?" cried a laughing voice from above.

"I am coming!" answered the stranger, as a young man answers a young comrade.

She turned and crept back into her chamber like a creature numb with cold, and cast herself across her couch, and lay there in a stupor.

What avail to take confidence to him now!

Truth now could look but Fear.

When her women, a while later, entered her apartments, they found her cold and stupefied, the passion-flowers crushed upon her hair, her bosom cut with the sapphires' sharp facets; and when consciousness revived in her under their terrified efforts, they heard her murmur—

"My sin has come home to me! It is just, it is just!"

## CHAPTER XXXI.

MIDWAY between the park and the dairies there was a cluster of acacias, now in blossom, and luxuriant as they only are south of the Loire. They parted two water-threaded meadows, and formed a thicket of foliage and blossom.

Under their boughs stood Annette Veuillot, with one hand on her hip, and the other balancing on her head the milk-pail that served to disguise her errand. Beside her stood the man whose feminine and languid grace had been so fair in her eyes, because of its utter unlikeness to her own coarse, robust, weather-beaten strength and ugliness. Her mouth laughed wide, her tawny skin was flushed with eagerness, her breast heaved against her leathern bodice.

"It was not madness in me, then!" she muttered exultantly. "Why were you so loth to believe?"

"I was not loth!" answered her companion, unable, through the bond between them, to resent her familiarity. "I was incredulous, indeed. The Duchess de Lira!—I have heard through so many seasons of her beauty, her fame, her extravagance. I could not credit that a creature so proud and powerful could be——"

"That bohemian's brat!" said the woman, with ferocious glee. "But she is, she is, I will wager; whatever millions of lies they may have told to screen her. You saw her well, my lord?"

"Twice. Once,—as long as I chose to look,—from the musicians' gallery, before any knew of my arrival; and again on the staircase. I do not think there is a doubt, though— Heaven!—who could have believed in such a change!"

"Fine feathers make fine birds! I knew her at a glance. Women never forget. Would you have known her, my lord, if I had not put this thing in your thoughts?"

"No; I doubt if I should. I should have been perplexed with some resemblance, but no more. The child was lovely, but the woman is magnificent as a goddess!"

There was a fervid longing in his tone that caught her ear, that told her with what quickness the died-out fancy for the child would revive in passion for the woman.

"Will she wed with your father?" she asked, savagely.

He broke a cluster of blossoms off the acacia with a gesture of impatience.

"He says so. I had speech with him late last night, concerning a question of some property, which he supposes is the object of my visit. I saw a change in him—there is a look in his eyes which is new there. I made allusion to his marriage as a rumor that I had heard. I asked if it were a true one. He answered, very briefly, that it was. No more words passed between us. I let him see that I was surprised and ill pleased, that was all; and to this he was indifferent. Now, you have no proof to give me that this persuasion of yours is a certainty?"

"None," she said, sullenly. "But if you are not answered, name old Virelois to her as I did; you will see then!"

"That is not what I mean. Myself, I have no doubt. But on anything less than some actual doubt, I cannot say to the Duchess de Lira, to the betrothed wife of Estmere, 'You are a foundling and a bastard; you are an imposture on the world you rule; you are the little fool that once took my jewels and toys, and was tempted, for my sake, to the house of Coriolis.' I cannot say this to her on mere conjecture, mere supposition?"

She understood, and stood thinking awhile; her strong teeth gnawing her nether lip. Then suddenly a dull, cruel gleam shot over her face.

"See here; there is one of her men who came down to Villiers with her, who has got into love with little Laure at my dairy. He is always there; after no good, but I let him come; I have heard a great deal of *her* so. And he told me one thing. There is a steward very bitter against her because she dismissed him, an old man who lives now with his son-in-law, Lobesq, the jeweler, in Paris. He might tell you somewhat? It is possible, my lord. I know Laure's lover said once that he believed the old man would hurt his mistress if he could, though he did not see what means he ever would be able to find."

He heard her thoughtfully.

"Lobesq? I have had dealings with him. I can learn this with ease. You are a wise woman, Veuillot. You see —since the honor of my house will be involved in both the past and the future of this dainty duchess whom my father loves—it is needful, as it would not otherwise be, that I should reach the truth, the whole truth, of her history."

She laughed grimly, with a sardonic appreciation of the sophistry in which he veiled his own vengeance in solicitude for the dignity of his race.

"No doubt, my lord," she said, curtly. "As for me—I am a woman—I want only to taste a drop of revenge for the pretty fashion in which that bastard called us once a set of senseless peasants! You great aristocrats are careful of honor, of course; a little vengeance does for us! And what is it you will do now?"

"I will go to Paris. I must leave my regrets and apologies to the fair duchess for quitting Villiers so hastily ere she has risen, and without presentation to her."

She smiled at the smile on his lips.

"When she is your father's wife you will see her oftentimes enough—you will be so welcome, my lord!"

Low, coarse, debased though her intelligence was, she had the shrewdness which took her straight to the means by which she would most surely awaken the worst instincts in this nature, which had long been her study.

"She will never be his wife," he made answer, with a sound in his voice that caused her fierce heart to leap with joy.

Then he slipped a roll of gold pieces into her palm and went his ways through the acacia-thicket. She looked after him with a hard, strange look in her eyes as she thrust the gold into her bosom. In her own brute-fashion she loved this delicate, indolent, womanish aristocrat, though she loved his gold still more; and her heart beat with great dull throbs against the leather of her bodice. A sudden fear touched her.

"Had I better have left her alone?" she muttered. "He will only love her again; and—who can tell?—he will have her secret, he may only use it to sever her from his father, he may wed with her himself,—who can tell?"

And she strode out from the acacia shadows, breaking their blossoms down with the swing of her great arm, and went across the meadows and through the lowing cattle with the glow of triumph faded, and the cloud of hatred settled on her face.

"Anyway, I have the gold," she thought, thrusting her hand into her bosom.

She did not notice, in a little shallow runlet of water that pierced the grass by the acacias, a child who was gathering water-cresses, and who hid himself among the reeds and bracken as she passed.

"Mother, I did evil to-day," said a lad of twelve, with soft, shy, brown eyes, and a tender, awed face, standing beside Ninette, who was busied counting the young apricots on her garden-wall.

She turned and looked gently on her son.

"Nay, thy crimes cannot be very dark, my Victor. What is this thing?"

"I did a shameful thing, mother. I was a spy!"

"A spy!"—she echoed the word in horror, thinking in an instant of the chevalier of the poniard, of whom her grandsire had told her in her infancy.

"Yes," murmured the lad, "I did not mean it, I had no thought; but I could not help listening. I heard without hearing,—you know?—and then I stayed and heard more, because I wished. It was very shameful, I know. But what they said seemed so strange."

"What who said?"

"Annette Veuillot and the young lord."

His mother's face darkened.

"The young lord? Is he come back? It was his carriage, then, that came through so late; your father had to get up for it. Veuillot—she was never a good woman. But what can she have to do with dainty aristocrats like Chanrellon?"

"I do not know, rightly. But I can tell you every word I heard, mother."

Ninette hesitated—spurred by intense inquisitive desire, withheld by a sturdy sense of honor.

"It seems wrong for me to listen," she said, at length. "Yet children should keep nothing from their mothers,

Well, tell me, then; I can tell Tricotrin afterward. He always knows what is best."

"It was just this," pursued the boy, in a rapid whisper. "You know the little brook that runs all through the dairy meadows? I was getting water-cresses in it at sunrise this morning. You know that great cluster of acacia-trees just behind the dairy-houses? They are so thick with bloom now, they would hide a hundred men. Well—as I was stooping in the brook after the cress, I heard Veuillot's voice. I crept nearer,—the rushes and the burdock grew so thick there that they hid me,—and I saw her, and my lord Chanrellon also. They were talking, and Veuillot had got her pail on her head. She is so ugly, mother, I wonder he does not talk instead to Laure? Laure is so pretty——"

"But what were they saying?" asked Ninette, impatiently, taking a slug from the wall.

"Well—all this," answered her son; and he told what he had overheard, confusedly enough, but giving it all the weight and emphasis he could in his wonder.

"And then he turned away," ended Victor, at the close of his long recital. "And she went too,—passing me quite close; and I heard her mutter, 'Anyway, I have the gold.' But is it not strange? What could it mean? Who is it they can think that splendid duchess is?"

"I do not know," murmured his mother, while her ruddy face turned pale. She did not know, but she guessed.

"*He* never said the child was dead," she thought to herself as she stripped a leaf off, so that a young apricot might get "gilded," as the people call it.

Then she turned and laid her hand on her son's forehead.

"Victor—promise me to speak of this to no living soul; not even to your sisters."

"I promise, mother."

"Right," she said, simply. "I fear there is wickedness afoot. That Veuillot was never a good woman. In the evening you get me the mule saddled, and I will go see Tricotrin."

But when in the evening she rode the mule down into the little hollow, where the sign of the Silver Stag swung above its hollyhocks and its fruit-trees, the keeper of the tavern lamented, with many regretful phrases, that his beloved guest was gone.

"Where is he gone?" asked Ninette, anxiously.

He shrugged his shoulders.

"Ah! who ever knows where Tricotrin is gone, or is going? He took his knapsack, and when he takes his knapsack he commonly goes for good. Besides, you know," he pursued, sinking his voice to a low whisper, and glancing around as though his straight, tall hollyhocks were officers of the law, "you know,—they say,—the students are up again in Paris; and when there is anything of that sort, Tricotrin is sure to be there ready for it."

Ninette turned the head of her mule sadly homeward, thinking nothing of the students and their riots, but thinking much of her foiled purpose. In her own heart she was certain of what the drift of the talk that her boy had overheard must have been. She had not forgotten the days when the Prince Fainéant had taken his golden gifts under the beechen-tree,—and she felt that when the Waif of the Loire had died to the peasantry, she had been translated to that marvelous sphere whereof they had only far-off glimpses, and vague, intangible, hazy conceptions.

"Tricotrin should have known," she said to herself over and over again as the mule paced slowly homeward, nodding his lazy head, and shaking his belled bridle, and stopping to graze at his pleasure on the wayside grasses.

Once she thought of going straight up to the great house, and begging audience of the one whom that wickedness of the woman Veuillot's menaced, and telling all to her with frankness and without fear. But she did not dare.

This duchess was so great a personage; she had no surety of her own suspicions being right, they were mere wild conjecture; she had but the word of her son, a child of twelve, with which to bear up her statement. And moreover, who could tell how her lord would resent such insults to his guest, such accusation to his son?

And Ninette, though generous and honest as the day, and in many things courageous, was a true woman. She thought of her husband's employment, of her children's welfare, of her happy home in the little, bright, ivy-hung lodge,—she could not endanger all these.

So she held her peace, and went sadly homeward in the hot, late evening time. In the porch there was a gay group, Victor and his sisters, and little Raoul, with his wondrous cuirassier, and Paulin, who, although an equerry, deigned to be not a little in love with the black-eyed elder daughter of the lodge.

The girl turned to her mother in unaffected concern—

"Oh, mère,—that beautiful duchess is ill."

"Ill!"—Ninette's eyes met her son's.

"Yes," interposed the equerry. "Her women found her in a swoon last night, and she has not risen to-day; though she will insist, I dare say, on going to Paris for that fête she is to give to the princes. The physicians speak of fever. Mademoiselle Marie's kind little heart is quite distressed for Miladi."

"Dost thou think because a woman is a duchess she must never suffer, Marie?" said Ninette, somewhat roughly, going within to lay aside her great cloak.

"There is evil against her, mère?" whispered Victor.

"Yes, I fear there is evil," said his mother, with a sigh. "And I could not see Tricotrin!"

## CHAPTER XXXII.

WHILE Ninette sought for him at the tavern, and rode her mule back in sorrow and perplexity, he was sitting on the oak settle within the porch of the little river-house, looking out down the reach of the stream.

All things were still. The cat slept, curled among violet-roots. The fowls and pigeons were gone to roost. The swallows had ceased their fluttering and murmuring among the ivy. The little Lorraine girl had gone to her own people. The dead had been borne out, by tender, reverent hands, through the green garden ways, and down the water-steps, and into the waiting boat; and grand'mère had been left to her last resting-place under the blossoming acacias of the vine country of her birth.

In the deserted house there was no sound; the gathered roses had withered, and hung their heads; the clock had stopped, for none had remembered to wind its works; on the brick hearth there was no fire; the evening shadows stole softly through all the little desolate chambers. On a chestnut-bough outside the door even Mistigri was silent, and very quiet, watching with her black sad eyes the flitting of the bats and owls.

His own gaze never wandered from the river, which was half in shadow, half in light, as the sun went down. His thoughts were with the old lost years.

Before his sight there hovered the gay and graceful shapes of a child at play among the tall scarlet bean-flowers; of a child swaying on the lithe earth-drooping branch of a beech-tree; of a child leaning over the side of a brown boat, and dipping her arms down into the water, and laughing when the keel grated on the rocky shore, and singing—singing ever like the birds at spring-time—from early dawn all through the day, till nightfall; of a child with the glad swift voice of childhood and the dark dreaming gaze of a woman, and all the fond, fair, innocent freedom of a forest-creature taught human love, but knowing naught of human fear.

The time had been when he, in his madness, had once dreamed that she like the young forest-thing would have returned to the hand that had fed and to the home that had sheltered her, as the fawn returns affrighted by the noise of the hunters, and by the bitterness of the water-springs, and by the gall of the collar, and by the width of the great plains in the new lands of its wandering.

But he had been in error. His fawn had gone where the pastures were palace-gardens, and the brooks were the wellsprings of pleasure, and the thickets bore the honey-laden buds of triumph, and the gilded collar was but a jeweled bauble by the chimes of whose bells she could lure all other herds to follow her.

And he sat alone in the little house by the river.

The sun set; the glow faded off the water; the dreaming hum of night-gnats was the only sound on the air; the dews fell thick on grass, and leaf, and blossom. He never stirred; he never took his gaze from off the gliding current. For him the hushed night-air was filled with the echoes of a young voice that never more would sound through that familiar place; for him the shadowy solitude was haunted by the vision of a young face that never more would smile on that deserted home.

And thus his recompense came to him; thus her debt was paid, in that common wage of bitterness and suffering whereby woman often requites the love of man, and fate ever requites the life that follows the law of mercy and forgets itself.

A step sounded on the rocky landing-stair. He started, and slowly arose; in the full, lustrous moonlight that now streamed over land and stream, he saw the one for whom he had waited.

He motioned his hand behind him.

"Go within, Gervase; all is yours."

The young peasant, hardy, sun-bronzed, strong as an ox of the field, trembled like a child.

"Ah! What can I say?—how can I thank you? Such priceless goodness!— —"

"Chut! Goodness to enable a man to marry! I never heard that before. Were it goodness to give you a knife whereby you could cut your throat?"

Gervase smiled; but his mouth quivered with strong emotion, which, save for his five-and-twenty years of manhood, would have found relief in tears.

"It is goodness that gives heaven upon earth!" he murmured. "You know—all her youth must have gone by; I am so poor, and she is only a little servant-maiden; and when one works so hard, so hard, the eyes get dim, and the hair gets gray, and the time of age comes so soon!——"

"I know! And you—you think there is naught upon earth like that little servant-maiden! Well—so best. Let it last."

"But how can I ever repay you?"

"Hush! Think you not that, when Napoleon Bonaparte lay dying, the memory of that Alpine shepherd whom he made happy with the gift of a meadow and a homestead, was sweeter to him than the memories of all his victories? Besides—you will pay me by taking heed of all these dumb things, all these birds, all these trees."

The young man bent before him, with tender, tremulous reverence.

"They shall be as sacred to me as *she!*"

"That is enough! And now—go within. I am late, and must lose no more time."

"Is it true, then?" the peasant asked, wistfully, "true that the boulevards have risen?"

"No. But it is true that the students may rise. Rise—to be massacred. Go within, Gervase—I would start alone."

"But—if there be massacres?" gasped the youth, mistaking his answer. "If harm come to you? If we see you no more?"

"Pooh! Do you not remember?—I am the Wandering Jew! Well—if harm do, if even Ahasuerus be given the divine gift of death, I have had a care that all this shall be for thee and thine. For you are gentle-natured and worthy of trust, Gervase. And when I die—if I die—make my grave yonder, under that great old beech, where I shall hear the singing of the river forever, and my people will know where I lie."

He smiled as he spoke; but there was that in the smile which only deepened the lingering and wistful melancholy of the words.

Gervase glanced up, and caught the look upon his face, and trembled with a vague sense of near calamity.

"Farewell," said Tricotrin, with another backward gesture of his hand toward the house.

The young peasant obeyed it, as a dog obeys a sign. He himself went down by the stone steps to the water's edge, and entered the little boat which waited there among the sand and sedges. He paused, with the oar resting on the bank, and looked long—as men look on what they leave forever—at the familiar homely place, with the stars of the midsummer-eve shining above its ivy-covered roof and on its ivy-shrouded casements.

He looked long: then let his oars fall, and drifted down the stream.

When the youth stole forth under the cover of the boughs, and gazed out down the course of the river, the little boat was far away, floating darkly, like a leaf adrift, upon the broad, white, starlit reach of the river.

He was gone—never more to return to the home which the Waif once had shared with the swallows.

## CHAPTER XXXIII.

In the dusky hot close of the late summer day in which he reached Paris, there met him one of the brethren of that religious community, who commonly called him their Alp-dog of travail and trouvaille, who brought them so many well-nigh lost lives, found, half frozen, under the snows of abject poverty, or in the crevasses of bottomless crime. Of creeds he had no love; of priests he had as little; but he knew that these men were of pure zeal, of sincere faith, and of a charity which labored unceasingly, and gave its ministrations without boundaries of code or cadence. He honored them, and aided them, and they—loved him in return, and felt before him something of that wonder with which the early leaders of their church saw the virtues of their own evangel surpassed in the pagan Julian.

In the sultry angry evening the monk paused to greet him.

"It is you, Tricotrin?" he said, with welcome shining in his sad sunken eyes. "You have been long absent!"

"Yes: who would stay beneath tile and slate, in this weather, if he could have the roofing of green leaves and pine-branches?"

"Well—there is ever work to be found and done in the cities."

"Doubtless; but there ought not always to be the doing of work in this life of ours; Nature gave us beauty and pleasure, we have a right to be still, and idle, and enjoy the twain sometimes. But—here you and I do not think alike. Tell me, how has it been with that poor wretch I brought to your doors, after the thieves' burning?"

"It is very ill with him. He has never recovered; he dies by inches. He has never left the bed on which we first laid him. His lower limbs are dead. But his brain is clear enough; he talks at times with a terrible wit and irony. He must some day have known the glittering side of the great world's vices. He has asked often for you,—not by name, indeed, but for the one who saved him. I have sought for you often; for at times he is hard to pacify, because we do not take you to his side. We have sent to all your usual haunts, but we could not hear of you. You will come and see him—now?"

Tricotrin made no answer.

"He cannot live," the monk pursued. "A few days—or weeks at uttermost—will close his life. You will come to him? It seems to me that he has somewhat on his mind that he desires to impart. You will come?"

"You are certain he cannot survive?"

"Certain. It is impossible."

Tricotrin paused some moments, silent still; then he raised his head.

"Yes: I will come to-morrow afternoon."

Then he bade the brother farewell, and went on his way with his knapsack on his shoulders, and the dust on his feet, and the monkey on his wrist; but, for once, with no song on his lips.

On the morrow he kept his tryst.

The great, dark, frowning pile of the hospital loomed through the gay sunlight of a lustrous and cloudless day. The bell rang dully through the stillness like a toll for a passing soul. The small postern door within the entrance-gates slowly unclosed. The brethren welcomed him with few, terse words, and led the way to the quaint, noiseless, cloistered nook where Paulus Canaris lay dying—a little naked cell, looking out upon a court where a single grape-vine, thrusting forth green leaves and green clusters, alone recalled the light and loveliness of the year's rich summer-time.

The Greek was stretched, exhausted and with his lower limbs paralyzed; maimed and disfigured still from the flames, yet killed, less by the fire than by the vices of his own past. The monk went to him, and said a few words; then left the cell, closing the heavy door behind him. The gaze of Canaris fastened with a great amazement, with a great awe, upon the face of his visitant. All his emaciated frame trembled like a leaf.

On Tricotrin the sun shone full.

"Great Heaven!" cried the Greek, with the dews standing on his brow. "Speak to me:—speak!—are you a living man, or only the wraith of the dead?"

"I was once the boy whom you wronged," he answered, simply; there was no passion in his voice, only an unutterable scorn—the scorn of truth and of courage—for a traitor.

"I knew—I knew!" muttered the dying wretch. "I knew that night when you dragged me from the fires; I never dreamed it until then. It was the look in your eyes that told me—that look!"

Tricotrin answered nothing; he stood at the foot of the pallet, while the midsummer light shone like an aureole on his head.

What could he say to this man?—whose whole life had been one long perfidy, whose whole existence had been one long assassination of peace, and faith, and honor?

The Greek shivered, and buried his face, and lay silent and sore afraid. It was to him as a resurrection from the grave.

"You know that I stole the jewels?" he cried, suddenly, looking upward at that sun-circled head as at an avenging angel.

"I did know it—I saw you in the act."

"Yet you never exposed me?—you never declared your own innocence?"

"I was falsely accused. Those who could so accuse me were unworthy of proof of their error:—as you were beneath vengeance when you stood by silent in your sin. Oh, my God!" he cried, a thousand memories awaking in him, and breaking forth in rapid, burning words. "I was a youth; I remembered only that I came of free races and bold blood, that I would never live beneath the roof where my honor had been outraged, that I would never bear the titles of a father who insulted and who hated me. I was too proud to clear myself of that foul, felonious charge; I was too full of scorn to harm so vile a thing as you;—I only longed for the sweet wild liberty of my mother's shores, for the sea-breezes of freedom and danger, for the joy of life untrammeled by pomps and untainted by hatred. I was only a boy; a boy full of chivalrous love of wounded faith, of thirst for a forest-animal's innocent, dauntless, wandering days. I never remembered that, in leaving you beside my brother, I left an adder in the purples I abandoned to him;—I never thought that, knowing how I spared you, you would feed and fatten on the bounty of my race in pampered luxury for years, and stain its honor, in return, by stealth, at the very hearth whose fires had warmed you. I never thought—I was a child, and acted in a child's headlong sacrifice and passion—I spared you, and you rewarded me a score years later by stabbing in the dark the only creature that I loved!"

The words died in his throat. Looking on this man, the bitterness of hate consumed him; the dead wrongs of his boyhood rose up from their distant graves.

The Greek cowered down, shuddering as under a rain of blows. He knew well what his sins had been against that lofty, generous, unsuspecting, northern race, which had fed, and clothed, and sheltered, and trusted him:—sins which, budding first in thefts of gems to sate the boyish avarice of a born gambler, had found their latest crown in thefts of a wife's love and of a husband's honor;—sins born at their earliest and their latest from one root, a devil's envy of the power and wealth and ease of those who had succored, and pampered, and lifted him from a hireling's servitude to a friend's estate. In that hour all the vileness of his life came out before his sight, and appalled him with an exceeding horror. His brain was giddy; his soul sick; he could only stare blankly at the face above him, and at the blinding light of a summer day's sun.

"You have lived like this!" he gasped. "And all deemed you dead,—dead in that ring of water. I wronged you—yes, heavily. I dared not say I stole the diamonds to pay a debt of the dice; and your father always smiled most on me when most I hurt you—so I kept silence. Tell me,—you have been content?"

A smile, that blinded him like the sunbeams, came on his listener's face.

"Content! There are greater things than contentment."

"But have you never regretted?"

"Never."

"What! Is it possible! Christ! how strange you are! All that men covet lay in your hands; and you—you flung them aside thus! Yet—since you do thus live,—*he* cannot justly own his lands, his gold, his earldom?"

"Silence! Dare you to speak his name?—you—the vile paramour of his accursed wife!"

The Greek made no reply: still staring at him with the same half-senseless, half-incredulous stupor of amaze.

To the Athenian—who had been born in servitude, and stolen his way to pleasure through secret sin, and sold his soul for the mere touch of gold, and risen by foul means into the light of affluence, and fallen again through the gambler's avarice and the traitor's crimes into that lowest deep wherein Death now had found him—this renunciation, this contentment, this abandonment of honors and riches for the mere sweet sake of freedom, were mysteries that bewildered and appalled him, half sunk in the stupors of dissolution as were his memories and his senses.

"And you have never regretted!" he murmured over and over again.

Tricotrin turned from him, and gazed out to where the late vine budded in its deserted home. He had never regretted—never save once, when he had seen the white and purple violets in the bosom of a woman.

His thoughts wandered far back, over the length of many years, to that long-perished time when of his own will he had forsaken the treasures, and the honors, and the luxurious ease, of his high heritage, to go forth to the freedom of his mother's people, to the simplicities of a life without ceremonial and care.

It had been a boy's wild generosity, a boy's vivid passion, a boy's headlong impulse, which had sent him forth from the home of his birthright, so that the child whom he loved might reign there in his stead; so that he should owe naught to a race which had scorned and had wounded his mother; so that he should be delivered forever from the trammels of greatness which galled the sea-lion's spirit within him; so that he should be freed forever to live his own life, and to roam wheresoever he would, unchained, unarraigned, uncrowned.

The daring, hardy blood of the sea-born Armorican races had been in him. There had lived in him the old dauntless hardy pride of the Bréton peasants, "*Me zo deuzar armorig,*" when they stood, loyal but equal, before their haughtiest seigneur of Rohan, Rochefort, or Rochejaquelin races. He had scorned the gilded cages of riches and of rank, and broken his silken bonds as a young lion-cub breaks its cords, disdaining to hold what was begrudged to him, craving only the open air, and the breath of the forest, the salt waves, and the sweep of the winds.

He had gone, leaving his crowns to other brows, his gold to other hands; gone, while they deemed him dead, to the liberty for which he was athirst. Gone to the shores where his mother's fleet feet had raced with the incoming tides, where her eyes had gazed at the sun like the eagle's; where the waves, and the breeze, and the storms had given her beauty their grandeur, and her courage their strength, and her soul their liberty, which lived again in his. Gone to those years of freedom, and gladness, and love, and mirth, and charity, which were uttered in one word to the people that loved him—the word of his self-chosen title—Tricotrin.

Poor, indeed, he ever had been in the coinage of worldly wealth. Some little gold stored away in the hollow of a rock, and bequeathed to him by one of his mother's brethren, to whom he was dear, and who alone knew whence the boy, who wandered to their western shore, had come, made all his portion. But he had been rich in every other thing beyond compare—rich as with the golden light of suns that never set.

A king without a diadem, a priest without a stole, a soldier without a sword, a leader whose hosts were unseen of the world, a poet whose melodies asked no answer from the trumpet of fame, a sovereign whose territory was meted by no measuring-rod, but stretched wherever men enjoyed or suffered,—he had lived his life.

And regret had never touched him. His years had been sweet and mellow, and full of color and melody, and fair to his sight and his senses. He had never regretted—never save once, when, out of the purest and holiest of his acts, there had arisen the greatest bitterness that he had ever known.

The Greek, still gazing at him like one half blinded, strove to raise his feeble frame and husband his sinking breath. He was not repentant, not remorseful; he had long ere then killed his conscience, and the sins he had sinned seemed precious to him; they were the relics of his youth, the laurels of his prowess, the things that told him all he had once been. But, in some dim sense, he felt the wonder and the greatness of this abdication, as he felt those of that mercy which, knowing him a foe so vile, yet had dealt with him as with one innocent.

"Are you a madman? or a god?" he muttered. "You must be one or other. And you have never regretted!—you must be made of other stuff than mere humanity. To lose all *that*—to lay it down—and never long to seize it once again! You must be more or less than man! Such a heritage! such a heritage!"

His hearer's voice crossed his words, with a grave eloquence of scorn in it.

"Whatever I be, you, of all men, can least appraise my act or motive. Speak no more of that dead time; all the issue of it lies with you. I do not care to raise reproach against a dying wretch; nor do I care to linger with you. You desired to see me:—wherefore, if there be no remorse in you toward Estmere!"

"There is none in me!" said the Greek, with sudden fierceness. "I hated him always! Oh, he was liberal, gracious, full of generous gifts,—I know that,—but I hated him. He was so just, so proud, so calm, so far above me, so wedded to stern truth. He was a living rebuke; I hated him. I stole his wife's love—yes; I stole her beauty, I made that highborn Austrian woman mine. But though I dishonored his name, I could not dishonor him: that was what went so bitter with me."

"Peace! If you cannot speak his name for pardon and repentance, do not dare to breathe it in my hearing!"

"You love him still? when he reigns in your stead, when he sits in your throne! But wait—wait an instant—and hear me. You have twice done good toward me: you, to whom I ever did evil in the time of your childhood. I have no remorse in me. With my last breath I shall curse the world and all in it. But I would tell you one thing ere I die; it may serve you. That child whom you reared——"

His hearer turned swiftly, struck as by a sharp blow.

"What of her?"

A cynical smile flitted over the blackened, haggard face of Canaris.

"Ah, there is one thing you regret, is there not? Well, that child is now Duchess de Lirà. How have I known it? Men, that live in the depths of infamy I have lived in, know all things. We are sewer-rats—yes—but we undermine palaces! Look you! after you gave me my 'chance' I watched you. I did not dream you were anything save what I heard; but I did not lose sight of your life. I saw that fair thing by your side one night in Paris. There was a look in her face, a glance, a smile, no matter what, that brought a fancy to my thoughts, a memory to my mind. I saw a likeness in her. It set me to seek out her history; more in idleness than aught else. I was miserably poor, and had not then taught myself the trades of coarser crime. I played long with this fancy;

at length I learned its secret. When I had learned it, it was of no use to me. The child was gone from you; I could not tell where. Years went by; I have been in the prisons, in the galleys. One day this winter, a great lady gave me a silver piece for lifting her little dog out of the mud as she went to her carriage; the face was the same face, the same fancy struck me. I watched and waited, and strung this and that hint together; I saw you once admitted to her hotel; I guessed the truth, though I did not know it till your look a moment since told me I had guessed aright. This Duchess de Lirà is the foundling you harbored—is it not so? Well, and of what stock did that stray child come?"

"If you know, say! say, for God's sake!"

"Stoop your head to my ear, then. Ah, what wealth this had been to me if I had lived, and owned my old cunning, and held it as a sword that might fall at any moment above that proud, delicate head! Bend nearer, that I may whisper it; a great lady's honor must not be tainted aloud! Now, listen; will you curse her, I wonder!"

"Speak out!" cried his hearer, in an unendurable torture. "If, for once, you do not lie—speak out, and say all you know."

"All I know!" echoed the Greek, with a dreary cynicism upon his lips. "Nay! I know so much—I was a slave, that mastered more than my lords; I was a pampered spaniel, that nestled in patrician bosoms; I was a thing that they spurned with their speech in the world, but caressed with their lips in their privacy: those lofty, languid, fair, sensual women! All I know!—pshaw!—would you have me tell lords they are bastards; would you have me tell virgins they are harlots? Well, well! be not angered, nor in haste. I would gather my memories,—let me think,—in peace. We spoke of the dainty duchess?—this foundling you fed on brown loaves and goat's milk, and who pays you by scattering the mud of her chariot-wheel upon you as she sweeps by? You would be told of the woman who bore her? Well, that woman is called Co. riolis."

A loud cry rang across his words—the cry of an unutterable horror. The hands of Tricotrin seized him where he lay.

"You lie! you painted snake! When ever yet did you stir save to poison? You lie!—oh devil! that you stood in health and in strength before me, that I could deal with you as you merit!"

The white lips of the Athenian grew paler still with fear as he heard; but for once he had spoken truth, and he had that courage which all truth confers.

"I have not lied," he said, slowly; "at the least, not willingly. She is the daughter of Coriolis. Take thought. Is there no kinship in their regard? They have likeness in unlikeness,—that bright glitter of hair, that mouth like a scarlet blossom, that smile that is so sunlit, yet so cold. They are dissimilar also, indeed, as are the water lilies of regal lakes and the poisoned lilies of Indian swamps; but, like them, they have likeness."

His listener's grasp fell from him; Tricotrin covered his face with his hands, and shuddered, and was still.

The vision of Coriolis rose before him as he had beheld it in her youth; and he remembered the enchantment of its smile, and saw in it what he had never seen, and knew that the truth had been uttered,—the abhorred, polluted, ghastly truth which broke in on him with the merciless flash of the electric light, that breaks the darkness only to leave it tenfold blacker, thicker, more hideous, than ere its gloom was pierced.

But still he strove for blindness, still he would not behold what that flash of light had revealed. He was as one to whom the glare of the lightning has shown some beloved and lovely face, stricken white and lifeless, floating on some deep and caverned pool.

"Likeness! likeness!" he echoed, wildly. "You dare say this thing on your mere sickly fancy, your mere delirious delusion! Your brain teems with vague shapes as you lie in your loneliness; and you dare thrust these forward as facts and as truths? Gold threads in the hair—a rose-bloom on the mouth—fine things indeed to be pointed to as warrants of kinship, as registries of birth——!"

"Wait," said Canaris, with his old malice gleaming in his eyes, tempered by a new emotion of pity and regret. "Do not think that I speak so idly, or that I give voice to deathbed vagaries. I tell you a fact that I learned, in case that fact ever may serve you. The likeness I saw; but that is nothing. How I know the truth came by pure hazard, as most things do after all, despite men's prescience and scheming. I knew Gérant, Coriolis' first lover,—you remember his fame on the lyric theaters?—knew him well. I was his confidant at the time when he took that pretty thing from her sea-cabin to bring her out on the stage. I thought her a lovely fool, and scarce saw, myself, what he would do with her; but Gérant knew better. He discerned genius, and—half a million of francs yearly, in her. Well, there was only one obstacle to her flight with him: her child by Bruno. Coriolis half loved and half hated it, so Gérant told me. He cursed it often enough, himself, and would have thrown it in the sea for his part. But she had a curious reluctance to leave it to her husband; she thought he would murder it in his first passion. She wished to be rid of it, but she wished to know all was well with it. It was a female child, called, I think, like her,—Madelon. Gérant, to content her, arranged with a woman he knew,—a chorus-singer, horribly poor, and who had a throat-affection, so that she could no longer sing, —to steal the infant herself when the house should be empty, in the first excitement of the fisher-folk over the disappearance of Bruno's wife, and get away with it out of the province. That was done. The simple people supposed the child was gone with its mother. Gérant gave the woman a large sum to do it, for it would have stood, of course, as a crime in the law. Some year or so afterward, when Madelon Bruno had made her mark upon Paris, and had become Coriolis, I asked Gérant how his contrivance had answered. He swore bitterly, and said the little wretch had died of fever, and he wished its mother was dead also! She had just broken with him for Prince Anatôle, and made mirth of him for all the money he had expended in insuring her stage-successes—money which he never saw back again. Now, I never once remembered this story of the child until I saw the face of the girl by your side one festival-night in Paris, and learned she was only a foundling whom you had taken the caprice of protecting. Then I said in my soul, 'That girl is Madelon Bruno: and the daughter of Coriolis did not die.'"

He paused, exhausted by his lengthened speech: Tricotrin's hard convulsive breathing alone stirred the silence.

"This is no proof!" he muttered, fiercely, at length. "This is but suspicion, conjecture, imagination. The child died; you heard that from Gérant; why should you dream that she—she——"

"I do not dream; I know," resumed Canaris. "I tell it slowly, for I am feeble. But patience—you will be contented! When I saw that girl in Paris, Gérant had been long dead. But I remember the name of the chorus-singer: it was Rose Léroux. I always taught myself to remember names: they are so useful. I inquired for her; I heard with difficulty, for people so soon forget, that she had been a long while out of the country, had returned, had committed a robbery with violence on an old woman, and was then at the galleys. Well—I went thither myself, not long after, for a more intellectual crime. I have not been many months released. I saw you one day this winter go into the Lirà palace; and I saw the face of its duchess. I said to myself, though it seemed like insanity,—is that his foundling throned there? is that Madelon Bruno among the sovereigns of the earth? I could not tell; but I sought out the woman Léroux. She was among the herd at Chaumont. We had many talks together. There were no secrets between us; we had the one bond of sympathy —we had both known the Bagne. By degrees I brought her to the subject of that child of Jean Bruno's. She laughed— she is horribly ugly, and ugliest when she laughs—and told me that the child might be dead, but had not died with her,

When she took it she never meant to be at the burden of keeping the child; but she wanted Gérant's money; and she always obeyed what he told her. She did not know well how to get rid of it; she kept it a year, as Gérant sent plenty of gold, storing the money up to enable her to get off to America, for she had even then done what made her uneasy of the law. Then, as he wrote her sharply word that she might look for but little in future, she tramped through half France on foot, with her gold and the child. She wrote back to Gérant that the little Madelon was dead of scarlet fever, and had been buried as her own natural daughter; but in truth she laid it down in the dawn one day, in the loneliest part of a wooded place by the Loire. Then she made her way swiftly to a seaport, and crossed the ocean westward. She said she should have sent the child to Coriolis; but she was afraid of rousing the wrath of Gérant, who had great power over her. She thought it no harm to leave the child in the wood; she had abandoned in like fashion one of her own, who had been picked up by a carrier and had thriven well. I asked her why she did not leave it at the foundling hospital; she said she had cause even then to shun cities; and besides—she hated Coriolis, she had loved Gérant—she desired the baby Madelon to perish, though she said she could not hold it under the water to kill it, its eyes were so pretty. I asked her what name the child bore with her: she said it could barely speak, but called itself Viva, from hearing the woman of the cottage, where she had hid all the year with it, call a spaniel dog by that name continually. I asked her also if she knew the fate of the child: she said no—she had not given it two thoughts since that time, until I recalled Gérant's name to her. That is all. Are you satisfied? If you want more, go to Rose Léroux up at Chaumont;. they know you there, though you have committed none of the crimes that are the common passports to its community. You see,—I spoke of no dream, no delusion. Well!—from Madelon Bruno the actress to Madelon Bruno the duchess, it is but a step! Both have sold their beauty, and one has her diamonds set round a marriage-ring, and the other her diamonds set round a drinking-cup; one has a little higher price than the other; that is all! It is a pity I lie here useless and helpless; what wealth I would have made out of this history! And you—and you—will do nothing, save strive with all your might to spare her its knowledge. You are the great spendthrifts of the world:— you men who throw away your opportunities to do evil. What fortunes you miss!"

## CHAPTER XXXIV.

THE doors of the monastic refuge once more unclosed, and Tricotrin passed out into the world of living men.

The full ardent light of the late day was about him as he went; but his eyes were blind to it, and he moved onward like one drunk and stupefied with wine.

There was no hope left in him that this thing were false. The words of the dying Athenian had carried the incisive force of truth with them. He had spoken as men do not speak when they lie, and his utterances had fallen deep into his hearer's heart, as aquafortis into metal. With less circumstantial precision than that which his narrative had borne, his listener would have felt that it was true, by the same ghastly sense of hopeless certitude wherewith the one who loves hears tidings of the death of what he loves.

A thousand memories, moreover, flashed on his mind that bore witness to their veracity; the strange dread witness of forgotten trivialities, from long-perished hours, which arise from their graves in the past to bear testimony that kills the peace of the present. Memories of sounds, and glances, and echoes of laughter; of a cadence in the voice, of a smile on the lips. Of a child's innocent nonsense among the wild gourds of a garden, and a woman's airy frivolities on the glittering stage of a theater. Of a girl's gay form fluttering over the clover and seed-grasses of a field, and an actress's radiant figure floating before the footlights. Of a young singer who sang like the goldfinch swaying high on a broken bough, and of a great singer who sang like the mocking-bird, delighting the ears of monarchs and princes:—all that likeness in unlikeness whereof the dying man had spoken in his cynical truth started out to his sight in witness that could not be denied, or disproved, or any longer doubted.

The bread that he had thrown upon the waters in pity for the stray fledgling bird left helplessly to drift upon their salt sea-tide, came back to him, and was bitter as ashes on his lips.

There could scarce have come to him a thing deadlier than this. He was even as a man who, gazing on the fair, sweet, gracious beauty of a woman he adores, sees, beneath it, the canker of a mortal and accursed disease, doomed, soon or late, to make it hideous in the sight of men, and draw it downward to the grave.

He had no hope. Every memory that returned to him was fraught with testimony of the truth of this history, whereby his enemy had recompensed him for rescue from the thieves' wild justice. Once when in the press of the populace at the theater of Coriolis, he had glanced, from the face of the dazzling mime whom the public applauded, to the face of the child in her little bright ruddy hood at his side. A certain sense of resemblance between them—vague, changeful, intangible—had stolen upon him, and he had thrust it away with repugnance and in contempt. The face of the woman was lovely indeed; but it was soulless and mindless as the face of a waxen, scentless, glowing-hued flower. The face of the child was careless indeed; but there was a soul in it, a soul dormant, dreaming, half awake, half lost in laughter; but still there,—in the great, soft, shadowy eyes, on the breathless, fragrant, caressing mouth. And he had chosen then to see only the difference,—it was the likeness now that recurred to him.

And was that likeness only of feature?—only of such slight surface-things as the hue of the hair, and the arch of the lips, and the tint of the skin? Was there none in the heart and the thoughts, in the passions and impulses? in the barbaric worship of gold and color, and sensuous pomp, and arrogant display? in the cold slighting scorn for all ways save the ways of pleasure and power? in the gay merciless mockery of all love that bore not its bribes of silver and gold?

The leaven of those women who had turned aside from innocence, and honor, and obscurity, to force themselves forth into the affluence of enjoyment, the furnace of passion, the paradise of wealth, was in her. It had been in her from her earliest hour, when she had broken aside the lily-leaves in eagerness for their yellow stamens; it had been, unknown to him, his subtle antagonist, his secret conqueror, when she had refused to dwell with him because he dwelt not among princes, and could not give her the gifts that her ambitions and instincts craved so blindly and so violently. Their desires, their impulses, their evil—the evil that had made no kiss sweet to them unless a jewel purchased it, no flower fair to them unless it were the poisonous laurel of notoriety,—had been ever in her, his foe, his rival, his betrayer, driving her from him on the spur of a vague discontent, seducing her from his arms with the whispers of that tempter which does the chief portion of Mephistophiles' work,—the tempter of feminine vanity and unrest.

These had been in her, as there had also been the poetic fancies of the peasant-girl who had made her friends from the robins of the pine-forests of Lirà, and the loyal, tender, generous temper of the sailor of the Riviera. These were in her also. And,—as in her physical loveliness, the fair hues, and laughing mouth, and dazzling graces of her mother were heightened and ennobled by the dark lustrous eyes, full of the sleeping fires of the south, that had once gazed from the pain-worn, sunburned face of Bruno, and told the tale of his desolated life,—so in her moral nature the higher and the baser instincts, the cruelties and the nobilities, the wanton weakness and the truthful courage of these conflicting and contrasted temperaments abode, ever in union and in disunion, forming the anomalous fluctuations of her life. The haughty blood of that patrician race of which Coriolis was the illicit offspring; the passionate, gentle, ignorant, heroic soul of the southern mariner; the instinctive poetry of the simple, harmless lives passed under the lonely skies of the mountain pinewoods; the ruthless greeds, the restless aspirations, the thirsty vanities of the women who had forsaken sinless love for gilded infamy;—all these lived in her. All these inspired her with those gifts, and graces, and sins, and follies, that she had once believed came from that more than mortal origin on which she had loved to muse in still sweet summer nights when her childish eyes had sought beneath broad burdock-leaves, and in dew-laden chalices of flowers, for the coming of the people of her nation, for the reign of the fairies upon earth.

He knew it; and there was no hope in him, as he went toward the dens of vice and misery at Chaumont: yet his chief thought still was of her.

If ever this truth came to her she would cry out that it would have been better that she should have been left to perish in the blindness and unconsciousness of her infancy than have lived for this shame to bow her proud head to the dust!

That absolute despair which paralyzes the courage, the faith, the strength of a man when he beholds his holiest acts change into his foes, and all his efforts as of no avail against the force of a cruel mockery of accident, came on him now, and broke the heroic temper in him, and killed the bright and clear philosophies which had withstood all lighter blows.

"He had never regretted," he had said to the man who died yonder; and he had spoken, not in the language of a sophist's hyperbole, but in the language of pure, straight, simple truth. He had never regretted, from the hour when a boy's ardent impulse for freedom and peace, and the joy of becoming his own law and his own leader, had made him abandon the heritage that was begrudged him, for the simple birthright of liberty that came to him from his mother's people. Chance had favoured him, circumstance had befriended him; he had cast greatness behind him, and he had found love; he had flung away dignities, and he had lighted on laughter; he had refused the rich savor of costly banquets since they were seasoned with gall, and he had discovered that glad contentment which gives sweetness to a cake of meal, and brings lotus-dreams with a draught of spring-water. He had owed no debt to any man; he had bound his will by no fetter; he had paid no slavery to custom; he had been yoked to no gilded chain of possession; he had shaped his own life, and had rejoiced in it; he had steeped it in the poet's idealism, the artist's color, the lover's passion, the gipsy's freedom, the scholar's meditation, and had found it exceeding fair.

It was not a life fitting for the multitude of men, but it had been fitting beyond all others for him. Because a million of field sparrows, and street sparrows, and reed sparrows build, and eat, and breed, and multiply in their low-lying nests, asking nothing better than food and wool, and all the small attainments and contentions of their communities, they will not understand that, because this is good and sufficient to them, it would be captivity and death to the bold, white-winged sea-bird that finds its joys in endless shores and boundless seas, in wild west winds and sun-flaked clouds, in rocky heights and ocean dawns, and would not change these even though famine, and peril, and tempest, be oftentimes its lot. For other men he left the city, or the field, or the duck-pool of the sparrows; for himself he took the sea-life of the gull: and he had never regretted, he had spoken the truth; never even though want, and conflict, and danger, and labor had been at times his portion; even though he had lived nameless and homeless among men. His life had been fair to him, infinitely fair; looking backward on its many-colored years he would not have exchanged it for any other, and he would not if he could, have undone the deed of his youth.

## THE STORY OF A WAIF AND STRAY. 281

Repentance, or disquiet, or ambition had never once moved him to desire the things that he had forsaken, to lament the act of his childhood, to desire to return to those pleasant places from which he had issued self-exiled forever. He had never regretted.

It was only now, when out of the gentle pity which he had felt for a stray child, his deadliest anguish came, that the desolation of dead hopes chilled his veins; and that he thought in the bitterness of his soul, "it was well said—call no life happy until its last day is seen."

The early evening had come by the hour he reached Chaumont; a stormy, crimson close of a midsummer day, with thunder-clouds rolling, unbroken, over the city.

"Where is Mi Minoux?" he asked of the people, giving them the password of their community. They answered him that their chief was there, in his own den; a lion whom no foe durst beard in his lair, a ruler whose word was as omnipotent, and vengeance as terrible, as though in lieu of his rage he had worn purples.

To that den he went straightway.

The Patron, heavy and spent from a night-long debauch to which a great robbery of alcohol and wine had given a rare power of furious indulgence, was stretched half asleep on a pile of sacks; his enormous limbs motionless like a gorged hyena's, his naked arms knotted above his head, his bloodshot eyes half closed. His cave was his audience-hall, his banqueting-room, his treasure-house, his shambles, his sleeping-chamber, his hall of judgment, all in one. Here and there gleams of smelted gold or broken jewels glistened out of the straw and ashes that strewed the ground; here and there a stain of blood darkened the bare rocky floor; a slaughtered lamb lay in one corner, a keg of wine stood half emptied in another. Watching him, there crouched, ready to spring up in obedience to his slightest sign, the half-nude form of the youngest of the women that he loved, with an Eastern look in her deep dark eyes, and a string of gold coins on her raven hair, and a jewel hung on her brown bosom. She was a greyhound that her master's whip lashed into abject submission, yet round whose throat he would lock a gilded collar.

He sprang to his feet as he heard a strange step; awake and alert on the instant with the vigilance of one who knows that his whole life is a crime, and that with every moment he lives free he robs the law of its rightful prey. As he saw who came he cast aside the knife that he had seized, and over his bloated face a gleam, that was a smile, passed for the instant. He raised himself almost on his elbow from his bed of sacks with a laugh.

"It is you! Do you come to beg another life? I will not promise you to let the next off so easily."

Tricotrin uncovered his head to the crouching girl with a grave courtesy, that made her eyes dilate in wonder. She was a thing that was alternately beaten with a whip and loaded with the fruits of theft; she knew only brutal blows and as brutal caresses.

"Do not belie yourself, Mi Minoux," he said, quietly. "Do not be ashamed of the one better action of your life. No: I come for a simple thing—to ask you if you have among you, as I have heard, a woman called Rose Léroux?"

Mi Minoux gave an indolent kick of his foot to the wanton beside him.

"Think for me, fool," he said, roughly. "Have we that name?"

"You call her fool!" said Tricotrin. "Well—truly she is one. To submit to your brutalities when she could steal out any day and sell your life to the law. Of such fools such men as you find many;—fools who love their tyrant, and are loyal, though their life is a hell."

Mi Minoux stirred uneasily. If any other living being had said this thing to him, his reply would have been to have lifted his club or drawn his pistol from his belt. Now, he felt a certain reluctant touch of shame.

"Oh, I am good enough to her—in my way," he muttered. "You would not leave me, Néra, because I kick you sometimes, or curse you a little?"

"Never!" she said, timidly and softly.

She did, indeed, love this man, whose wooing had been a union of violence and fraud, and whose kiss was commonly followed with a blow.

"Well—well!" he said, hoarsely, moved despite himself. "I never want to hurt you; you know that. It is only—you see, Tricotrin, it seems natural to beat dogs and women. They will not do well without. If they have not the stick, they want their own way. Léroux, you ask me?—Léroux? Yes; we have her, I know. What has she done?"

"I wish to speak with her; that is all."

"You do not want to give her up to the tribunals?"

"No. I do not want to do so."

"It must be for something bad she has done, that you ask after her? The brute has no friends."

"Poor wretch! Yes; it is for a wrong that she did once, but very long ago. I only require to question her; and I shall be glad if you can force her to tell me only the simplest truth."

"It is a hard matter to get them to tell the truth. You see—it is so much easier to lie; and they all get in the way of it. But I could order her, and she would hardly disobey, to be frank with you. You are sure it is nothing that will bring one into trouble?"

"Nothing. It cannot possibly concern you."

"Then I will take you to her. It will do me no harm to stretch myself; I am as sleepy as an owl." With many curses on the brandy that had made his eyeballs so hot and his throat so parched, he shook his ragged dress together into some sort of order, and went forth from his den to seek the lower part of Chaumont, where the woman, asked for, abode.

Mi Minoux knew all who came into this hive of crime whereof he was the center.

"You ask what Léroux is?" said the Patron, as they went along. "She is a dull, uninventive beast, with a tough will and a hard courage, but a stupid head; a woman that robs at mid-day, and lies drunk on church-steps, and is never two months out of the hands of the police. A chorus-singer!—oh, I dare say she was once; all the brains of those people lie in their lungs. Up yonder—to the right of the stair--where the red shirt hangs to dry."

Up where the tattered shirt hung on an iron spout that served as a linen-pole, was a wretched black den, full of squalor and filth; the recent rains had beaten through the hole that served as window, and drenched the floor. The only seat was a heap of rags; there was some water in a cracked pitcher, scores of mice were scampering to and fro, scores of spiders wove their gray webs in every nook, a toad squatted in a corner; blowing on some sticks to get fire was a disheveled, scarce-clothed, black-browed woman.

"Léroux, he wants to hear something; tell him all he wishes," said Mi Minoux, in their own tongue. "This is Tricotrin; answer him as you would answer me, without lies, or it will be worse for you. If I find you tell him one falsehood, you shall have a bullet down your throat."

The woman muttered a promise of obedience. The Patron's word was law at Chaumont. She stood staring, with her black eyes lusterless but savage. She had no apprehension; she was in the lowest deep; there was nothing worse to come.

Without preface he asked her straightly, when Mi Minoux had left them:

"You are Rose Léroux, to whom the child of Madelon Bruno was confided?"

"Ninie spoke of that to me this winter," she muttered, calling the Greek by his name in that quarter. "Ninie, whom they tried to burn as a spy. What is that thing coming up for now?—it is long enough ago!"

"You are the woman who took the child? Answer me that."

"Yes; I took the child," she assented, sullenly, mindful of her chief's injunction.

"And abandoned her?"

"I left it in the wood; that was nothing. Somebody always finds them."

"Where did you leave her?"

"In a knot of trees, aside from habitations, in the Loire valley. I have forgot what village it was near. It was distant from the highroad and the plain. I tied the child down, so that it should not crawl about for anybody to notice it until I had got away some leagues. That was nothing; that did not hurt it."

The sullen self-extenuation was half-ashamedly, half-ferociously urged,—pleaded against accusations that had not been made.

"What was your motive in her exposure?"

"To get rid of it."

"Why did you wish to be rid of her?"

"I wanted to get off to the west with all the money I had had for it. I could not be burdened with the little brute. If it had been Gérant's child, it would have been different; I would have done well for it; but he would not pay me more for this thing of Jean Bruno's; and I would not go to Coriolis. I hated her—the yellow-haired, lily-skinned, laughing thing! Gérant had told me she cared for the child; and I thought it might sting her to think it was dead. I had thought of that some time before; but where I kept it the woman of the house was a fool over it, and would have made an outcry if it had been missing. She thought I was miserably poor; and she fed the child almost for nothing. I had to spend none of the money on it. Else I should not have kept it a whole year. It was pretty, very pretty; I remember it. It had great black eyes like that sailor—its father: and all her yellow silk of curls. I remember it. What can you want to ask about it now? this is a score years ago, all I tell you. I never starved it, nor beat it; it was well enough with me. And as for leaving it in that wood,—it was warm weather, and I knew some one would find it; it was reaping-time, and there were people about. What have you come to me for when the thing is so old?"

She spoke with a restless, dogged, smothered dread and impatience, which, but for the command of Mi Minoux, would have found vent in wild ferocity and brutal defiance. She smote one of her bits of wood upon a mouse, and killed it; it was a relief to the violence in her, which she dared not let loose on her questioner.

He stood silent. The vague hope he had cherished was dead in him. The words and the accent of the woman bore the impress of truth. He could doubt no longer. And his heart was sick within him.

She looked at him, and spoke again, in irritation at his long silence.

"What is there to tell of that baby? You cannot have come here for nothing. I did not think any creature knew its name. It could hardly talk when I left it: and it called itself Viva—after a dog that it liked. It lived, I suppose; or this noise would not be made. I always thought it would live; it was a child that always laughed—laughed all day long,—never whimpered and whined. Those children always fare well; they are born with silver in their mouths. That is why they smile. What do you want of me? I have done things much worse than that since."

He roused himself from his silence, and resumed his examination of her. She told the same tale in all points that the Greek had given, more fully, and with many touches that proved its veracity. There was no falsehood, no contradiction, in the narrative; it was brief, strong, naked in its wickedness;—the wickedness, old as the world, of jealous hatred, and penurious greed, interwoven and reacting one on another, and bearing their common fruitage in crime. She felt no remorse, and but scant shame. To herself it seemed as a virtue that she had not drawn a knife across the child's throat, or held its head down in the mill-stream. All things are comparative; and, by comparison, this abstinence was marvelous and deserving of praise in her sight.

He endeavored vainly to shake her statements, or confuse her memories. She was speaking the truth, and he saw it:—saw that all hope was dead; and that for the life that he loved, there was no birthright save the dishonor of Coriolis.

"You will not harm me for this?" said the woman, doggedly, when she had ended. "I have told you the truth, as Mi Minoux bade me; you will not go and use it against me?"

He sighed in weariness and sickness of heart:

"Poor wretch! Is treachery so common with you? No; you are safe with me. You did a great crime,—whose roots and branches stretch where you never dream,—but you shall have no chastisement for utterance of the truth."

She regarded him with curious, dull wonder. She did not understand, but she felt vaguely that the law would not be summoned to deal with her.

"Does the child live?" she asked, abruptly.

"Yes—the child lives."

"And it is well with her?"

"Very well."

She bit her stick, that had killed the mouse, savagely with her strong teeth.

"Ah!—she thrives; she has Madelon's blood in her. Look,—Madelon drove that sailor mad; and sent her child away to perish; and fooled Gérant, and cheated him of all his wealth, to make her triumphs; and robbed her lovers in a day of more than I robbed from the streets in a twelve-month; and all she does prospers. She is called Coriolis: she is rich; she eats, and drinks, and laughs, and takes her pleasure; she is wooed by princes, and fingers the purses of kings. She thieves, and she cheats, and she murders;—but she prospers. And we—we go to the galleys!"

And she slew another little brown mouse with her billet of wood; the contrast of crime proscribed, and crime rewarded, was bitter.

What made the difference?

She herself had been handsome in the time of her youth, though now disfigured by drink and disease; she had been willing to sin in any fashion that came to her; she had been without scruple, without mercy, without remorse; she could not lay to her charge one fault of the weakness of virtue, whereby she had deserved less the successes of vice. Why then had life buffeted, and proscribed, and scourged, and starved, and imprisoned her, while it had lavished all fair things upon her rival?

She did not remember that she had once had one fault from which Coriolis had ever been free:—with all her brute nature she had been unwise enough to love.

She had loved the actor Gérant with a blind, furious, once generous, once unselfish, passion, that had borne her to wreck and ruin; and which, when it had been cast aside upon itself, had made her savage, and dull, and brutalized, and cunning.

She had been at one time his devoted mistress. The weakness had brought its vengeance. She dwelt here in squalor and horror, in ignominy, in starvation: it was only the woman who had never loved aught save herself who lived in perpetual ease, perpetual laughter, perpetual delight.

And she slew the little creeping mouse in the violence of her envy. When life has become unutterably horrible, unutterably irredeemable, unutterably hopeless, it finds its only luxury in cruelty.

A beggar can wield the same terror over his chained dog as an emperor can wield over his fettered nation; the equality in dominion has its sweetness for the fallen.

A fox, pursued by the hounds, once turned aside as it fled for its life, to seize a barn-door fowl by the throat:—the hunted human creature, with the baying of the law behind it, will also pause in its flight to enjoy the sweet sense of power that lies in the action of slaughter.

## CHAPTER XXXV.

The den above that which the woman Léroux tenanted in this hive of criminality — honeycombed with innumerable cells, that were filled with wretched famished idleness, or with the industry that only labors for guilty ends — was occupied by an old, feeble, sickly man, who was by trade a forger of false coin. He was a timid creature, who trembled if a leaf blew against him; he scarcely dared to pass his portion of the base money that he had worked; and he was very poor and miserable.

It had not always been thus with him: there had been a time when he had been a dramatic author and musical composer of no mean merit; when he had heard the sweet music of public applause; when the fair eyes of actresses had smiled on him; when his little, slight, airy, fantastic pieces, full of a sparkling mirth, which passed as wit, had been very popular in Paris.

There had been a time when the world had held for him pleasure, and love, and ease, and years of bright folly, and childlike glee, and ignorant extravagance; and, in a certain sense also, the charmed delusions of fame.

But then, on that time had followed another, when the tastes of the volatile public altered: when the weather-cock of popularity no longer pointed his way; when the same audience that had applauded with so much enthusiasm, hissed with equal acerbity; not because there was change or was fault in the thing that he gave them, but because they had tired of it themselves.

And then he, being weak and heart-broken, and ill made to do combat with the stern foes of censure and ridicule, of bankruptcy and ruin, had succumbed to his fate, and had sunk gradually down, step by step, into wretchedness, and at length into crime.

He never ceased to abhor the evil ways to which he had yoked himself, the evil comradeship to which he had become bound. He was never anything save a pitiful, trembling, faint-hearted servitor of sin. He had been harmless, generous, and of innocent though inordinate vanity, in the season of his successes; he was scarcely more harmful now, though the degradations of poverty had driven him into the acceptation of crime. For the rest, the world had forgotten even his name; none remembered it, save when some restless young tyro of the theaters turned over a repertory of old theatrical pieces; and he would have killed himself if he had only had the courage to inflict the one final, unknown, dreaded pang.

As he sat now, huddled on his bed of straw, and shivering, though the evening was sultry and full of storm, he heard the voices below him. A rat had gnawed a hole through one of the beams of the floor; and through the chink the sounds ascended distinctly to his ear. An instinct, that was the remnant of his earlier and higher life, moved him to plug the hole, and shut out the sounds; but as he was about to thrust a piece of wood in it, a word caught his ear that made him pause, and listen eagerly. The word was Coriolis.

He had been at the height of his own renown when the yellow-haired mistress of the singer Gérant had first appeared to the world of Paris. Her first effort had been made in one of his own slender, graceful, burlesqued comic operas. He remembered the night so well. He had the name of Coriolis interwoven with all his sweetest successes; and in a fond feeble fashion he had loved this gay creature from the far southern sea-shore, who had mocked him, dazzled him, and made him ridiculous in her boudoir, but who, on the stage, had conceived and represented to such perfection his own fancies. In his way he had a tenderness for her yet; though she still basked in the sunlight, and he had sunk into nethermost darkness.

Moreover, a few years earlier, ere he had lent himself to the forgeries which now made him fearful of venturing out in the daylight, he had timidly stolen to her one day, as she loitered in her villa gardens, and recalled himself to her recollection, and begged alms of her, weeping piteously at his own abasement as he did so.

Coriolis, who would be very generous with gold not her own, and liked to play patronage, had been good to him, and given him the contents of her purse, and sent her servants to him with choice meats and wines; and he had never forgotten these gifts. He had never gone to her again, for some touch in him of his better life had made him shrink from trading on a liberality that had so willingly befriended him. But he had never forgotten. Therefore he listened eagerly, setting his eyes also to the rat-hole, and peering down into the den below.

He recognized Tricotrin; and he heard all that was spoken.

And he remembered, as he heard, one night in the autumn of a year that had long died out from his memory,—one night, when he had been full as poor, but not as criminal as he had now become, and could move as he chose among his fellow-men at liberty, and had joined the throng of a Café Chantant; all the old inborn love of melody that he possessed urging him to spend one of his few copper-pieces on the hearing of song. Now, his own music had almost, by that time, ceased to be heard in Paris; it had not possessed the strength that lives; it had caught the crowds for awhile, but had speedily died off their lips and their ears. Still, here and there a chorus, a burden, a snatch of its tones, was sung by many who were ignorant of their author; and this night they had been sung at the café.

He had listened to them with the tears hot in his eyes; and at the light, buoyant mirth of their melodies, he had seen a child near him laugh, and clap her hands, and move with delight and ecstatic sympathy.

She had recalled to him the many faces that he had once seen reflect his harmonies thus. He had turned to her as it ended, and asked her, gently, "This pleases you?" She had answered, "Oh, yes! I never heard lovelier music!" and he had felt grateful to her. The people had begun hissing the song as old; and clamoring for a new favorite.

He had noticed the child, and the man who had been with her. The man he knew by sight as a friend of the artists, a peripatetic of the boulevards, an idol of the people; and he had asked who the young girl was that was with him. "Oh, that is only Tricotrin's Waif," had answered the painter whom he had questioned. "A foundling, I think they say; — his daughter most likely."

The memory of that night came back to him as he leaned over the rat-chink, watching and listening. With the subtle penetration which the suspicions and the expedients of his present mode of life had developed in him, he connected his remembrance of the girl who had then listened to his music, with the inquiries which he now heard asked.

"That Waif of his was the child of Coriolis," he said to himself, where he cowered on the floor. "Else why should he ask this of Léroux now? She is well in the world—that is all he will tell to this woman. It is well with her; she lives in happiness then, in greatness even, perhaps, who can say? Would Coriolis feel aught at that?—aught of regret or rejoicing?—if she knew?"

The sound of Tricotrin's footfall as it passed away down the crazy stair; the sound of the woman voice as it raised a tempest of oaths in fierce feud with her neighbor; the sound of the sullen heat-drops of the coming tempest beating on the broken roof; the sound of a young child's shrieks as some one beat it with furious blows in the court below;—all these came on his ear where he sat by the rat-hole, huddled in his rags, and thinking.

"Would it be any service to tell her that her child lives?" was the thought which revolved to and fro in his feeble, tired, vacillating mind. And the hunger of his body, and the extreme wretchedness of his estate, made a baser, meaner, lower thought, from whose coarseness and selfishness he shrank, intrude itself, and twine in with the first,

It was:—telling her, would he be likely, or unlikely, to receive some gratitude, some gift, some plate of food, some coin of gold?

## CHAPTER XXXVL

A MYRIAD of lights were glittering under the trees and upon the waters, in the place where the sailor of Riviera had fled, as from a devil, from the face of the woman who had dishonored him.

Gilded gondolas and boats, like many-colored shells, floated over the little lake. Lanterns of every hue glowed and beamed under the branches, and at the prows of the miniature vessels. Music, and laughter, and song, and the murmur of the cascade crossed each other on the stilly night air. The roll of carriages sounded ceaselessly through the darkness of the avenues beyond. In the houses on the lake there were crowds of gay idlers, and of women in their richest appareling, jesting, eating, making love in the coarse and witless fashions of modern dissipation. There were color, blaze, luxury, extravagance, pleasure, everywhere; even amid the deep, green, quiet woods, where ever and anon there broke the chorus of a song, or there flashed the sparkle of a lamp, or there glistened in a break of moonlight the hues of a woman's robes.

In one of those little caïques, with Chinese lanterns suspended at its prow, was a woman who leaned over the cushions of the boat's side, as she had leaned over the balcony of her mansion to watch the passage of the troops.

A glitter of green and silver enfolded her; there were huge gold serpentine coils upon her arms; there was a wondrous bloom of art, delicate as any sea-shell's, upon her face; she was smiling, and listening to a lover, in whose hand the oar rested idly. And she was pondering how little or how much he would be likely to pour into the bottomless pit of her debts; and thinking of the flavors of new sauces, and of the strange old wine a prince had sent to her; and of an oriental burnous, all interwoven with pearls and turquoises, that an oriental ambassador had given her at her asking; and of a torch-lit fête wherewith she had astonished the eyes of nobles at her villa the night previous.

For these were the things for which she had fled from Bruno; these were the things that to her made the paradise of life; these were the things which to her filled the whole soul and sense of a woman with never-ending, ever-renewing delight.

To Ninette, the gardener's wife, it was the fatness of fowls, the plenteousness of bread, the ripe abundance of plums and of gourds, the presence of many gold pieces in the earthen pot buried under the apple-tree, that made the measure of life's perfect peace. To Coriolis, the actress, it was the worth of the emeralds on her arms, the cost of the yellow wines in her ice-pails, the gigantic size of the mirrors in her supper-room, the weight and worth of her lovers' ability to bear her share in their fortunes. To Madame de Lirà, the Duchess, it was the magnitude of her proud estate, the supremacy of her power at the courts of the nations; the perfection of her diamonds, of her lace, of her horses, of her palaces; the extent of her subjugation of all the coldest and haughtiest that came near her sway.

But it was the objects alone that differed; the passion in all was the same; the one dominant feminine passion to possess, to surpass, to be rich in the possessions of life, to be content with the sweetness of the senses. The passions that kill their own souls, and make them kill the souls of their lovers and of their children—strangling them with a noose of satin, stifling them on a bed of roses.

The boat glided across the lake that is in summer so gay with its plaything freight, and in winter so gay with the evolutions of silver-heeled skaters; the spherical Chinese lanterns glowed rosily through the gloom; the answering laughter of challenged friends came mirthfully across the water from other lamp-lit vessels; the little skiff came lightly to the shore, touched by acacia-branches. She threw aside her green and silver covering, and stepped with careless feet on to the land, and went up, still with laughter, and love-words, and malicious jests, all intermingled, to their midnight dinner at the house beneath the trees.

There were crowds of guests, of equipages, of men and women sauntering to and fro. It was midsummer; the theaters were about to close; foreigners formed the chief part of the throng; but there were still thousands who thought nothing so well became those balmy night-hours under the blue starry skies, in the full beauty and fragrance of the year, as colored lanterns, and brandy, and high-seasoned dishes, and loud laughter, and music taken from the Taverns, and women begotten on the Walpurgis-Nacht.

Out of the gay, amorous, motley crowd, a young man glided, and came to the side of Coriolis, and murmured in her ear.

She left her own group, and went with him up the staircase and into a little chamber looking on the wooden balcony of the house: a chamber all gilding, and mirror, and velvet, and color, filled with the scent of burning perfumes.

She cast herself down on one of the couches, and folded her hands on its carved back, and looked up with her blue innocent eyes.

"What is it?" she asked.

There had been love once betwixt this man and woman: "love," as in lack of better language that is called which is, on the one side, a youth's ambition to be named in the mouths of gossipers with one of the loveliest and most notorious women of her day; and is, on the other, an adventuress's amusement in entangling and despoiling the boy who is, for the hour, as a gold-mine to her pillaging hands. There had been this love betwixt them; but, when its season had passed, there had come neither alienation nor distrust.

Neither had, in love, ever believed the other; but each had served the other, love having passed, with as much sincerity as was possible to their natures. He had been, indeed, a child in years to her, but she had found him no child in subtlety. She had seen that it was best to be well with him, a pretty snake, that had learned how to sting mortally ere he had reached maturity. He had seen that this woman, without principle, or conscience, or weakness of any sort, save the weakness of her own vanity, could serve him in fashions wherein he often needed service. They had been friends ever, in that unacknowledged bondage to each other which the knowledge of mutual sin and mutual use makes binding and inviolate on those who smile at oaths and laugh at loyalty.

Leaning against the window, he answered her now:

"You know the Duchess de Lirà?"

A steel-like glitter came into the blue serenity of her watching eyes.

"By sight—yes."

"My good Coriolis!—you only can know duchesses by sight. The gulf is so wide betwixt your practices and theirs! You seem to hate her by that look; do you, and, if so, why?"

"I hate them all!—why?—pooh! how can I tell? I hate them—just as cats hate dogs—so! The dog goes grandly past as if no cats were in existence,—well! the cat spits and scratches just to show it is not safe to ignore her, even though he may be a dog, legally registered and honored by men, while she is down in the law as vermin, and can only mouse for a living!"

"You are very candid."

Coriolis laughed again, her rich, light-hearted, contemptuous laughter.

"I always am. I do not mind being a cat at all; it is generally well with cats. They get the cream, and the butter, and the warm fire, and the soft cushions, if they get them surreptitiously; now your dog,—if it be legalized, it is taxed and muzzled, and if it have a place in the laws, it has seldom bones in its platter! As for the 'grandes dames'—pshaw! they are only copies of us; they copy our slang, our costume, our manners, every one of our amusements! One always scorns a *replica!* And now and then they give one a look—ah!—a look in the passages of the opera, in the crowd of the carriage-drive, the dog's look at the cat, see you; and then one could kill them! As for this de Lirà—this daintiest of duchesses!—I have hated her ever since she was first pointed out to me years ago at the theater. She looks so insolent, so cold, so arrogantly well-content! The other day a rose fell from my balcony into her carriage—ouf! she cast it from her as though it were plague-stricken! She shall eat of that rose some way ere long; and it shall be death to her!"

A look of cruel meaning passed over the mirthful clear radiance of her seraphic face, changing all its happy indifference, its sea-shell bloom. It was scarcely ever that this bitter passion disturbed the easy sunny temperament natural to her, but she had the feline instincts in her. She could resent, and wait, and deal her vengeance with sure aim.

He smiled.

"You have studied this duchess well, it would seem," he said to her. "Do you see no likeness in her?"

"No."

She saw none; she was not swift to combine indications; and she had that curious torpor of the imaginative powers which appears so often to characterize those whose career lies in the embodiment on the stage of the imaginations of others.

"Think twice," he urged, softly.

She obeyed him, ruffling her pretty yellow hair as her habit was in the torment of thought, and beating restlessly with her fan on the gilded wood of her sofa. She did not see, she did not guess; the resemblance which had sufficed for the coarse hatred of the dairywoman, and for the subtle intuition of the Athenian, escaped her. Coriolis had lived without thought, and she had little power of mental conception.

"Think twice," he urged, once more, "of a stray bird that once escaped you and me!"

She started.

"What! what! The child Viva!"

"Yes—the child Viva!"

"It is impossible! This woman is an aristocrat by birth!——"

"By marriage only. The duchess who cast out your rose from her carriage is the foundling who befooled and escaped us both at once."

Coriolis gazed at him with utter unbelief.

"It is impossible," she cried, afresh; "she came from north Europe, the daughter of noble people. She was an orphan in her infancy, and was adopted by their friend, the old dead duchess—so the story runs, as I have heard; and that man—half-fool, half-hermit—married her——"

"Oh, yes, he married her. I do not deny that. She is all that he could make her, and—she has forgotten that she was ever anything else. Nevertheless, it is true. This magnificent Cleopatra is the young fool that fooled us. How have I learned this?—never mind how, at first. When I saw her, I knew her; just one look on the stairs, and I read her face, and she mine. We have met with courtesy, parted with compliment; my lady is almost as fine an actress as you! But I know, and she knows that I know. Do you think she has slept in peace one hour since? I do not!

"I should have only suspicion in the stead of certainty, save for one false step of hers. It is this. It seems a year since she dismissed a steward of her late lord's from his rule at Lirà. He had been trusted, respected, well treated by the family for near thirty years, but—he displeased miladi. These hereditary sovereigns are so used to implicit submission, they cannot brook disobedience! He differed with her,

and neglected a command; she gave him his dismissal—
carelessly, as she would have brushed off a fly!

"The old man took it ill. But fair spoiled women never heed how they make such an enemy. People I have, who are skillful, told me this when I bade them gather all histories of miladi's victorious reign. The old man dwells now in Paris with his son, a jeweler. I have seen him. You can believe how little love he bears to this new mistress, who banished him from a thirty years' well-feathered nest because he combated one out of her thousand caprices.

"With some persuasion, and some payment, I got the truth from him. He told me, when I asked him straightly if it were not so, that she was what I thought. There had been only three persons of the whole Lirà household who had known whence she came—himself, his wife, and one of their sons, who was chasseur to the duchess. All three were devoted to their master, and would have perished rather than have displeased or babbled of him. The wife and son both died some years since; the old man only lived, to be subject to all the vagaries of his new mistress's will. She dismissed him; and the thorn rankled in him. Miladi was wise when she turned him away; those servile worms never turn! Well! —you see I speak on no fancy; I tell you a fact. This woman who gives you a 'dog's look' on the opera-stairs, this great lady who flings your rose into the dust, this duchess who goes to stare at you as a spectacle, is Tricotrin's Waif and Stray—is the baby Viva, who has proved herself wittier, wiser, keener in the strife of life than you!"

Coriolis heard him, breathless, and with her hands tight clinched. The treacherous, murderous glitter in her forget-me-not-hued eyes grew colder and more brilliant; the soft curves of her mouth straightened and grew hard; the laughter on her lips was merciless. Scathing, mocking words of hatred rushed to her utterance. It was bitter as gall to her—this thing that he told.

That child who had once gazed at her with such rapt admiration, that little bohemian in her red gipsy hood, that nameless creature that she had played with, and dressed up, and tossed sweetmeats to, in careless patronage, that young fool who had fallen so readily into her nets, and who had worshiped her as some divine being, was now this haughty woman, this superb patrician, this leader of fashion, who gave her the glances that kill, who swept past her as though naught of the same humanity could be in them!

"What—what!" she cried, aloud, while her sweet silvery voice became harsh and dissonant. "What!—that beggar-child a great duchess? that thing of hazard a court beauty? that golden-curled bastard a lawgiver of fashion? It is not true—it cannot be true. It is ridiculous to talk of rank in the same breath with her! What! a creature that a vagabond picked up on the highway, lifted on high like this? A baby that should have gone to the foundling houses, to the public charities, a Duchess de Lirà?—a little wretch that should have been reared in the hospitals and made into a sempstress, a fruit-seller, a flower-girl at the best, turned into a million-aire, a lady-of-honor, a glittering princess like this! Pshaw! you talk fables. We are not in fairy-land, to see such trans-formations!"

He smiled, and waited in patience till the tempest had spent itself.

"Am I like one who speaks idly?" he said, at length. "No: what I say now is true. It is the same face; only, what was Gretchen then, is Cleopatra now. That is all. Trans-formation! Is there any transmuter like the magicians of wealth and ambition? Down at Villiers, a woman—stupid, heavy, and coarse as any one of the cattle she tends—knew her; knew the features that failed to tell you their story. If I had no proof, I should not be less sure of the past that be-longs to her. It is true, however much you may doubt it. And I fail to see why you should doubt. Is the story of a man's infatuation, of a girl's ascendency, so rare? She had beauty, pride, tact, ambition,—these have kept her feet sure on the giddiest heights."

"But a duchess!—a duchess! It is ridiculous—incredible—intolerable!" she muttered, with something of that childish petulance with which she ever opposed what displeased her, deepened by an acrid envy and hate against this life that had once been in her hands like a fluttering, unfledged, caught bird, and now had soared to such vast heights above her. "A duchess!—that little, friendless, vanity-eaten, ignorant, superstitious, insensate fool, who adored me first as an angel of light, and then thought me a fiend out of hell! What! You tell me that imperial woman, who carries her head like a stag, and has a glance like an eagle's; that woman who sits at the opera covered with jewels like an empress out of the old world of fable; that woman who has every man who looks on her, her lover; and has palaces, and castles, and lands, and all that her soul can desire—is the child that I robed in my laces, that you sought as your mistress, that lived in an attic with a republican vagabond, that asked no better of heaven than to tread in my steps!"

And she laughed aloud, her eyes shining like the steel of a sword.

She no longer disbelieved, though disbelief was on her lips.

She had ever hated the child who had been tempted by her, with the hate that the wrong-doer ever bears to the wronged; hated her, if only for the sudden force, and loathing, and perception of her own evil life, that had broken in upon Viva at the last hour of her temptation, and released her from the fatal bewitchment of her sorceress.

Coriolis had supposed that swift punishment in the shape of poverty, and privacy, and hardship, and heart-sickness had overtaken the venturesome creature that had dared to defy and resist her. She had supposed so—whenever she had given thought to the matter: and it was like iron in her soul to believe that in the stead of these, all gracious things, and all proud glories, had fallen to the lot of this life in whose pollution and betrayal she once had failed.

"I tell you this," he said, slowly, in answer. "Do you imagine it is so welcome to me that I should dream it out of pure desire for her good?"

"You told me she was dead," she said, with a certain ferocity that crossed strangely the soft and even tranquillity of his own tones.

"I told you as I believed: they said so about Villiers; it was the popular belief in all the southern country of the Loire. It was certain, too, that she had disappeared from her home, and was no more seen by the side of that man, Tricotrin. I did not doubt what I heard; moreover, I was scarcely in the country—I lived chiefly at the Austrian court —I was soon consoled. I soon forgot her existence, although I did not forget——"

"That you would have your vengeance one day on the man, if the girl had perished," said Coriolis, with a certain impatience of his discourse. "No! we forget to love very rapidly: but I doubt if we ever forget to hate as long as there is any breath in us! Then you believe that when she fled from us, and disappeared from her garret, she went in all honor to those Lira?"

"I do not believe. I know," he made answer: and recounted to her all that the steward had told him, which was a simple history enough, and essentially truthful.

Coriolis heard him, still impatiently; beating her fan upon the gilding, loosening and tightening the gold coils on her wrists, leaning restlessly out over the wooden rail of the gallery, and breaking off the white clematis buds and throwing them out into the moonlit shadowy gulf below.

She could doubt no longer: and where the rays of a lamp from above caught her face, and made bright the gleam of the eyes and the smile, both were cruel as men never are cruel—cruel with the cold, slow, wakeful, deathless, unsparing hate of a woman.

For some moments when he had ceased to speak she was silent; only the rapid working of her hand, as it tore up the stars of the clematis, and scattered them out on to the darkness, told the fret and the rage of her soul.

Suddenly she flashed her glance on him.

"Look you!" she said, between her set teeth, with a violence he had never seen wake from under her sunny indifference. "I might have been greater than she, once. Anatôle was all mine; a fool who adored me, and who was in my power, and who would have wedded me, all prince though he was, because I know so much,—so much that he feared the world ever should know! And I lost all *that* because I was the wife of the madman who died at my feet,—on my stage,—this winter-time only, while this duchess of yours sat on high and looked on! I had as much beauty as she,—ah, God, there was nothing on earth so fair as I was!—I had in me the blood of the noblesse; I had the skill that holds a populace spell-bound; I had the charm that drives men to madness. And yet this bastard, found stray in a thicket, is throned in honor because she had the wit to be earlier faithless than I!—this nameless thing who was reared on the bread of an old peasant's alms passes me by in the passages of the opera-house with the cold calm of the aristocrat who does not even deign to perceive that such women as I are near, though the same hands make our robes, the same workers fashion our jewels, the same purses feed our fancies, the same lips caress our cheeks!"

In the passionate utterance of the words, Coriolis was transformed; she was for one solitary moment of her actual life possessed and moved by the emotions which she so long had counterfeited on the stage.

Her eye gleamed, her mouth trembled, her voice rang, under the inspiration of hatred, and envy, and of a vague shame that fought against her life-long repulsion of it; some feeling wakened in this careless, callous, mindless thing, some inarticulate pain stirred in her and found voice.

It was low, it was venomous, it was born of envy, and bitterness, and many an evil thing; but it was pain,—the first that Coriolis had ever known, save that which had dully smote her conscience on the night when a dead sailor lay in the house by the theater with a knot of sea-grasses and a woman's azure ribbon on his breast.

He who heard her now had perception of this; but no pity. He mused how best this would further his own desires.

"Well," he said, slowly; "well—if you have this against her, you can repay it now."

"How so?" she muttered, restlessly, breaking down the clematis flowers. "How can that ever be? She is what she is by law, you say; how can one touch her, or despoil her, or hurl her down?"

He leaned over the wooden railing by her side, and looked down into the gray soft night shadow broken with gleams of color and rays of light where the people moved below.

"You can do none of these; true. Her possessions, her titles, her dignities she must keep all her life through. But you can do almost as much as though you stripped her of these; you can make her subject to the world's contempt. You can fling her story to the hounds of slander, you can give all the women whom she has rivaled a poisoned dagger against her; you can leave her in solitude among her splendor."

Coriolis gave a fierce gesture of denial.

"If we leave her her riches and her titles, we leave her a herd of lovers, a crowd of friends! Does the world ever forsake what can feast it?"

"That is true. Nevertheless, you can deal her such bitterness that she will be lonelier in her eminence than any famished beggar that has ever asked her alms. She loves at last;—she is again about to wed:—one breath of disgrace cast on her, and the man she worships will let her die rather than ever trust her with his honor."

Coriolis looked quickly up: her eyes caught their look from him, her mouth laughed with ruthless joy, her breath came eagerly.

"Ah! that is well put. This man is——?"

"Estmere."

She laughed softly still, under her breath.

"I see! I see! How strange it is! Yet if he love her will he care? Men are such fools!"

"For her story? No. But for her shame he will leave her forever."

"Her shame! What is it?"

His smile was slow and very full of meaning, as he answered her.

"Forgive me; but—can we not say she was once beneath your roof? you see!"

She crushed a snowy cluster of the clematis blossom violently in her palm, and flung it forth into the gloom, and laughed still,—with her teeth hard set, and a warmth of sudden color on her face.

"I see," she murmured back to him. "Yes. It will serve —it will serve! She lies in the hollow of your hands; and— only the other day, I thought if I could see her mount the guillotine! For she threw my yellow rose in the dust—in the dust under her carriage-wheels!"

## CHAPTER XXXVII.

As the light silvery robes of Coriolis swept through her moonlit garden toward dawn, a frail tremulous creature, hiding beneath the myrtles and hydrangeas, stole forth and touched her timidly.

"Madelon—Madame—may I have one word with you?"

She turned and gazed at him in surprise. None save those who had known her in her earliest years ever called her by that name.

"It is you, Fleurus! Hiding there like a thief! What is it you want? money?"

He quivered a little. The time had been when his aid and his heart had been passionately craved by the young, unknown, ambitious mistress of the actor Gérant.

"I am no better than a thief," he whispered. "Still, I do not come for alms. I come to tell you something that may be of service. For the sake of the past——"

His voice broke down. That past was so sweet, so irrevocable, so utterly forgotten by the world! She smiled, and carelessly motioned him to follow her through the glass doors of a lighted chamber that looked on the gardens.

"Speak quickly," she said, casting herself on a couch. "I am tired, and it is almost daylight. I will do what I can for you—short of reviving your little operas!"

He winced under the contemptuous laugh. Those slight, airy, sparkling, world-forgotten pieces had been the stepping-stones to her fame!

"It is not that," he said, hurriedly. "It is—do you ever think of your child?"

Her eyes opened in amaze.

"What child?" she muttered.

"The child of Jean Bruno."

She started slightly, and her face clouded.

"Fool! what do you talk about?" she said, with impatient contempt. "A child dead a score years ago!"

"She is not dead——"

"She is. What are you driving at?—I do not understand—speak out plainly."

"I do. She never died. She lived to womanhood—she lives still——"

"That is folly! What impostor has cheated you into this nonsense? Why do you bring these stupid things up?—I hate them. They make me feel old!"

A certain sense of remorse stole on her. She had never thought of this child twenty times in as many years; but she thought of it now, as she had last looked on it, asleep in its boat-shaped cradle, with a plume of sea-weed in one hand, and its fair curls tumbled and tossed in the summer heat.

The wretched Fleurus was frightened; he had hoped to pleasure her.

"It is true, indeed," he murmured. "I thought you might wish to know. And all is so well with her, they say——"

"Who say?" she said, fiercely, for the bitter passions awakened in her that night were still in the ascendant. "You are a fool, and have been told some ludicrous lie to chicane you. Who has been talking to you of these by-gone things? Answer me!"

And he told her: omitting no word that he had heard by stealth in his garret at Chaumont. Coriolis listened, with a tempestuous shadow on her face, and her eyes by turns incredulous, contemptuous, startled, angered, and wondering. She felt neither joy nor sorrow; she was only moved by a restless sense of impatience against these things of her long-buried past, that would thus arise and pursue her, and force her to think, and remember, and, in a vague sense, to regret.

In a vain, gay, childish fashion she had been pleased with her infant's beauty. She had been amused to put its fair face and limbs in contrast with the brown sunburnt children of the neighboring cabins; she had been willing to toy with it, and be painted with it as Venus and Love, Mary and Christ, by traveling painters. But in a sense, also, she had hated it as an emblem of her bondage, as a type of her obscurity, as a constant reminder of the passion of which she was so unutterably impatient. She had forsaken it willingly; she had never thought twice of its fate. She listened in indifference, touched with anger, and with scorn.

"So!" she said, with a laugh that was bitter; "the woman lied to Gérant, and Gérant lied to me, and the child was left to grow up a living lie—if your tale be true. Well! that is all very fitting as the world goes. She ought to have prospered. Where is she now?"

"Ah! that is more than I can tell. The man did not tell that to Léroux."

"But who is the man? You saw him?"

"Yes, I saw him. He is a bohemian. The people care for him. They call him Tricotrin."

"My God!"

The cry of habit broke from lips which ever mocked in their sport at all deity and all faith. She rose impetuously from her indolent rest; there was a look on her face that terrified the timid soul of the old dramatist.

"You lie!" she cried, with that ferocity which had only arisen in her that night, transforming all her soft, gay grace. "You lie! You are sent here to blind me with this story, to disarm me against her, to seal my lips as to her past! He has put his wretched stray thing on high among princes; and because I know and can ruin her, he sends you to baffle me, and unnerve me with this fable about Bruno's child. You are his tool—his mouthpiece—confess it! This is a wretched, senseless, baseless lie!——"

The old man quailed before her; bewildered and wholly ignorant of her meaning.

"As Heaven is my witness," he cried, desperately, "I tell you the simple truth. I have never spoken with him in all my life. And as for her—I know not what she is; whether princess or beggar. It seemed bitter to him; and only freshly learned by him. I tell you only that which I heard. Why do you doubt, only because I have said the man's name? You did not seem to doubt while I told you. You seemed to know that it was to the woman Léroux that Gérant gave the child when you fled with him."

"Silence!" hissed Coriolis. "What if I knew—what if I knew? I thought the child dead. I believed the tale that they told me. Why have you stirred my belief? Why have you brought me this accursed truth now? Why have you not told me this thing either sooner or later! She—she—that woman who loathes me, that creature I hate, is the child that I bore, and suckled, and held to sleep in my bosom! The daughter of Bruno that cold empress, who passes me by in the height of a great lady's scorn! Ah, devil!—beast!—that you are to have told me! Out of my sight—out of my house! or I will give your body to the tribunals, and your soul to hell, if a hell there be! Off—do you hear me? My child—mine! Great Heaven, if only you had held your peace for one day later!"

The miserable Fleurus, gathering his rags about him, gazed at her trembling still, but with a dignity in his look, a passionless rebuke in his eyes.

"I might have known it," he said, slowly. "The woman who dishonors her husband, forsakes her lovers, and forgets her friends, can have nothing of womanhood left in her save its passions and its cruelties. I have told you the truth; seek Léroux if you doubt."

And without another word he turned and passed away.

When the morning came, a dead body was found floating in the river above Surennes, in which none of those who saw it recognized the man whose melodies once had echoed from all the laughing crowds of Paris.

Coriolis stood motionless where he had left her; she had no memory of him, she was paralyzed by the truth which had come to her from his lips. She strove to doubt, but she could not. Truth for once was stronger than this fair liar, whose art it had been through so many years to breathe life, and substance, and power, into the falsehoods of fictitious woes, fictitious joys, fictitious passions.

That vague horror which had moved her when her husband had fallen lifeless at her feet, returned on her now. She did not feel remorse, nor regret, nor yearning, nor shame. But she felt fear,—a shapeless and nameless fear,—a fear of her own sins.

In her lighted chamber, in her festal robes, in all the gay costly glitter of her summer-night's appareling, she stood cold, numb, stricken—appalled by the specters of her past.

There was not in her tenderness, or pity, or repentance. There had been no place for them in the supreme egotisms of her youth; there could be no place for them in the seared sensualities of her maturity. She had never loved aught save herself. Husband, or lover, or child, had never been more to her than the flower worn in her bosom one day, to be tossed aside unremembered the next. She hated with deadliest hate the woman who had passed by her with that cold disdain, who had thrown her rose into the dust of the street with that gesture of loathing aversion:—hated her but the more because the tie of this close union was between them, because the blood of Bruno flushed those scornful lips, because those eyes that had swept over her in that chill scorn were eyes which once had smiled in hers the dreaming smile of infancy.

She hated her but the more; she had cried out in her fury against the accident which had revealed this truth to her ere her vengeance had struck its blow; she had no mercy in her heart, no yearning for the pardon of the creature she had wronged,—only hate, hate—the bitterness of hate, for the little child she had forsaken when it had been sleeping in the hot summer noon down by the southern shore, as for the superb patrician who had smitten her with the pang of dishonor by a look. Yet there was that in the horror of this,— —their mutual fate,—which daunted and terrified even her hard, light, wanton nature. There was that in this destiny which brought her face to face with the guilt of her earliest youth, that froze the life even in this frivolous, inconsistent, mindless, merciless courtesan.

In this very chamber she had spread her nets for the unwariness of innocence, and tempted the guileless faith that saw in her such divinity, and sought to draw down to destruction this soilless life that had sprung from her own, as the purity of the lotus springs from the corruption of the river.

She had been the temptress of her daughter's soul.

And there was that in the unnatural horror of her sin which overcame her, and was stronger than all her levity and all her wit, and cowed her with a ghastly sense of crime that made her crouch as beaten hounds crouch to the lash. She had no fear of chastisement, no fear of a future life, no fear of man or God; but this at length she feared,—the infamy of her past.

Suddenly she started, and looked up at a clock above her; it was not yet dawn.

"There may be time—it is a chance," she murmured, and she threw her cashmeres over her, and bade them bring forth her night-horses once more, and drive back whence she had come.

There was scarce a league betwixt her gardens and the park-gates of Boulogne. They took her swiftly as the winds. In the house by the lake there were still lights, and music, and noise, and carriages rolling away in the gray of the breaking morning. The last embers of its revelries still glowed.

She alighted and moved toward it, her eyes glancing hither and thither; a group of men and women, wild with hot wines and mad vice, reeled out in the soft shadows, chanting boisterously a chorus of a new opera: she saw among these rioters the one whom she needed, and went among them and drew him away. He was not drunk like his companions; he understood and obeyed her. He went passively where she led,—into solitude, under the trees by the lake. They were as utterly alone as though they had stood in the heart of a western forest. A wall of green enshrouded them, the still water lay at their feet; the only sound of the life that was around them was the sound of the rioters' chorus growing fainter as they passed farther away.

"What is it? Why are you come back?" he asked, hurriedly, noticing the strange colorless intensity upon this face that had never known grief, nor shade, nor thoughtfulness.

Her hands clinched on his arm.

"We must let her be!" she said, sullenly. "We must leave her to her honors and glories; we cannot touch her--we cannot."

He looked at her in amaze.

"And why not? A woman's vacillation in *you?*"

She laughed; and the laugh was as mirthless as the dreary dull mirth of the singers.

"We cannot!" she echoed; and there was an accent in the word that told him the renunciation was very bitter to her, wrung from some other power in her than her will or her pity. "We have wronged her enough—you and I. We must let her be."

He gazed at her, in incredulous scorn.

"Coriolis!—are you mad? An after-thought of remorse from *you!*"

"Pshaw!" she said, fiercely, in her shut teeth. "Remorse! Who talks of remorse! I am not a fool. There is nothing to repent of;—I have enjoyed, I have always enjoyed. I would not change any of it if I could. It has been sweet enough all these years. Remorse! you prate like a poet! There is none in *me.* But we must leave her alone, I tell you. Listen, listen:—she is the child of Bruno!"

"Of Bruno!"

He repeated the name without comprehension. In his world the past of Coriolis was scarcely known. She had abandoned some husband for Gérant; she had come from obscurity; she had been once the wife of the mad fisherman who had died on her stage; this he knew, but indifferently, and with indifference. What to him or the world was the early life of a woman who, having none who cared for her future, had none who asked of her past?

"Well! do you not know now?" she muttered through her teeth that were still shut. "I was his wife!——"

He started from her side as the light broke on him, and stood gazing at her by the clear rays of the morning stars. Cold and cruel though his nature was, it was a shock that went home to him.

"*You* are her mother!" he said, breathlessly, while his voice was drowned in the drunken song of the revelers that came to them through the depth of the trees.

She laughed, that laugh which made even him shrink and feel a sense of fear. Not because there was in it any great grief, or any sort of despair,—these were not possible to her,

—but because it was so utterly without these; so entirely the laugh that rang over her wine, her wit, her lovers' flatteries.

"Her mother—yes! It makes one feel old. That sea-cabin down in the south, so dark, and narrow, and wretched, —ah! it was all very well for an actress's nest, you think, but unfit for the birthplace of that great duchess! I can smell its salt scent; I can see its nets and its creels; I can remember its steep leaning roof, and its path cut in the rock, and the eternal sough of the waves down below. Ah, God, how I hated them all! He was her father—Bruno. She has his great, dark, dreaming eyes. I ought to have known them when they looked at me first!——"

"But—great Heaven!—how have you learned this? I cannot comprehend——"

She told him. He heard in silence, as she had listened to Fleurus.

"There is no doubt, then!" he said at length, with lingering doubt in his accent.

"No doubt!" she said, as she stood looking straight at the still starlit water, with that curious look of scorn and of pain, of passion and of levity, on her face. "It is the daughter of Bruno that gave me that look in the opera! Things are strange! When I first saw her face in the gray dawn, on the day of her birth, I did not think;—pshaw! if women ever did think of their children's future, they would strangle them the same hour that they are born! I left her—oh, yes! She was his child, and I was so weary of him! So it comes back, you see—things do. I do not hate her less; I think I hate her more. She is on such heights; she is so cold, so proud, so pure, so great—and she shudders when a rose that has touched my hand touches hers!"

When she had sunk down on a bench by the lake, she gazed fixedly at the gleam on the water; forgetful of her companion. Some sense of the dreary unnatural horror of this destiny that had thus enfolded these women held him silent.

The chorus of the rioters had ended, the lights were out in the pleasure-places, there was no sound save the sighing of the trees, the trembling of the wind upon the water.

"I hate her more," she muttered. "That creature is mine, and yet scorns *me!*" I hate her more. But I cannot hurt her. I dare not. She must never know what I know— never. She was in the theater that night when he died; she was laughing, and covered with diamonds. God! how strangely things work!"

Her voice fell again; he said nothing. A sense of terror oppressed him at the ghastly fate which thus had brought, in her utter unconsciousness, the daughter of both to be witness of the death of the one, of the shame of the other; yet a sense of exultation moved him also at the added vengeance given to his hands.

"You will keep this secret?" she said, fiercely, as she suddenly looked up. "I have many of yours in my keeping! Answer me: you will leave her in peace—now?"

He made no answer.

"You will leave her in peace?" she said, again. "We owe her that—you and I. How we strove to net her, and chain her, and drag her down to our depths! And she was mine all that while! Is there really a devil, I wonder? You will let her be—now? Answer me—you will let her be?"

The slow, soft smile she knew so well stole over his face.

"Coriolis:—if you have your daughter's honor to keep, I have my father's honor to save."

And almost ere the words were breathed, he had glided quickly from her, and was lost in the blackness of the woods.

She did not stir, she did not cry out; she sat still, with a scared look in her eyes. For the first time in all her many seasons of success, she had been deceived. Her secret was his, to deal with as he would. She had only brought to his hand the poison wherewith he could make mortal the dagger-thrust he already was free to deal!

"Oh, fool—fool—fool!" she said in her soul. "When did you ever know him spare!"

An hour earlier, she had mourned that her vengeance was stricken from her grasp; now a sickly horror of what she had done possessed her. Husband and child—had she not wronged these both enough already?

The gloom of the trees inclosed her; the wind sighed wearily over the water; the stars faded, and the dawn came. When the morning broke, Coriolis still sat there, with her eyes still fastened on the stillness of the pool, and the red flush from the east tinging as with blood the opals in her bosom.

She had not remorse; she had not pity; she had not grief; but she had fear—fear of the dead sins of her dead years, that broke from their graves, and came and faced her here.

## CHAPTER XXXVIII

THAT night there were tumult and tempest in Paris. Though the jests passed, and the jewels glittered, and the buffoonery rioted, and the equipages rolled in all her light places of pleasure, none the less in the dark lairs of want, and of woe, of restless thought, and of fretting passions, was the lust of revolution making keen the eyes of men, and heating their blood as flame.

Children glowing with the stories of Hellas; youths burning with youth's noble madness; man lashed to fury and blindness by some friend or some brother's prison-agonies; students sick with the dire disease of the old world's endless corruption; these again, as times countless before, were eating their hearts out in weariness, and feeling helplessly in the darkness for truth, and counting no possible wrong in the future could be so great as the wrong of the present, and willing to cast their lives in the dust under the wheels of the cannon, if only from out of their death deliverance for their people might come. And again, as times countless before, these—the world's divine madmen—were foiled, and spurred on, and beguiled, by the brutes of sleek tongue and strong sinew, who desired to light the torches of freedom, only that they might toss them into the stores of the rich, and who crazed with their lips for the seizure of tyrants because in their hearts they were thirsting for the seizure of treasuries and granaries.

It was the story, so old and so weary; the story that would break the strength and the spirits of men if they paused too long to muse over it; the story of high thoughts, and pure dreams, and impossible hopes, fused in with base greed, and base cant, and base envy; the story of idealic ambitions, soilless as snow on the mountains, finding no better comrade and issue than the charlatan's screech to the mob, and the demagogue's rage against power. The eternal story, without an end—young as the days of Mentana, old as the Hellenic ages.

"There will be work to-morrow," said Mi Minoux, showing his great wolfish teeth with a laugh of grim joy, as he passed down, through the evening shadows, from the den where Rose Léroux dwelt.

"Work!" Tricotrin echoed, wearily, not thinking at that hour of his meaning.

The Patron touched the knife that hung at his waistband.

"They say the students are rising!" he said, with indifference as to who might hear; in his own kingdom he was above the law. "They will be shot down, of course. The government is strong, and they are fools; but while they are up, it is high jinks for us. We have always a good time of it. For my part, I wish they would have a game of barricades every week."

And he drew his hand across his throat with a significant gesture; he had drawn it across other throats than those of lambs.

"It will be an affair of children," continued Mi Minoux, his tongue still loosened by the lasting fumes of the alcohol. "Nothing else. They are wild because their darling has been arrested for that demonstration at the Lycée. They are fools! The government knows of this—oh, yes—but it lets them go on a little while. They will rise, and they will arm, and they will sing the Marseillaise—all very fine for a few hours—and then—ponz! the cannon will clear the streets of them. It is always so. And meantime we—we shall plunder the houses! Oh, I like that trade of yours, Tricotrin—what you call it—patriotism! It is very much like ours—when everything is said. They work together amazingly well!"

Tricotrin made him no answer; his heart was heavy with a bitter sense of utter weakness against the mailed might of circumstance, the merciless cruelties of chance.

He knew well that the rough reasoning of Mi Minoux had its germ of a terrible truth in it; he knew well that the coarse wisdom of the law-breaker foresaw the sure issue of the unequal conflict with which the time was pregnant. But he heard only dully; he had not the strength left in him to reply.

The dead weight of his own pain numbed in him all other sorrow for all other things. The power of sympathy was numbed in him by the deadness of hopeless regret. The impersonal was for once killed in him by the force of the personal; as it is oftentimes killed, from birth till death, in many lives.

He gave the Patron a brief good night, and went down through the long steep road that led back into Paris. Evening had just fallen, and the first drops of the coming rainstorm, the first sullen roll of the thunder, gave their warning of the tempest that was gathering slowly in the west. It might break that night, it might drift away for a brief season and leave the skies in semblance clear again; but it was in the atmosphere—hot, sickly, terrible; making the air troubled, and the wind winged with pestilence, keeping the parched earth waiting like a captive bound and athirst.

As he passed through the quarter, the people stood in groups before the doors of their wretched dwellings. The women, ragged and filthy, leaned out of their windows with their eyes gleaming in exultation from under their shaggy brows. Here and there, one had twisted up her unkempt hair under a red kerchief; here and there, one shrieked fierce, foul invective against the decent and the rich. In general they were very quiet, and had the still, dogged, watchful look of those who pant for action but wait perforce for a word of command.

They were the terrible daughters of terrible mothers,—offspring of those women who once rose at the beat of the drum in the quarter of St. Eustache, and poured out down the roads of Versailles, till even in the voice of the lion there was fear as Mirabeau muttered—"Paris marche sur nous."

He never looked up at them; he never noted them, as he passed through their streets and their lanes. His head was sunk, his eyes saw nothing; his thoughts were filled only with this lineage of evil, this heritage of shame, that were all the birthright of that proud, scornful, fearless life which believed that it had sprung from the purple bed of a Porphyrogenitus.

One of them placed herself in his path, a woman of thirty years, with a head fit for Pallas Athene, and a body strong and sinewy as the frame of a cart mare, with her bosom bare, and her arms akimbo, and her garments all in rags.

"Tricotrin!" she cried. "What ails you?"

He started, and gazed at her like one awakened from a trance.

"Your own malady—unrest," he answered, curtly, and strove to pass her. But she would not let him go.

"Tricotrin!" she muttered, with her lips close to his ear as she reached up to whisper, "you know?—you know?"

"Yes. I know."

He knew that she spoke of the insurrection seething in embryo in the minds of many.

"And you are with us as of old?"

"I can never be against you."

"But you will not take leadership, they say?"

"No. I will not. Not to lead children into a pit of hellfire. But why are you in it—you,—a woman?"

Her eyes glowed like those of a lioness.

"Women have made many revolutions!"

"Ay; they have. Revolutions merciless, murderous, narrowed to personal wrongs, mad with the rabies of hate, inspired by the lack of bread on their platters—revolutions that recoiled in the end on themselves; like all revolts on all women!"

Her dark face grew full of rage.

"Why should not women be patriots as well as men?" she muttered. "We can stab!"

"Ah, truly! And you never think that when the stab lets the life out of a tyrant, it gives him in return all the might of martyrdom. Women can be patriots?—yes. By other ways than the dagger. You are a patriot—you—Athénaïs Var?"

"To the death!"

Her black eyes flamed; her mouth set. She believed what she uttered; she was drunk with desire to be one with Corday and Théroigne in the memories of the people.

"That is well. And what is your calling?"

She flushed under her dark skin; her infamy was in rags, but it was the same that Coriolis covered with satins.

An infinite sadness, half pity, half scorn, wholly sorrow, was in his gaze as it dwelt on her.

"Ay! A patriot!—and your trade to lead your country's sons into evil! Can you give tyrants better mockery of patriotism than that? When women gather no more in the bagnios, and drink no more in the taverns, and flaunt no more in the ways of vice, and no more lure and lead the youths down into ruin, then will it be time for women to talk of politics and patriotism."

A strange emotion flitted over the woman's handsome face.

"Théroigne was vile," she muttered; "and she helped shatter the Bastile! That was something?"

"It was. But to purify and make honest her own life had been something also,—something greater and something harder. Having some germ of genius in her, she would do something—poor wretch! It was easy to inflame the mob; it would have been severe to bridle her licence. So she rode astride of a cannon; and left all her vices to flourish. Do you the other way;—leave the cannon to soldiers; and go combat your passions. Be not a coward who leaves the near duty that is as cruel to grasp as a nettle, and flies to gather the far-off duty that will flaunt in men's sight like a sun-flower."

She looked at him with a look like the look of a dumb beast that is half savage, half timid, and hung her head.

"You are right," she said, sullenly, as she turned away. "Women are cowards; they are afraid to starve!"

He went onward, losing all thought of her as his memory drifted back to the fate of the creature he loved. Many strove to arrest him; but he waited with none any more. Yet he walked on without aim, without destination; walked on merely in that wanderer's impulse that was in him to find his way out into the open country, and to lose all pain in motion, and air, and the sweep of the winds, and the width of the heavens.

The streets were crowded. The lamps were hung for the festival of the morrow. The populace were taciturn, feverish, gloomy; watching the preparations with angry, sullen eyes. Every face wore a look of hushed, vague, unquiet expectation, save the faces of the indolent idlers, whose carriages swept in endless motion through the gaslit avenues. Every now and then, there passed some student, or artist, or workman, who wore in his shirt a spray of the gray lavender that was piled in such odorous heaps in the flower-markets:—it was the rallying sign of the morrow.

He went through them, on and on, noting nothing until,

as he took his way without thought, he came close to two bronze gates set in a massive wall. He looked up, and shuddered. They were the gates of the great Lirà Palace.

There were many people about them, many laced liveries, many hurrying pages; and men were lighting the lamps that would make the frontage one blaze of light.

"Is your mistress in Paris?" he asked of one thus busied.

The man, garrulous and good-tempered, turned and laughed.

"She came an hour or two ago. It is her fête to-night to the princes. I thought every one knew that. Look at these lamps, three thousand of them. And each one cost five francs a piece! Fine times, are they not?—for the lampmakers!"

"Is she well?—your mistress?"

"Well? I suppose so. She can eat and drink silver and gold if she likes! I saw her go through to-day. She was very pale, now you speak of it. You know she is to wed with that foreign lord—what is it?—Estmere? So her women tell me. They say it is a love-marriage; that is rare among these people."

And he turned again to the lighting of his three thousand lamps.

Tricotrin went onward.

The lamplighter looked uneasily after him.

"Look you," he said to his comrade, "that man moves like a man I once saw struck by a bullet; he walked like that, with the ball in him; but twelve hours after he was dead."

## CHAPTER XXXIX.

"THE storm passed?" said the carver of ivory, standing out in the hot sulphur-scented night before his threshold.

Tricotrin glanced at the skies; they were starlit and very clear.

"For a season," he made answer. "It will be but the heavier when it falls."

The carver regarded him in anxiety.

"Is it true," he murmured; "true that the students to-morrow——?"

Tricotrin pointed to the skies.

"Who can say when the tempest may break? It is in the air. It may pass—it may come."

Clerot shuddered.

"Tempests kill?"

"Ay. They kill. But more mercifully than the corruption-born plagues that they sweep from the earth. Is it worse with Jacques Bénoit?"

"It is worse. He sinks surely, and he is light in the head; he talks foolishness."

He asked no more; he went up the dim stairway to the place where, high in air, pent among the peaked masked roofs, was the attic where the old man lay, slowly dying, and muttering foolishness,—of the old mill-stream, and the sweet pine-woods, and the shining yellow sands, of his birth-country. These were all that he saw now; though for sixty years he had stitched, and stitched, and stitched, till his eyes were blind, over the black foul-smelling leather in the garrets and workshops of Paris.

His mind was gone; but over his face glimmered a smile as he heard the voice of his only friend, and his withered hand crept feebly forth to meet a grasp that it could return but for a moment.

"Thou comest from Leuzarch," he muttered, thinking still of his birth-hamlet in the west. "Thou hast the scent of the pines, and the song of the lories, with thee——;" and with that he ceased his feverish babble, and was very still, with the smile yet about his mouth, and a curious, listening, happy brightness on his face.

Tricotrin watched by him through all the hours of the night;—a heap of straw his couch; the only light a wretched flame upon the hearth that warmed a little iron pot of soup for the sick man; above, in the sloped ceiling, the narrow space they called a lattice, through which the blue and starry skies gleamed curiously. By instinct—the instinct taught by many such vigils as this, which had been common in a life that men had deemed wholly of pleasure—he served all the few sad needs of this death-bed, whose disease was simply age. But, for himself, he had no other consciousness than that of the keen, hard agony within him, that still dulled all his senses to all other things.

To that little garret, so high in air, so far from the lighted streets, so near to the starry skies, there came no sound of traffic or of speech to call his thoughts to the ways and the wants of men. All the day, and the night preceding the day, he had spent among the attics, and the cellars, and the painting-rooms, and the secret haunts of Paris, arguing with those whose young souls were set on impossible dreams, whose young lives were eager to be thrust forward to the slaughter. All the night and all the day, until he had heard the Greek's tale, he had bent all the strength, and the mind, and the suasion, and the genius in him, to hold back from their madness these children who dreamed of a millennium, and rushed on to the mouths of the cannon; who murmured of Harmodius and Aristogiton, and stumbled blindfold to the bench of the galleys.

But now, where he sat in the narrow, dusky, moonlit garret, with no sound on the silence save the slow, gentle breathing of the old man, who had ceased to babble of the pine-wood and the lories, and who slept on his hard knotted

bed as he had used to sleep in childhood on the moss under
the firs,—he had forgotten these; he had forgotten the things
that had been nearest and holiest to him through all the
years of his life; he had forgotten all except the passion
which consumed him.

When she had gone from him in her youth, his rivals
had been riches, and vanities, and all the manifold temptations of the senses—rivals he had scorned while he had
cursed them. But now—in her womanhood—his antagonist
was that love which he had bade her follow; his spoiler was
the man whom he had bade her honor.

All his life long no taint of greed had darkened his
thoughts against the possessor of his heritage; no pang of
grief had stirred in him for all that he had forfeited. When
the calm wisdom of maturity had surveyed that rashness of
boyish chivalry, no single desire, no solitary envy, had made
him wish the past undone. There had been but one regret
in him—the regret that with all the affluence and power
which his act had conveyed away to Estmere, it had not
been his also to give with them the four-leaved shamrock of
perpetual joy.

The passage of the years—which kills all things—had
never killed in him the tenderness of early memories, the
nobility of early impulse. Envy had never touched him—
can the king who voluntarily abdicates, envy the successor
whom he has of his own will lifted to a throne, that he, himself, may roam the earth unchallenged, and live in the sweet
peace of unwatched freedom!

It was only now,—now when the beauty of a woman was
the thing of his desire—that he cried out against this fate
which made the holder of his heritage, the owner of his
treasures, lord even of this also.

Above the little casement, in the roof, the stars grew
larger with the coming of the dawn; the flame of the cold
hearth died down, and left but the gray sickly ashes there;
the rats, growing bold in the silence, stole forth and rustled

beneath the straw on which he sat. There was not even on the stillness the breathing of the old man in his slumber.

For, once, when he himself had arisen, and had gone to the pallet where the cobbler lay, he had listened and heard no sound, he had put his hand to the sleeper's lips and felt no warmth, he had looked closer by the clear light of the moon, and had seen that the deep tranquillity of death had stolen over the grim, dark, wasted, withered face, which had a smile upon it as though in his last hour he had heard the lories singing.

He had closed the lids softly over the old dim eyes that through the mists of dissolution had once more seen the purple hills and the wide woods of the country of their youth; and he had gently folded together on the breast the aged hardened hands that had worked on in ceaseless toil for the bare needs of life, but never had been outstretched for alms since their palms had been soft and rosy in an infant's years, catching in mirth against a mother's skirts. Then he had gone back to his place, beneath the roof-hole, where the stars shone through; and thus he still kept vigil there,— alone with the dead old man, and with the knowledge that was bitterness passing that of death.

He held in his hand the truth that would tear these lovers asunder.

But—to use it? He recoiled from the power as men recoil from thoughts of murder.

A season earlier, truly, he would have forbade her to enter the life of a man with any lie left in her own. When she had been his, he had not suffered her to go to her chosen future with one false thing to stain her innocence. By every law that binds the consciences of men, he knew that to withhold her history from one who should stand to her in a husband's place was to do dishonor, treachery, and a craven wrong. He knew this;—a day sooner he would have forced its truth on her without mercy, and compelled her to obey its dictates. But now,—this severity of justice looked no better than the brutality of vengeance.

The stern simplicity of perfect truth which he had ever followed, as men lost at night upon the moorlands follow the polar star, was leading now to that way whereby the baser part of passion in him would be likewise obeyed; and he no longer dared to yield himself to its guidance, lest desire clothed itself in honor, and the longing of jealousy made itself look fair in the guise of duty.

He was even as the Syrian who beheld his single vineyard seized by the monarch in whose hands were all the breadth, and beauty, and plenteous increase of the land; and he had more than the Syrian's pain. For he had of his own will given the scepter from his hands, and of his own will descended to a wanderer's estate; and because it refused to bloom and ripen in the shade, he had turned his young vine toward that sun-glow which, gilding it, had drawn upon its luster and loveliness the robber's sight. He held in his hand, indeed, the power by which he could lay bare the canker at the root of this fair vine, and make it worthless in his spoiler's eyes, even as a plant poison-fed and breathing poison. But the strength and the love in him alike forbade him that power's usage.

The vine had once been his,—the vine was now so exquisitely fair, so laden with all golden fruitage,—should his be the vengeance that should tear it up by the roots because it blossomed within the walls of palaces, and his hand no more could touch its glories?

The worm was at its root, indeed; but none knew this. The vine might flourish, and grow exceedingly, and die at last in age and honor, with rich rare fruit borne by it and begot on it: and the worm might never waken, never gnaw, never be discerned.

The worm might be forever mute and numb: the vine live on,—if left in peace.

He could not, of his own hand, break down its glorious crowns of bloom, even though these bloomed for a prince's pleasure, for a despoiler's delight.

## CHAPTER XL.

WHAT he would have seen could his gaze have pierced through the dark mass of crowded houses, and across the reach of the river, into the Palace of the Lirà, would have been a woman standing in the midst of a vast painted chamber, that was all aglow with gold and silver, and white and amber, and the marvelous chromatic hues that stole from a million blossoming flowers—standing, amid that luxury and wealth, as a stag upon the bare gray moorland, in the raw winter dawn, stands at bay for life.

A woman, erect as a desert-palm, fierce as a desert-beast, with one hand clinched against her breast, as though she drove a dagger into it to end a life made unendurable by shame; with her head drawn back, and her face bloodless, and in all her limbs the frozen horror that sculptors give to those who gaze at the Eumenides.

What he would have heard, could any sound have stolen on the air from the mansions of the princes to the attic where he watched, would have been a soft, smooth, cruel voice, that murmured:

"You tell me that I lie? Look! is there no memory in her face? Ask her, my lord, if this thing be not true? if she never lived on the mercy of alms, if she never was a stray thing of shame, if she never took my gold toys one glad summer; if she never owed bread to the man she forsook; if she never laughed under the roof of the actress whom she and you call Coriolis? Ask her!—only ask. See! how her eyes answer you, though her lips are as dumb as the dead. She is a great duchess, no doubt; the world has done her honor to-night; there is no beauty to compare with her beauty; and there is no pride so proud as her pride! She will be also your wife, you have said?—then her honor must be pure as the snow!—is it I who am dreaming these things? Nay, ask her—she surely must know! And her birth-name, too; you would wish to hear that. Can she tell it? I fear not! She was a foundling, you see! Well, I—I who thought of your honor, over-much, it may seem,—learned this also an hour ago. Marriage made her a duchess,—the world has made her a queen,—and you, you would make her wife, as you say. But birth (a mere accident this, as democrats show us!)—birth only made her,—Madelon Bruno. Madelon Bruno! —the world knows that name; the world thought it scarcely poetic enough for her mother who bore it. Madelon Bruno, the daughter, is the Duchess de Lirà: Madelon Bruno, the mother, is—Coriolis."

## CHAPTER XLI.

The night slowly waned, and grew into morning. He never moved, but sat there with his eyes fastened on the ground, and his teeth ground upon each other, and his face gray, and dark with bloodless shadow like that of the dead man, yonder, on his narrow bed.

In a sense there seemed a fitness to him in this companionship of Death. He, who had so often loved the fullest crowds of men, the laughter of the fair and wake, the humors of the streets, the gay eccentric follies of humanity in herds, found, in a measure, sympathy and friendship in that old, worn-out, lifeless frame that rested there—at peace at last, —after its fourscore years of travail, pain, and want, and thankless labor.

Death!—was it, after all, the only mercy that life brought?

Surely;—since those whom the gods love, die young; and they who live, live to cry wearily, soon or late, "O that we were dead!"

Life, to him, had been sweet, and luscious, and ever pregnant with flavor, like a paradise-apple, God-given; but now at its close it grew hateful, and bitter as wormwood, and empty as ashes; and he would fain that he had died in the years of his youth.

As the first beams of the daybreak stole through the lattice in the roof, and the warmth from the sunrise awakened the street swallows under the eaves, there came a swift soft movement like the brushing wing of a hastening bird. Through the unlatched door, into that shadowy place, another shadow came, the shadow of a woman that glided to his feet, and fell there.

"Is it true?" she cried. "Oh, God!—is it true?"

Her voice had no likeness of itself; her face had the startled ghostly horror of those who have beheld unnatural crime; her whole form sank and crouched like the body of a spent and dying stag. All the rich color and undulation of robes fit for an empress swept about her, crushed and torn; on her breast and among her hair great jewels glittered; beneath her bosom a girdle of precious stones coiled like a serpent; and all their glow and splendor made only deadlier by their contrast the whiteness of her gasping mouth, the stricken horror in her eyes, the convulsive helpless trembling of her limbs, as she dropped there.

"Is it true?" she cried, clasping him with her arms as though in him only were her strength against this shame which killed her. "Is it true?"

"Is what true?"

The words died almost as they passed his lips; his face was bloodless as her own; his hands shook like hers as he strove to raise her. To gain time—breath—thought—he asked her this; but without answer he knew what this thing was which drove from her all her glory and her power, and sent her here to crouch like a fallen and accursed creature thus.

"You know!—you know!" she gasped, reading that knowledge in his face. "Look at me,—meet my eyes,—if it be a dream, a lie, a hideous device of hatred, look at me; look long and pityingly as you used to look, and tell me *so* that it is false!"

She clung to him as she used to cling in the brief sorrows

of her childhood, and gazed up in his face with eyes that sought to pierce his very heart.

There was a great agony in his own; and they looked out, not at her, but at the morning stars that shone beyond the lattice.

She was answered.

Her head dropped; her arms let go their hold; she fell as the dying stag falls beneath the last death-shot.

He stooped and raised her, and bore her into the empty attic near, which had been the dead cobbler's place of labor, and laid her down upon the heap of leathern shreds, that served there as a couch of ease.

She lay like an animal stunned; her arms flung out, her head bowed on them, her hair unloosened, with the jewels braided in it, sweeping the bare boarding of the garret-floor.

He stood above her, his eyes filled with an infinite love, an infinite pity, an infinite love such as never again would be hers, let her lovers gather by thousands as they would.

In the years of her gladness he had been forgotten; in the hour of her misery she had remembered him. He had his vengeance.

There was silence in the chamber; the city still rested from labor; the sun had barely risen; the shadows of night still hovered where she lay. He never spoke, he never touched her, he never wondered why she had come to him thus, or who had borne to her that secret which he thought was his own alone. He only gazed at her with an unutterable yearning love;—and, as the diamonds on her robes glittered in the gloom, he shuddered as though he saw in them the smile of those devils of vanity and desire, who had been his rivals, and her tempters, in the old years that were gone.

Suddenly she lifted herself, and looked up at him with blind eyes.

"Is it true, then?" she asked, still.

He stooped over her, and his voice had that tenderness which had survived in him through all the wrongs and all the cruelties her wanton, thankless egotisms had dealt to it.

He bent over her and laid his hand with the pitying touch of old upon her head. He was silent; he could not answer her in any other wise.

"Oh, my God, my God!" she moaned, aloud. "If only you had left me to perish in my infancy!"

He still answered nothing.

The bitterness of this reproach was all that paid him for his martyrdom!

She raised herself with the fierce gesture of a wounded leopardess.

"And you knew this? Always?——"

"Never till yesterday."

"Yet it is true, you say? Speak! answer me! Tell me all you know,—all,—no matter how hideous or how vile!"

"But what brutes have borne it to you?——"

"No matter! Tell me all—worse than I have heard there cannot be. Quick,—for the love of Heaven, or you will drive me mad!"

Half risen from the floor, with her hands clinched on his wrists, and her dilated eyes gazing up into his face, she forced the truth from him with imperious, delirious command. Resistance maddened her, as she had said;—this woman who awoke from dreams of the heritage of kings to find her parentage in poverty and shame.

He obeyed, and told her all.

She heard in unbroken silence; crouching, as the magnificence of the leopardess crouches under the throes of pain, a dumb, passionate, breathless terror on her drooping face.

"And I saw him die—die at her feet!" she muttered.

The horror of her fate consumed her as with fire—fire wherein that staff of life, her pride, withered, and fell in ashes, as a reed held in a flame.

The shame of her mother was upon her like the weight of her own shame; the foulness that was her inheritance seemed to taint her like a plague; all the haughty, rejoicing scorn of her high estate had vanished as the prophet's gourd vanished in the space of a fleet summer night.

In all her glory she was desolate.

And in her desolation it was not to her friends, or her lovers, or her courtiers, that she turned, but to the man whom she had forsaken, and forgotten, and abjured.

"It is just," she murmured, dreamily, gazing at him with her hot, wild, tearless eyes. "I sinned against you;—how could I choose but sin, having been born of *her*? This is just vengeance on my crime to you, vengeance sent of God!"

"Hush! Are His weapons a frail woman's vices? And what vengeance have I ever asked of God or man on you?"

The grave, sweet patience of his voice stilled the passion in her as it had once stilled the wayward and rebellious spirit of her childhood.

She was silent, lying there with her head still bowed down on her arms, her eyes still hidden from the rays of day.

His face grew dark with wrath—wrath against her destroyer; his breath came sharply and hardly, as he bent over and asked:

"What devil was pitiless enough to tell you?"

She lifted herself upon her elbow, and under their swollen lids her eyes flashed with a blue light like flame.

"A devil! yes; a devil who came in angel's guise to save his father's honor! My young lover whom I thought the fairies sent me—the tempter to whom she would have sold me, body and soul, in my child's ignorance."

"What! his son?"

"His son. You know it, then? Oh, Heaven, why not have warned me? Ah! hush! I dare to reproach you—I!—when my whole life has been a crime which you have never wearied of forgiving! Listen! I saw him once, five nights ago, at Villiers, only for one instant as he passed me by. I knew him then, and he knew me. On the morrow he was gone, leaving a gracious message of regret. That very night I promised to be Estmere's wife; that very night I had sworn to myself that nothing on my part should be hidden from his sight. But where was the use to take him truth that only could have seemed to him a fear? Once having looked on his son's face, I held my peace. I let my doom come as it would. I kept, so long as fate would leave them to me, his love, his trust, his honor. I knew how soon they would be struck and perish. This was madness? I think I have been mad since the night I saw that smooth, soft, devilish face; I have been like a creature in a dream;—the dream has broken; I am wakened now—wakened to see, and hear, and feel all things—my misery, my wickedness, my shame."

Her hands clinched on him as she spoke, and drew him down to her, seeming thus to keep hold upon some strength, some reason.

He shuddered as he gazed on her.

"Those are wild words," he murmured. "The shame is another's, not your own, and—you forget. Your father was poor indeed, but he had honor in his simple, bitter, martyred life that no wife's sin could touch. You are his, no less than you are hers. He was a rude, unlearned seaman, it is true, but he had in him honesty, heroism, truth. Are these mean birthrights?"

A shiver ran through her crouching frame. To the woman who had believed herself born from the secret nuptials of some Porphyrogenitus, the sea-bird's nest looked foul as any vulture's; and the strength and the simplicity of this compensation to which he bade her turn were on heights beyond her reach.

The man, nobly bred, could recognize the nobility that lies in character apart from all circumstance and all chances. The woman, basely born, could measure by nothing save the visible symbols of dignity and greatness, of poverty and shame.

"Birthright!" she echoed, with a laugh that had in it the sound of the laughter of Coriolis. "Do not say that word, if you would bid me keep my senses. To-night I was in all my glory. Kings and princes were under my roof. I had his love and the world's honor. In all Paris there was not a creature greater or more envied than I. All splendors, and all follies, and all graces that my wealth could give, I gathered there. I knew that some evil would fall; I knew that his son would come there; I knew that the days of my peace were numbered. I chose that he should behold me at my greatest, my highest, my proudest; I chose so to score myself into his heart and his soul that he should never be able to put me away from them, strive how he would. I had my victory—so far. He loves me; oh, God, he loves me; but it is passion only; not such love as yours. Listen! to-night has been the most brilliant night of my life, and this is how it has ended."

Rising, and pacing to and fro, like a chained leopardess infuriate with its wounds, or cast down upon her rude couch in the exhaustion of despair, shrinking from the light of day, she told him how its horror had come to her, stealing like a thief in the night into her palace.

Every word that had been uttered had cut her like a scourge; she could number them as the quivering creature numbers his stripes by their separate sharp agonies.

He heard her in silence, his face hidden in his hands. What solace had he to give this woman to whom his love was nothing?

Once only he asked her—

"And he—he whom you are to wed? he loves you still?"

She laughed once more, the laugh that was so terrible in that silent place.

"Still! Is he like you, that evil and shame should only be titles to his pity and his pardon? No woman is loved so *twice*. He forced his son from my presence; he refused to believe, while others hearkened; he was generous, noble, great. It is his nature. But, once in solitude, I saw the look upon his face. How is it I live yet? It maddened me; I knew that I was dead to him—worse than dead—forever! I told him the truth of you and of myself. I told him everything my life had known. I prayed, I begged, I knelt to him,—not for his love, or his forgiveness, but only for his belief. It was his doubt that killed me."

"He doubts still?" His voice was stifled as he spoke, his hands were locked over his eyes.

"Doubt! oh, God, what is there for him to believe? I am a living lie to him and to the world. I implored, I conjured, I tempted him. Again and again he almost yielded; again and again I saw love, and love only, in his eyes; and yet I knew he would never yield utterly. There was such scorn in him, such dread of me, and such disdain. 'Not for your birth,' he cried to me; 'not for your mother's shame would you be less pure, less honored in my sight. It is your life, your lie! You tell me the truth now? it may be so. But it is told too late!' And then I grew mad, I think, and broke from him, and got out into the street unseen, I know not how, and came to you, as beaten dogs come to the only creature that has pity for them."

And the love which she had slighted, and mocked, and trodden on so long, had vengeance on her, and grew in might and majesty before her sight, and was her only refuge now, her only friend, her only mercy. And yet! more dear than this, was that love which had disbelieved, which had scorned, which had repudiated her.

"What is my life worth if he be lost to me?" she cried. "What are my rank, my lands, my titles, my dignities, to me without him?"

In the intense self-absorption of her anguish, she never heeded what blows her words might strike upon the heart of her hearer.

All she remembered was that one great horror which enfolded her—the horror of that destiny which had hung over her when in the fair fancies of her infancy she had dreamed herself the daughter of the old dead kings of Gaul; the destiny which had seized her in the attained ambition of her womanhood, while she laughed in her glad scorn at fate, and love, and death; the destiny which clung around her, stifling her life as the fireweb of sorcery clung around Glauce.

He never spoke, where he stood against the open lattice, through which the hot air of the stormy and oppressive dawn poured like the fumes of a slaughter-house.

She, flung down upon the heap of leather, with her arms

outstretched, and her face hidden on them, longed to bury herself from that searching light of coming day.

She thought that never more could she go forth into the sunshine, and meet the eyes of men, and be as she had been. Her past was branded, her present was laid waste; her future was accursed: the greatness that she had said could never pass away, was polluted and without worth; her dignities and her possessions, and all her glories in which she had exulted, as in a strength that made her godlike, were now of no avail.

They endured indeed, they were unchanged, unchangeable: but they could not cleanse the life whence hers had sprung; they could not give her back the pure and fragrant peace of honor. The shame of her mother was upon her—upon her for evermore.

## CHAPTER XLII.

ABOVE the million roofs of the city, the flush of the full day came. From out its nook the little monkey crept, and gazed at her with wondering, sad eyes. In the stillness, the great black door of the garret was thrust open—in its embrasure her lover stood.

He had tracked her hither.

The fairness of his face was livid, his voice was strangled in his throat, his eyes had the fury and the woe that men had seen once in them,—once—in the days of his youth, when the dishonor of his wife had been revealed to him.

He threw one glance on her,—one glance of unutterable horror,—then went straightway to the place where Tricotrin stood.

"She has fled to you!"

Tricotrin shook off his grasp; and stood silent: facing him, with the light of the dawn upon them.

She had fled to him!—well, who to her had so great a

right, so high a title? All the hatred he bore to this man, as to her owner and his spoiler, stirred in him, and prevailed, and killed the old soft tenderness of early memories and of boyish love.

She, with a great cry, sprang from her wretched couch, and dragged herself to her lover's feet, and threw herself there in piteous abandonment, calling out to him to believe —to believe—only to believe.

He did not heed her, even while all his frame thrilled at her touch and burned under her beauty; he did not answer her; he did not raise her; he only looked still at the man in whom he saw her closest friend, his deadliest foe.

"What have you been to her?" he cried, aloud,—"her husband, her father, her paramour? Answer me! What tie binds you? What bond unites you? Is it sin, or secrecy, or marriage, or blood? Answer me! What is this woman to you?"

Tricotrin, standing erect, with the gleam of the dawn on his face, and the darkness of evil passions in his soul, looked him in the eyes with a keen, hard, changeless gaze, and still kept silent.

"Answer me!" Estmere cried again. "Answer me! or——"

She sprang up and caught his lifted arm, and drew his hands into hers, and clung to him so that he could not move unless he cast her off from him with violence, and trampled her aside.

"Wait, wait!" she muttered. "Strike me, not him. What guilt there is, is mine—mine, to you and to the world. There has never been anything on earth greater, gentler, more long-suffering, than his life to mine. I have been base to him, faithless, cowardly, unworthy; but he!—he has never once reproached me, never once deserted me. I was a wretched stray thing—you know, you know!—nameless, homeless, desolate, utterly; and he had pity upon me,—pity, when I was a little lost child dying of hunger save for the bread he gave me. Ah, God! call my crime what you will; curse me, loathe me, leave me,—that is just; but believe,—only believe. Give him justice, and give him honor. In my vanity and my sin I have refused him both so long."

The evil of the world had fallen from her, the false shame of her false pride had perished; truth and courage revived in this soul, wherein they had so long been dead; her voice rang clear and strong in all its suffering. He, whom she conjured, shuddered under that passionate appeal, and gazed down into her eyes, staggered, confused, unmanned, knowing not what to doubt, nor what to believe.

"If this be true," he murmured, "your sin to me weighs nothing beside your sin to him."

"No!" she cried, aloud, as she loosed her arms from about him, and sank down at his feet with the hot blood burning over all her drooping face.

"No. To you I sinned indeed, because I gained your love upon a lie; but you were a stranger; I owed you no debt, I bore you no allegiance: you were free to seek me, and as free to leave me. But to him my whole life has been a crime —a crime when I forsook him because ambition bribed me; a crime when I repaid him for his charity with discontent and with ingratitude; a crime when I was too base to let the world know all I owed him; a crime when I heard you slight him with your satires, and held my peace because I was too base a coward to dare lift up my voice in his defence and honor. It is hard for you to believe me,—yes!—I have forfeited belief. But, as God lives, I will not cease to kneel to you till you believe in him."

He looked down on her, blinded, bewildered, pierced to the heart, confused with a crowd of half-formed thoughts.

"Your love is so great for him!" he asked, the passion in his own soul jealousy seizing on that which smote it the most cruelly.

Her eyes met his in one long look, then turned and rested on the man whom she had wronged.

"Yes, my love is great, now," she said, slowly; "but what is great,—great as eternity,—is my remorse."

He was silent; the force that lies in perfect and unflinching truth was in her now; it conquered him, it was stronger than he, it bore in on him with a witness he could no longer doubt, the purity of this passionless love, the intensity of this vain remorse. He knew that there was nothing in this love which he, as her lover, as her husband, need envy, or could suspect; he knew it, as men in such hours know truths that their colder reason would mock, their worldly scepticism would scorn. But he saw also that this remorse was for a guilt none the less base, none the less craven, because in its shame it was still chaste as ice, because in its selfishness no sensual stain was found.

He believed; but belief was as deadly to him as his doubt had been. She was as worthless, in his sight, as though she had been the faithless and dishonored wife of the man whom she had forsaken—of the man who stood there, in the radiance of the dawn, motionless, wordless, urging no claim, seeking no justification, giving no sign that he heard or that he saw under all the passionate invocation, the violent despair, of this woman who had abandoned him for the treasures and the triumphs of the world.

It was at him, and not at her, that he himself looked, as he spoke.

"This is true?" he asked of him.

The eyes of Tricotrin met his own with a strange weariness, and scorn, and pity, all in one, in their regard.

"It is true," he answered, briefly. His voice was cold and harsh, and all its melody was gone. For once he did not seek to aid her; for once he did not stir to lift her burden from her; for once he left her, alone, with the love that she had chosen in the stead of his. If it failed her, if it scorned her, if it repudiated her, it had been her choice. He left it to deal with her as it would.

She, kneeling there at the feet of her lover as a criminal at the feet of her judge, looked upward in his face.

"You believe now?" she cried to him.

He bent his head.

"Yes, I believe."

In the assent there was a colder, a more hopeless, a more unyielding condemnation of her sin than could have spoken in the uttermost ferocity and abandonment of upbraiding. He believed; and because he believed in the truth of her history, he believed also in the cowardice and the falsehood of her life.

She rose up, slowly, and stood before him; her arms were crossed upon her bosom that heaved and swelled beneath their pressure; her face was like the marble mask that sculptors take from a dead loveliness; her eyes were full of an unutterable woe.

But she prayed no more for mercy, she implored no more for pardon; she had asked for belief, and it had been given her; it was all, she knew, that she could claim; and the superb pride which had been her idol for so long, and which that night had been stricken down as a stately palm is struck by lightning, was in her still, though broken and stilled by the bitter shame, the abject humiliation that her birth had brought.

All her life through, she knew, she had wronged Love. If now Love had its vengeance, and had forsaken her, was the crime hers, or Love's?

It was only from his look that she cowered and shrank, as from a thing unbearable.

"Have you no pity?" she cried, suddenly, the one appeal wrung from her by her utter desolation. "My mother's shame I knew as little as you until to-night. I wronged you; yes, but not one tithe as I wronged him. He has forgiven—shall not you forgive?"

Estmere turned from her with a shudder, as men turn from the dead disfigured body of the beauty they have loved.

"Forgive! forgive!" he echoed; "what is it to forgive? My pardon cannot give you back your honor and your truth."

"Oh God! you said you loved me!"

"Loved you! Men love women that are foul as they are

fair. I gave you tenfold more than love; I gave you—trust!"

A shiver shook her all down her slender, supple, lofty frame. She knew that never more could this man trust her with the one sweet, full, idolatrous, and perfect faith with which he had believed in her when his first kiss had touched her lips. For faith is as the white pure crown of the century aloe, which, once cut down, can bloom no more within the space of the same lives that first rejoiced in it.

He, drawing his gaze from her as one tempted beyond his strength draws it from the loveliness that assails him, moved away slowly, with his head sunk on his chest.

"The woman false once is false always," he said, briefly, with a quiver in his proud clear voice that no manhood and no pride could stay. "Men, younger, happier than I, might give you their faith still—I cannot. You have killed my life, you shall not beggar me of honor."

And without one backward look at her—one look whereby that exquisite and sensuous loveliness might steal his strength and make him the mere slave of passion,—he thrust the great door backward heavily, and passed the threshold of the chamber.

She let him go without a word, a cry, a gesture. She never changed her posture, but stood there, drawing her costly gem-sown robes together, as a beggar, perishing in winter cold, draws his rags around his frozen limbs.

Only once she looked at him whom she had wronged—at him by whom, even yet, she had not been forsaken.

"You have your vengeance," she said, slowly. "It is just."

He had his vengeance,—the vengeance which the old dead Loirais woman had foretold, the vengeance which broke his own heart as it fell.

She stole backward with slow numbed movement to the rude couch of skins, and crouched on it once more. She had no memory of her home, her rank, her household, her dignities; she had no memory save for this one thing,—that she was the daughter of Coriolis. The hours passed; time was nothing to them; the noon came; she still lay there, as Magdalen beneath the cross; and he had never stirred from where he stood beneath the lattice, with his arms resting on the wooden sill, and his head bowed down upon them.

Since the sun had risen there had been a low, hoarse murmur on the air: a sound like the sound of the depths of the sea. But here it was dulled by distance, and it smote their ear,—unheard.

It was the sound of conflict:—it was the sound of the hymn of blood.

Suddenly it deepened, and came upon the silence in loud fitful gusts, and pierced his lethargy as the war-note rouses the stupor of the wounded charger.

He heard the Marseillaise.

"God forgive me! I forgot them!" he cried, aloud: for the only time in all the many years since first he had elected to be one with them, and make their dwelling and their portion, their pleasure and their suffering, his, he had forgotten the people.

"Wait you here," he murmured to her. "It is the children only who have risen. But there is danger, there is slaughter. God forgive me,—I forgot!"

And he left her, and went swiftly through the house, that was deserted as though pestilence had swept it bare, and passed out into the hot noontide—into the streets where the students had risen.

It was a revolt of the children,—an outbreak of youth's noble madness, a passion of boys' futile frenzy; but the massacre of the children had begun, and would not cease till the sun had its setting.

A woman, weeping and frantic, threw herself in his passage:

"Oh, friend! save my son!" she cried to him. "You are as a god to these children! He is all I have upon earth,— you know! A creature of seventeen summers. And he is there at the barricades! Ah!—they die in their madness, proud of it. It were harder to live for mere duty!"

He put her aside; and went onward.

"God forgive me!" he said, still in his heart. "I had forgot them—I had forgot them."

## CHAPTER XLIII.

IN one of the streets of the city, in one of its white and golden palaces, there was a balcony hung with scarlet draperies for the festival that had been a baptism of blood.

Many a time there had come thither a woman, sunny-haired, laughing, full of gladness, tossing sweetmeats and flowers to the crowd, leaning there with roses in her breast, and her arms indolently folded, to watch the spectacle beneath of military pomp, or of imperial entry, or of the masked fooleries of the idle carnival time. And many a time the passing multitudes had looked up, and laughed back to her, and shouted their acclaims, and caught her tossed flower-buds and kissed them: for they had loved her, since she had been clothed with the divinity which this age beholds in Vice.

The scarlet folds hung stirless on the breeze; the gilded butterflies upon them sparkled in the sun; the Eastern birds murmured merrily; the exotics bloomed in every hue, above in that bright balcony, while the slaughter raged beneath.

But on its marble floor the woman lay lifeless, with the slow blood welling from her breast—a stray shot had found her where she leaned to watch the pageantry of strife, and she had fallen here among her flowers. Below, the populace had paused one instant in the tumult of their passions, and had murmured—

"It is Coriolis—killed!"

For fate was still merciful to this woman, who had been merciless to all, still tender to this spoiler, who knew not tenderness, still full of gifts to this assassinatress, whose hands had ever been outstretched for gold. It slew her when fear had begun to touch her; it slew her when her past sin rose against her; it slew her ere her beauty perished, ere her power waned. And Coriolis—a creature soulless as the butterflies that were her emblem—had the noblest requiem that a human soul can have;--she had the sorrow of a people.

Verily, men are just.

## CHAPTER XLIV.

In a dim, gray, ancient street, outside the passage-way, where the town was still old, in the heart of the students, where no cannon could sweep and no squadrons deploy, but each combat perforce was fought out hand to hand, in the old fierce, fair fashion,—there the first barricade had been thrown. A barricade barring the entrance: a barricade that already had served to repulse the soldiery sent up against it, though held only by youths,—goaded on by their comrades' imprisonment; blind with dreams of impossible worlds; lashed to action by agitators and demagogues; beholding only the excellence of liberty, not seeing the excellence of patience. Youths of all ages, all tempers; some gay with zest for the devil's dance of a riot, some grave with a purpose too hard for their years; some drunk with their own evil passions, some with pure longing for freedom; some the ignorant poor tools of conspirators; some the ardent young prophets of truth.

They filled the narrow windings of the street; they climbed upon its roofs, and its ironwork, and its lamp-posts; they knelt at its windows with their muskets at rest on its ledges; they defended its stones as though they were the altar-stones of their holiest temple. They shouted; they sang; they dealt death and they took death; they fought shoulder to shoulder; they mounted, and dived, and hid, and charged; they swarmed over the timber mountain that they had cast up betwixt them and the world; they tasted blood, and were even like young hounds whose tongues are whetted by a dead deer's gore.

And ever and again as one among them was shot down, they lifted his corpse upon the timber to raise the pile higher, and sang more loudly their Marseillaise.

Above the hiss of the bullets, above the cries of the women, above the roll of distant volleys as the musketry sought their quarter, above the din and the tumult of carnage, the great chorus rang out, dominant and triumphant: as it first rang over the crowds of Paris, and over the battle-plains of Europe, while its creator fled through the mountains, proscribed, and desolate, and friendless. The chorus of the hymn that is deathless, because, while men shall live, its passions, and its woes, and its agony of vain desires must live also, unquenched, unstilled, and unattained,—born half of hell, born half of heaven.

Yet above even that divine and devilish chant of the nations' liberties, his own voice rose as he forced his way through amid them, and sprang up on to their topmost pinnacle of the jammed mass of wood and stone. A great shout welcomed him:—ever since the day had broken, men in the paroxysms of fear, or in the heat of conflict, had asked of one another, Where was he?

"Ah! faithless and strengthless!" he called to them. "And only a day since you pledged me your word to keep peace!"

They were the people of his own quarter; the youths that came round him like dogs round their keeper; only a brief space earlier, he, who had come to save them if they would be saved, had spent the days and the nights among them in their cellars, and clubs, and workshops, and painting-rooms, striving to hold them back from destruction, striving to make them wait, for the dear sake of that liberty in whose name they were mad for war. And these,—these few at the least, —these two hundred and more who fought here, had listened, and given way, and vowed to keep from the snare spread for them and their kind by men to whom rivers of blood were as the waters of Pactolus.

They had promised: and thus they redeemed their word. Thus, with the knives at their waist, and the steel in their hands, and the lust to slay in their eyes.

He stood unarmed in their midst; on the highest place, where the sun's rays came fullest and the bullets fell fastest. His eyes swept the crowd as the eagle's the earth; all the warmth, and the light, and the passion had flushed back on his face at the sight of the gleam of the steel, at the sound of the anthem of revolution.

On them a sudden hush fell—a sudden humiliation smote.

They had promised him peace,—and at his feet the dead already lay three deep!

"Could you not be faithful one day through?" he cried to them, in the reproach which all those who love and serve humanity are driven to cast against it, by the weight of its own measureless ingratitude. "You promised me—you, my own people!—and your promise is kept thus! I knew that you were betrayed; I knew that you were drawn down into a pit; I knew that they left your sting in you, only that by it you might slay yourselves, like the scorpion in the flames. I warned you, and you heard, and you swore to keep in your homes and be untempted. And this is the fulfilling of your oath!——"

The youths, pausing, and taking breath, and crowding one on another about the barricade, heard him, and were ashamed. One lad, the youngest of them all, the child of whom his mother had spoken, lifted his fair and glowing face with reverent love upon it, and gripped his rifle closer:

"It is for liberty!" he murmured. "Have you not taught us,—without it life is worthless?"

The eyes of Tricotrin rested on his with infinite tenderness, infinite anguish:

"I have taught you that? No! Life without it is joyless; but life without joy may be great. The greatness of life is sacrifice; is sacrifice liberty, think you? Oh children, you are blind and astray! You spend your strength following shadows. This is love of your country, you call it; and heroism, and all things that are noble? It is but the froth of your passions, the rage and the fret of your boyhood."

A storm of hisses broke across his words. They loved him, indeed, but in that moment of exultant fury, of unappeased bloodthirst, they would not hearken even to him. He waited, patiently and unmoved, until their fury had in some measure died out from its own violence.

Then again he spoke, with a gesture that awed the loudest, the fiercest, the most turbulent, to silence.

"You lift your hands against me?—you think your yells and your threats will make me deal you a demagogue's flatteries? Pshaw! men who dread death scarcely come hither. All this while have you known me so little? Demagogues, to delight you, would lash on your passions. I displease you because I bid you have patience.

"To die, when life can be lived no longer with honor, is greatness indeed. But to die because life galls, and wearies, and is hard to pursue:—there is no greatness in that! It is the suicide's plea for his own self-pity. You live under tyranny, corruption, dynastic lies hard to bear, despotic enemies hard to bear—I know. But you forget, what all followers of your creed ever forget, that without corruption, untruth, weakness, ignorance, in a nation itself, such things could not be in its rulers. Men can bridle the ass and can drive the sheep, but who can drive the eagle or bridle the lion? A people that was strong and pure, no despot could yoke to his vices.

"Against the foreign foes of your country die in your youth if she need it. But against her internecine enemies live out your life in continual warfare. When I tell you this, do you dream that I spare you? Children—you have yet to learn what life is! Who could think it hard to die in the glory of strife, drunk with the sound of the combat, and feeling no pain in the swoon of a triumph? Few men whose blood was hot and young would ask a greater ending. But to keep your souls in patience; to strive unceasingly with evil; to live in self-negation, in ceaseless sacrifices of desire; to give strength to the weak, and sight to the blind, and light where there is darkness, and hope where there is bondage; to do all these through many years unrecognized of men, content only that they are done with such force as lies within you,—this is harder than to seek the cannons' mouths, this is more bitter than to rush, with drawn steel, on your tyrants.

"Your women cry out against you because you leave them to starve and to weep while you give your hearts to revolution and your bodies to the sword. Their cry is the cry of selfishness, of weakness, of narrowness, the cry of the sex that sees no sun save the flame on its hearth: yet there is truth in it,—a truth you forget. The truth,—that, forsaking the gold-mine of duty which lies at your feet, you grasp at the rainbow of glory; that, neglectful of your own secret sins, you fly at public woes and at national crimes. Can you not see that if every man took heed of the guilt of his own thoughts and acts, the world would be free and at peace? It is easier to rise with the knife unsheathed than to keep watch and ward on your own passions; but do not cheat yourself into believing that it is nobler, and higher, and harder. What reproach is cast against all revolutionists?—that the men who have nothing to lose, the men who are reckless and outlawed, alone raise the flag of revolt. It is a satire; but in every satire there lies the germ of a terrible fact.

"You,—you who are children still, you whose manhood is still a gold scarcely touched in your hands, a gold you can spend in all great ways, or squander for all base uses;—you can give the lie to that public reproach, if only you will live in such wise that your hands shall be clean, and your paths straight, and your honor unsullied through all temptations. Wait, and live so that the right to judge, to rebuke, to avenge, to purify, become yours through your earning of them. Live nobly first; and then teach others how to live.

"Lay down your arms—you have not won the title for

their usage—lay them down, I bid you; and when you shall be able to point to high deeds done by you, and high thoughts born from you, then come forth so armed again; and none shall dare to cast at you the jibe that because you knew not how to live, therefore, and therefore only, you would die!"

They heard, and were very still; and paused, half sullen, half afraid. They knew that he spoke truth, but that truth was cruel to their pride. Their souls were moved and disquieted; but their self-love was stung into rage. They could not hear his voice without the instinct of honor and obedience, as children hear the voice of their father. But they were hardened against him, and they murmured loud and deep.

One young boy alone, standing by his side,—the son of the woman who had besought him in the street,—lifted his bright, flushed, kindling face.

"Do with us as you will," he said, softly—and he laid down his musket, and loosened from his breast the badge of insurrection.

Tricotrin smiled on him.

"That is well. Remember your mother now—in the days of your youth—you will not serve your country less, but more, when manhood comes to you."

The action broke the spell of awe and reverence that had held entranced the throng around them: as baffled hawks, missing the heron, swoop on fieldfares harmless among the corn, so their baffled, stifled rage turned upon the lad.

"He would forsake us! He turns traitor!" they hooted against him, and they rained the stones of the streets at the child. One—more drunk than all with the passions of the hour—heaved up a great block of granite, dislodged from the edge of the pavement, and hurled it hurtling through the air to strike to earth the slender figure of the boy.

The square gray block sped on its way as from a catapult; winged by the force of hate.

Tricotrin looked upward: he saw its darkness betwixt him and the sun, he seized the boy and drew him backward, backward into his own place. The stone descended:—the boy stood erect, unharmed; his deliverer fell with the weight upon him.

The wail of a people's agony broke from all the multitude below, then hushed into a dead dread silence,—the silence of a speechless terror.

He lay there with the great stone upon his chest, where it had struck him, and had felled him at a stroke, as lightning fells the tree. From beneath it the blood slowly welled: the bones of his chest were crushed in, and bent, and broken.

The boy, for whom he had thus met death, sank on his knees, and covered his eyes with his hands, and cried out to God to slay him also, since through him this martyrdom had come. Those about him, youths likewise, trembling, and weeping, and afraid as with the fear of crime, thrust off the brutal weight, and raised him, and called on his name with piteous outcries, and forgot every other thing on earth, save that this man who loved them had died for them;—died thus; in the hour that they had revolted from him, and disobeyed him, and refused to hearken to his voice.

Then all that breathless stillness broke up into an awful tumult:—the multitude, mad with grief, and with rage, and with remorse, flung themselves on his destroyer, and seized, and choked, and tore him limb from limb, while through the crowded quarter there rang, from mouth to mouth, the cry that Tricotrin was dead.

On the pile of the barricade the noontide sun poured down. They lifted him up on a shelf of timber, beneath the drooped folds of their flag of liberty. His head was sunk, his eyes were sightless, the blood welled slowly from his breast:—for the first time in all his life amid them he gave no answer to their prayer, no pity to their anguish.

Yet, even now, voiceless, motionless, senseless, he was still their deliverer from evil; for, farther onward, as the troops came up to the massacre, to the ruthless mowing down of all these lives that were as ripe corn for their sickles, the artillery were checked and forbidden to advance, and dimly heard those in authority above them murmur that the people would no more have soul or strength for combat, since Tricotrin was dead. And the soldiers halted, afar off in the noontide heat, and came no more against them, but left them alone with their remorse.

They trampled under their feet, in the insanity of vengeance, the body of his murderer; and spat upon the corpse; and stamped its features into a hideous mass; and left it, battered and shapeless, in the gutter of the street. Then, raving, weeping, tearing their hair, shrieking his name aloud, they closed once more upon the barricade. They were as children whose father had perished;—he had loved them so well, death would have no power to make him deaf to their cries, merciless to their despair!

As though their voices called him, indeed, back to this earth on which they lingered, desolate and bereaved, his consciousness returned, his blindness passed, his eyes unclosed and rested on them. Each breath was torture, each moment numbered; but his thoughts were for them, not for himself.

He signed to those who strove to rouse him, to let him be, to let him lie in such peace as was still left him. He knew that before the sun should have declined from its zenith he would be no more amid the world of men; no more live this life that to him had been ever so fair, and so rich, and so worthy the living. His bloodless lips smiled still as he looked on them.

"Children—do not grieve for me. Death is gentle and generous. See! it spares me sickness and age."

His voice sank; each word was a pang, as he drew breath through the lungs on which the crushed breast-bone pressed as with the pressure of an iron vice. The throngs around him only answered with a great sob that came as from one heart. The tears rained down their cheeks, they stretched their arms to him as though to seize him from the hold of death. The women rent their robes and wailed as the women of Rome at the tomb in the Campus Martius; their little children were trodden under their feet forgotten; from mouth to mouth, from house to house, reaching those that fought in distant streets, reaching those that crouched in vaults and catacombs, this one cry rang—that they had slain him.

The full sun was upon his face; he looked upward at its noonday glory;—and the smile that had come ever on his lips when he had beheld the gladness of its rising, over plain, and lake, and forest, came there still, in this, his deathhour.

"It is well," he murmured. "Why will you grieve? It is well. I die at noon;—ere the darkness of night sets in; ere the night of age overtakes me. My people—if you will that I die content, let my life purchase yours; leave bloodshed, and go in peace. Shall it be that you will refuse me this, the last thing that I shall ask of you?"

With the strength that so long had been in him, he lifted himself on his arm, and conquered the physical pangs that devoured him. His voice was low and stifled; yet never in all the hours of its eloquence had it reached so far to the hearts of the people, had it stirred their innermost souls so deeply, as the wind stirs the depths of the ocean.

"Answer me!" he cried to them, strong in that moment through the love he bore them, and victorious over the power of death. "Answer me! Will you grant me this because you have killed me? Will you go in peace, and save your bodies from fruitless slaughter? Answer me, if ever you loved me!"

They were silent, pierced to the quick; then, still as with one mouth, they lifted up their voices.

"We say as he said,—do with us as you will!"

A glory that was greater than the glory from the sun shone in his eyes as he heard.

"It is well," he said, softly, once more. "Forget not your word when I be dead."

And they cast down their weapons, and broke them asunder, and wept sorely; as children weep, refusing to be comforted, because their hearth is cold, their bodies are famished, their hearts are desolate, their lives are fatherless and friendless.

His eyes wandered dreamily over the crowd, seeking hither and thither, seeking for a face that was not amid them. Then, suddenly, they rested on a far-off gloomy place, where, in the shadow of an arch, one watcher stood aloof, and gazed upon the conflict. He stretched his hand out, and pointed thither.

"Bring him!" he muttered to them. "Bring him,—yonder, —do you see?"

The throng surged closer together, then rolled asunder, and parted, and left a passage free.

He whom he had summoned came, and stood, with the light on his fair, cold, weary face, against the black piles of the timber of the barricade, against this death-bed of wood and iron whereon the man who had died for the people rested content,—as on a prince's nuptial bed.

Tricotrin, leaning still upon one hand, stretched out the other to him.

"Brother,—you may know *now*."

Death, ere it laid the seal of eternal silence on his lips, let them breathe once more the name that by Life had been forbidden them.

And the people drew back, and left them alone, and gathered together, hushed and frightened, as dogs that gaze, helpless, at human passions and human woe, and vaguely thrill with the despair and the divinity of both.

\* \* \* \* \* \* \* \*

The words that passed their lips none heard. That recognition in the shadow of death none watched. The people stood aloof, wondering, and still afraid.

All that they saw was the proud head of the great noble bent down lower, and lower, and lower in reverence and awe: all that they heard was one futile reproach that broke from him and pierced the stillness.

"Oh God! Why have you been lost to me so long?"

The voice that answered him was too faint to reach their straining ears:

"Why? why? Because I loved my freedom; because I knew that not one hour would you have kept your state and station if you once had known. It was a child's quixotic folly —yes; but it never brought me one regret. Let no regret be with you. That old Dante—you had forgot it. Yet you might have remembered;—it was the priest's gift to me for my quick learning of the Latin that he loved. Ah!—you recall the day now? You believe?—yes; you believe. If you doubted, there are papers in the attic yonder, that would vouch to you. Is my life strange in your sight now? Do you see mystery in it, or shame?"

His brother's hands closed upon his.

"I dared to judge you! I dared to condemn you in my pride and my blindness. Oh Christ, if only I had known!"

He smiled; the old soft ironic humor laughed still in his eyes, even through the mists that dimmed them.

"Ah! You thought me astray in my ways and my creeds, you thought me a wanderer and a profitless idler. You were right,—from your view. Dignities have befitted you well: I would not have borne the burden and heat of the ermine; I could not have lived unless free. My mother was sea-born, you know, and perished,—stifled under your pomp."

His listener's frame shook like a woman's. All the chillness of long habit and of social eminence was shattered in him as a glacier shatters in its fall. The bitterness of this hour was infinite; and, by its very force, burned out that canker of a too hard scorn, of a pride too pitiless and too incredulous, which so long had marred the nobility of his temper.

His justice, that he had deemed so pure, had proved but warped opinion. His vision, that he had deemed so clear, had been but purblind prejudice. He scorned himself; and was crushed under that anguish of self-reproach with which he surveyed his own fallibility and condemned his own injustice. And there was no atonement possible for him; he learned all that he had lost, all that he had misread, all that he had missed, only in the moment when to learn them was too late, only when they passed away from him forever.

"And all these years I have but thieved from you!" he muttered. "All I gave you when we met were suspicion and derision! One look—one accent—should have sufficed to me."

"Nay—reproach not yourself thus. What remorse can there lie at your door? Yet if you think that you owe to me aught—pay it in one fashion."

"Demand of me what you will! Is not all that I possess your own?"

"No! you possess your will and your pride—those are not mine to bend. If you will indeed give me what I desire, yield me these——"

"Yield them? You have killed them! Before your life, how can I see any other thing save a usurper's fraud and falsehood in my own?"

"Hush! you were in ignorance. If you had known, you would have beggared yourself in an hour, sooner than have continued to enjoy. Give me these—your passions—nevertheless. Give me them, and take *her* back to your pardon, to your love, to your life. You will not?"

"Will not? I dare not!"

"Because she is the child of Coriolis?"

"Because she is faithless, and without truth."

"She will be true to you, and to you faithful. I have forgiven; shall not you forgive?"

His brother was silent: his face was hidden on his hands.

"I have forgiven," he who pleaded for her urged again, "and what is your wrong to mine?"

"As she wronged you, so will she wrong me."

"Not so: you have her love. I never had it."

"That you had not is her guilt?"

"No. She loves me as a gay child loves—no more. To you she gives the love no woman gives save once. Dying here, I swear to you that she has purity, and honor, and a soul that through you may be lifted to all high things. If you heed not the shame of her birth, no other shame is on her. In my letters you will find her dead husband's witness to her perfect innocence—men, dying, do not lie. She suffers, she is crushed under brutal humiliation; shall you also strike her, now that she is prostrate? Great God!—how shall I plead with you? You tell me your pride is broken, and you resist me thus? Look! all her years through I have guarded her from pain, and found her joy. Will you make my life a failure at the last, because you will condemn and put away from you this only creature that I love? For my sake—not for hers—give her your pardon! I have forgiven,—I!—I tell you that you shall not refuse to her what I have yielded. I tell you that you shall not dare to judge when I already have declared her sinless!"

He lifted himself upon his arm; his voice rose strong and sonorous; his eyes flashed with the passions of other days. He spoke no more as a suppliant; he spoke as a sovereign speaks, against whom there is no appeal.

There was a long silence.

Then, at last, his brother raised his head and looked at him with one long, weary, reverent gaze.

"For your sake be it," he muttered, while his proud lips trembled. "I believe—I will strive also to forgive."

Tricotrin smiled: the smile of one victorious, but whose victory is wrested from the grave.

"You have paid me all your debt. Be merciful to her; keep her in gladness and in honor. This legacy I leave you—Viva's life."

His head fell back, his lungs bled inwardly, exhaustion overcame him; and through the throngs a loud wail went, and echoed once again through all the passage-ways, and over the close-standing roofs; till its reverberation shook all silent inmost places into sound, and startled sleeping infants in their cradles, and awakened old and helpless men from their shivering lethargy by their dull hearths.

There were movement and agitation in the crowd below;

through them there forced her way, in blind, fierce passage, the lofty, slender form of a woman, who flew with swift sure feet up the side of the barricade, and came, and threw herself beside him where he lay. She saw no other face than his in that burning glow of sunlight; she heard no other sound in all that tempest of emotion, save the cry that he was dead.

"I am too late! too late again—my God!" she cried, in her delirium. "Oh people of Paris!—have you no shot, no steel for me? What was I once among you!—a stray and homeless thing, fed on his alms, saved by his mercy, reared in honour and in innocence through him alone. And I forsook him, I denied him, I was ashamed of my debt, I was apostate to his love. Kill me with him if you have pity in you. I am viler than the vilest in your streets!"

In her madness, the truth seemed to her all the atonement that was left; in her remorse, the vengeance that she forced upon herself was wider, deeper, more cruel, than any vengeance that men take on guilt. There was a terrible justice in her expiation:—to the people whom she had scorned with all the gay scorn of her proud life, from the childish days when she had trodden on her vine-crown, her confession and her humiliation were now rendered.

To the multitude the words bore no meaning; and her voice was drowned in the moan of their own lamentation, that was loud as the moan of the sea. But he heard, and his eyelids unclosed, and his gaze dwelt on her in that speechless and immeasurable love of which never in one hour of her life had she once been worthy—until now.

"Viva mine," he murmured, in the old, sweet, familiar phrase of other days, "thou dost wrong to thyself. Thy sins have been but a woman's foibles. I forgave them long ago. Truth is with thee now, let it abide with thee forever. Where truth is not, how shall there be peace? In his love thou wilt have no need of mine. Have no memory of my life save such as may be glad to thee. I made thy happiness—once. Remember only that. I die content. I have saved all these from slaughter,—these children,—they may yet be great men, and free. Life has been sweet,—ah, God!—but death is welcome. Stoop down and kiss me once—once—it will leave no shame on thy lips for him."

For awhile he rested, motionless, breathless, with his eyes blind to the light, and his ear hearing no more the wail of the anguish beneath him.

Then suddenly he raised himself erect, and looked upon the great, still crowd below, and upward at the summer skies.

Earth had been ever so fair to him, and men so well-beloved: and never again would his sight behold the greenness of the summer world, or the faces of his brethren.

"Let my death be the ransom of your lives," he cried to them, while all the strength and sweetness of his voice returned, and rang over the stricken multitude. "Keep my memory in your hearts a little while. If it come ever between you and any guilt, I shall not have lived my life in vain. You suffer for me now?—ah! how soon will you forget? Stand back, and let me see the sun once more—once more: it is the smile of God."

And, looking upward to the last, he died.

Over the whole city a great silence fell; and with that hour the slaughter ceased. Even as he had loved them in his life, so in his death he saved them.

And the people mourned, refusing to be comforted.

THE END.

www.ingramcontent.com/pod-product-compliance
Lightning Source LLC
Chambersburg PA
CBHW020243240426
43672CB00006B/618